2ND EDITION • COMPLETELY REVISED AND UPDATED

Patrick W. Miller, Ph.D.

GRANT WRITING

Strategies for Developing Winning Proposals

GRANT WRITING: STRATEGIES FOR DEVELOPING WINNING PROPOSALS 2ND EDITION

Patrick W. Miller, all rights reserved.
Library of Congress Catalog Card Number: 99096197
ISBN 0-9673279-5-4

Printed in the United States of America
10 9 8 7 6 5 4 3

Preface

Grant competition is rigorous. Each day more organizations vie for the same external dollars. Many institutions view grants as icing on the cake, while for others grants are the only revenue source they have to maintain and improve programs. Most institutions, however, are *not* prepared to respond to grant solicitations. They generally: (1) lack knowledge about the funding agency's rules and regulations, (2) lack knowledgeable and prepared staff who can respond to Request for Proposals (RFPs) or Request for Applications (RFAs), and (3) lack upper administrative support. The typical grant proposal submission is seldom awarded funding because it is an unorganized knee-jerk response to an RFP or RFA. Funding seekers often respond to grant opportunities without considering the institution's mission. Without this direct tie to the institution's major goals, grant awards often become more of a burden than a solution to a problem.

Funding seekers who win grants on a consistent basis usually follow a series of comprehensive activities that can be broken down into six fundamental phases of proposal development:

- activities before the RFP/RFA is released;
- prewriting activities after the RFP/RFA is released;
- writing, reviewing, rewriting, and editing narrative;
- preparing budgets;
- producing, reproducing, packaging, and delivering proposals; and
- postsubmission activities.

Grant Writing: Strategies for Developing Winning Proposals is designed to walk funding seekers through the major phases of grant development. The second edition of this book represents more than twelve years of ideas and techniques used in the development of grant proposals. It includes eight chapters with more than 75 exhibits. Review questions and exercises are presented at the end of each chapter to reinforce learning. Exercises in this book were developed to teach proposal writing and budget development skills to new and experienced grant writers. A glossary, list of resources, and a comprehensive review are presented at the end of the book. Chapter and comprehensive review answers, as well as exercise answers, are located in the appendix.

About the Author

Patrick W. Miller, Ph.D., has worked as a Director of Grants and Contracts, Proposal Manager and Contract Administrator. He has served as national grant reviewer and panel leader for the U.S. Department of Education. In addition, Miller has been a grant and project consultant to school districts and a mentor to college and university faculty and staff on methods of completing and submitting grant applications.

Miller has been a university professor and academic administrator teaching professional and technical courses, advising graduate and undergraduate students and serving on numerous departmental, college, and university committees. He has written more than 100 articles and authored five books.

Miller frequently speaks about grant writing at conferences for professional associations. He teaches grant writing classes to faculty and graduate students at several universities and conducts proposal development workshops throughout the United States for members of nonprofit organizations. For more information, please visit www.pwmilleronline.com.

Patrick W. Miller is listed in *Who's Who in American Education, Who's Who in America* and *Who's Who in the World.* Dr. Miller holds a Ph.D. in Education from The Ohio State University, as well as a master's certificate in Government Contracting from The George Washington University School of Business and Public Management.

Acknowledgments

Many people helped me formulate my thoughts about developing grant proposals to win funding. Early in my career, discussions with Robert Stanton helped me understand the complexity of the proposal development process and government contracts. During the same time, Richard Kulka taught me the significance of paying attention to detail. Michael Kwit gave me an appreciation for clear and accurate budgets and Susan Erfurth and Francie Margolin taught me the importance of editing for style. I thank all those individuals above for their mentoring.

The author also wishes to acknowledge Marshal Chaifetz, J.M. Duff, James Skaine, and Maggie Steinz for reviewing the 2nd Edition of this book. Their invaluable comments and suggestions were greatly appreciated. The author is also indebted to Robert Deloughary for always being there to solve my computer problems and listening to me struggle with each chapter. I also appreciate my daughter Joy's layout and design work, which greatly improved the appearance of this book. Finally, the development of this book would not have been possible if it were not for the support and understanding of my wife Jean. Jean always encouraged me to write this book, even when the task seemed impossible.

Acronyms

ADA	American Disabilities Act
CBD	Commerce Business Daily
CEO	Chief Executive Officer
CFDA	Catalog of Federal Domestic Assistance
CFO	Chief Financial Officer
CO	Contracting Officer
EOE	Equal Opportunity Employer
FAR	Federal Acquisition Regulations
FBO	Federal Business Opportunities
FEDIX	Federal Information Exchange
FOIA	Freedom of Information Act
FR	Federal Register
FTE	Full Time Equivalent
F&A	Facilities and Administrative
GAN	Grant Award Notification
GPO	Government Printing Office
GPRA	Government Performance and Results Act
GSA	General Services Administration
NARA	National Archives and Records Administration
OMB	Office of Management and Budget
PD	Proposal Director
PDF	Portable Document Format
PI	Principal Investigator
POC	Point of Contact
RFA	Request for Application
RFP	Request for Proposal
SGA	Solicitation for Grant Application
SF	Standard Form
SOW	Statement of Work
TOC	Table of Contents
URL	Universal Resource Locators
WBS	Work Breakdown Structure

Table of Contents

List of Exhibits

Chapter 5
Writing, Reviewing, Rewriting, and Editing Narrative 73

Chapter 6
Preparing Budgets 103

Chapter 7
Producing, Reproducing, Packaging, and Delivering Proposals........... 125

Chapter 8
Postsubmission Activities 137

Chapter 1

Funding Sources

The U.S. government provides funding in the form of: (1) grants, (2) cooperative agreements, and (3) procurement contracts. Although similarities exist among funding types, each has a distinct purpose. These funding opportunities are presented as Request for Proposals (RFPs) and Request for Applications (RFAs). The primary functions of RFPs/RFAs are to: (1) solicit proposals, (2) specify proposal content and format, (3) provide procedural information, and (4) describe selection criteria. The government's goals are to maximize competition, minimize solicitation complexity, ensure impartial evaluation of proposals, and select the best proposal(s) that meets the funding agency's requirements.

Grants

Grants provide financial assistance to eligible recipients to accomplish a proposed project where there is no substantial involvement between funding agencies and recipients during performance periods. Many grant seekers look to grants for external funding to support and enhance organizational programs. Grant funds are often used to: (1) conduct research, (2) implement project ideas, (3) complete inservice training, (4) purchase equipment and supplies, and (5) hire new staff members. Grants are administered through various government agencies and as such the requirements can vary greatly.

The *Catalog of Federal Domestic Assistance* (CFDA) includes a comprehensive listing of grant funding programs. The CFDA is a government-wide summary of federal projects, services, and activities that provide financial and non-financial assistance or benefits to the public. The CFDA's primary purpose is to assist users in identifying programs that match the needs of potential applicants. The CFDA is issued annually (in two editions) and is available at most public libraries (information is available in hardcopy, floppy disks, or CD-ROM) or online at www.cfda.gov. The CFDA is a good starting point for funding seekers to locate information about grant opportunities offered by federal government agencies.

CFDA programs provide a wide range of benefits and services, which have been grouped into 20 basic categories and 176 subcategories that identify specific areas of interest. **See Exhibit 1-1.**

Exhibit 1-1

Catalog of Federal Domestic Assistance Categories

- Agriculture
- Business and Commerce
- Community Development
- Consumer Protection
- Cultural Affairs
- Disaster Prevention and Relief
- Education
- Employment, Labor, and Training
- Energy
- Environmental Quality

- Food and Nutrition
- Health
- Housing
- Income Security and Social Services
- Information and Statistics
- Law, Justice, and Legal Services
- Natural Resources
- Regional Development
- Science and Technology
- Transportation

CFDA programs provide benefits and services in 20 grouped categories.

Each CFDA entry includes the following information:

- Name of federal agency overseeing the funding program
- Legislative act that authorized the program
- Goals/objectives of the program
- Type of assistance offered (financial or non-financial)
- Uses and restrictions placed on a program
- Eligibility requirements
- Application and award process
- Funding allocations for a fiscal year (October 1 through September 30)
- Regulations, guidelines, and literature relevant to a program
- Information contacts at the headquarters, regional, and local offices
- Related programs
- Examples of funded projects
- Criteria for selecting proposals
- Policies and directives pertaining to a program

Funding seekers should use a six-step process in searching the CFDA for federal assistance:

1. Browse the CFDA using the index or keyword search to locate assistance for your specific needs. A review of the CFDA may or may not identify programs that provide funding for specific proposal ideas. Both the applicant and funding agency should have similar interests, intentions, and needs if a funding seeker is going to win.

2. Read potential funding opportunities and carefully consider the program eligibility requirements, program objectives, type of assistance, restrictions, and application procedures required for each federal program listed.

3. Consider the reality of preparing a proposal in relationship to the deadline date. Deadlines for submitting grant applications are not negotiable and are usually associated with strict timetables for agency reviews. Some programs have more than one application deadline during the fiscal year.

4. Review the "Information Contacts" section of the program description and identify the funding agency's *Point of Contact* (POC) and phone number.

5. Phone the POC and determine: (1) if the proposed project is applicable to the program agency's needs, (2) the availability of funding, and (3) answers to other proposed project questions. During this telephone conversation, ask for suggestions and advice about your proposed project.

6. Based on responses from the POC, decide to apply or not apply to the funding agency. If feedback from the POC is positive, the funding seeker should consider the grant requirements and deadline date before deciding to submit a proposal. Funding seekers must also consider the reality of implementing the proposal in terms of award notification and project start dates.

Funding seekers should contact the CFDA staff with specific questions about project ideas and possible federal assistance.

The *Federal Register* (FR) is the primary document used by funding seekers to locate information about grant opportunities. The FR is a legal document published every business day by the *National Archives and Records Administration* (NARA) that lists all federal agency regulations and legal notices, including details about all federal grant competitions. The FR publishes a wide range of federal funding opportunities and is available in most major libraries that house government documents. Individuals may also purchase an annual subscription by contacting the *U.S. Government Printing Office* (GPO) at www.access.gpo.gov.

Each issue of the FR has a table of contents organized alphabetically by agency, which lists each document and span of pages. FR announcements include the full grant *application notice* (including necessary forms) or provide information about how to obtain these forms online or from the government agency that is responsible for the particular program. Application packages or kits usually include: (1) program rules and regulations, (2) guidelines for proposal development, (3) application forms (coversheet, certification, assurance, and budget forms), and (4) mailing instructions.

The GPO also allows funding seekers to search and download FR notices and other documents at no charge. The FR online edition has the same table of contents as the paper edition with hypertext links that take users directly to each document in the current issue. The FR online table of contents provides easy access to documents published since January 1, 1998. Funding seekers can also search past issues of the FR by category, subject matter, and date to retrieve documents in current or past issues from 1994 through the present day. The FR online via GPO is available at www.access.gpo.gov/su_docs/aces/aces140.html. FR documents are available in summary format (abbreviated text), full text format (with graphics omitted), and Adobe PDF (Portable Document Format).

Numerous publications are available that provide guidance for proposal development and identify potential sources of funding. Many newsletters, journals, reports, and other publications disclose information about upcoming grant solicitations. These publications provide a summary of the grant's purpose, deadline date and time, funding range and number of awards, eligibility requirements, project areas, and contact person. **See Exhibits 1-2 and 1-3**.

In addition, almost all funding agencies (e.g., U.S. Department of Education, National Science Foundation) have Web sites that serve as excellent up-to-date sources for learning about funding opportunities. Comprehensive resource lists also exist on the Internet and provide links to other Web sites that are extremely useful to funding seekers. For example, the *Internet Resources for Nonprofits* (www.ai.mit.edu/people/ellens/Non/online.html) and *Links for Fundamentals of Grant Writing* (www.tecweb.org/funding/grant.html) include dozens of links to other *Universal Resource Locators* (URLs). In addition, the Web sites for University or College Offices of Sponsored Programs and/or Grant Offices contain valuable links to funding information. Refer to page 201 for a list of additional funding resources.

Other sources of funding information include: (1) past and present RFPs/RFAs, (2) past and present grant agreements and contracts, (3) agency-published information, (4) agency reports in public domain, and (5) funding agency meetings minutes.

Exhibit 1-2

Selected Grant Funding Publications

Funding Publication *	Description
Chronicle of Higher Education www.chronicle.com	Provides funding information about grants and research competitions.
Federal Assistance Monitor www.cdpublications.com	Provides information about federal funding announcements and legislative actions.
Federal Grants and Contracts Weekly www.aspenpub.com	Provides early alerts about funding opportunities from federal agencies.
Nyquist Report www.nyquistassoc.com	Provides information about funding opportunities for two-year colleges.

* See page 203 for additional funding publications.

Numerous publications provide information about funding opportunities.

Exhibit 1-3

Sample Grant Solicitation Summary

Title: Higher Education Challenge Grants

Purpose: The Department of Agriculture is inviting applications to improve postsecondary education in specific areas to strengthen the nation's food and agricultural scientific and professional workforce.

Deadline: February 14, 20XX; 4:00 p.m. EST

Funds: $4,000,000 for grants of up to $100,000 for regular projects and up to $250,000 for joint projects. Awards are for one year.

Eligibility: Land-grant and other U.S. colleges and universities offering a baccalaureate degree or first professional degree in at least one discipline or area of the food and agricultural sciences.

Areas: Projects should have the potential for high impact, innovation, multidisciplinary effort, and generating products and results. Projects must address one or more of the following: curricula design, faculty preparation, instructional delivery systems, and student experiential learning.

Contact: Jeffrey Smith, 987/654-3210, e-mail: jsmith@reeusda.gov

Grant summaries provide specific information about upcoming funding possibilities.

The U.S. government awards grant funding through two types of grants: (1) discretionary and (2) entitlement. *Discretionary grants* are competitive and funding agencies have the authority to determine the award amount and recipients. With discretionary grants, agencies base award decisions on peer review conducted by panels of experts or readers. Awards are based on how well applicants respond to solicitation criteria. Funding agencies allow applicants to indicate how they respond to grant announcements. Most small grants (under $250,000 for example) are for one year, while large grants (over $250,000) are for multiple years. Continued funding is awarded to recipients after the initial year of a multi-year grant if applicants meet the agency's terms and conditions specified in the *grant award notification*. Funding is not automatic and agencies may impose conditions that must be met before further funding is awarded.

Entitlement, mandatory, or formula grants are only available to state agencies. These general revenue or federal pass-through funds are allocated by state agencies to institutions and organizations based on pre-determined formulas. State agencies give awards as long as recipients meet statutory and regulatory conditions. Once these conditions are met, state agencies must make awards available. State agencies can refuse to award grant funds only when grantees fail to comply with requirements under which the entitlement program was established. Award recipients develop and submit written project/budget reports periodically throughout the performance period.

Cooperative Agreements

Cooperative agreements provide money to recipients in order to accomplish a proposed project where substantial involvement is expected between funding agencies and recipients during performance periods. Substantial involvement means agencies will participate in the management of projects. Cooperative agreements are primarily used in large clinical research trials.

The Office of Management and Budget (OMB) provides government-wide guidelines and policies to state and federal agencies regarding the administration of grants and cooperative agreements through circulars included in the CFDA. New circulars are published in the FR. The OMB Web site is located at www.whitehouse.gov/omb/grants/index.html. OMB circulars are indexed by the following categories:

- Budget
- State and local governments
- Educational and non-profit institutions
- Federal procurement
- Federal financial management
- Federal information resources/data collection
- Other special purpose

Procurement Contracts

Procurement contracts acquire services or products for the direct benefit of or use by the federal government. In one of the earliest procurement contracts issued on December 23, 1907 the United States Army Board of Ordinance and Fortification published Signal Corps Specification No. 486 for "a heavier-than-air flying machine." On February 28, 1908 the United States War Department signed a contract with Wilbur and Orville Wright at 1187 West Third Street, Dayton, Ohio for $25,000 to manufacture and deliver one flying machine on or before August 28, 1908. Complete requirements concerning this contract as well as additional information is found at www.b-26marauderarchive.org/RP/RP2217/RP2217.htm.

Procurement contracts are governed by the *Federal Acquisition Regulations* (FAR). The FAR (www.arnet.gov/far) contains uniform policies and procedures for governing federal procurement *acquisition* activity. The FAR requires that government agencies post all public notices about federal procurement actions over $25,000 in *FedBizOpps* (FBO) (www.fedbizopps.gov). Please note that prior to January 2002, these procurement opportunities were published in the *Commerce Business Daily* (CBD). The FBO is the single point of universal electronic public access to government-wide procurement opportunities.

Procurement contracts are grouped into two broad categories: (1) *fixed-price contracts* and (2) *cost-reimbursement contracts*. Specific contract types range from *firm-fixed-price*, where the funding seeker has full responsibility for the performance costs and resulting profit or loss, to *cost-plus-fixed-fee*, where the funding seeker has minimal responsibility for performance costs and the negotiated fee (profit) is fixed.

Procurement solicitation synopses are categorized by letter codes "A" through "Z" to represent services (e.g., the letter "A" is used for Research and Development" and the letter "U" is used for "Education and Training Services") and number codes "10" through "99" to represent products (e.g., number "22" is used for "Railroad Equipment" and number "52" is used for "Measuring Tools"). The FBO publishes between 500 and 1,000 synopses each business day. **See Exhibit 1-4.**

The *General Services Administration* (GSA), which manages the FBO, provides files that can be downloaded free of charge (vsearch1.eps.gov/servlet/SearchServlet). You can use the FBO search engine to locate synopses or awards by solicitation number, date, classification code, and/or government agency. Questions regarding the site can be directed to support staff by calling toll free at 877-472-3779. Potential bidders can request copies of RFPs (noted in FBO synopses) from funding agencies by writing to the POC. **See Exhibit 1-5.**

Exhibit 1-4

Sample Federal Business Opportunities (FBO) Synopsis

TITLE: National Youth Risk Behavior Study (publication date: November 14, 20XX) RFP #200-96-0503(P), DUE: December 14, 20XX, POC: Dale DeFilipps at (404) 842-8467. The Centers for Disease Control and Prevention contemplates awarding a contract to implement a biennial national school-based Youth Risk Behavior Survey (YRBS) for 9th to 12th grade students during the spring of 20XX and a national YRBS for selected populations of high risk youth during fall, 20XX. The YRBS System monitors priority health risk behaviors that contribute to the leading causes of mortality, morbidity, and social problems among youth in the United States. The six categories of health risk behaviors are behaviors that contribute to injuries; tobacco use; alcohol and drug use; sexual behaviors that contribute to unintended pregnancies and sexually transmitted diseases; dietary behaviors; and physical activity. The contract period of performance for the base period is 12 months. In addition, there are four optional periods for a total performance period of 60 months. Requests for the RFP must cite RFP #200-96-0503(P). Centers for Disease Control, Procurement and Grants Office, 255 East Paces Road, N.E., Room 507, Atlanta, Georgia 30305

FedBizOpps (FBO) provide synopses about procurement contracts.

Exhibit 1-5

Sample Letter to Order RFP From Funding Agencies

November 15, 20XX

Centers for Disease Control
Procurement and Grants Office
255 East Paces Road, N.E., Room 507   ⟵ **RFP Number and Title**
Atlanta, GA 30305

Re: RFP #200-96-0503(P) – National Youth Risk Behavior Study

Dear Mr. DeFilipps:

John Jones and Associates requests a copy of the above-referenced solicitation, which appeared in the *FedBizOpps (FBO)* on November 14, 20XX. Please mail a copy of the RFP to:

> Daniel Fairman   ⟵ **Where to Send RFP**
> John Jones and Associates
> 596 W. Jackson Blvd.
> Chicago, IL 60606

Sincerely,

Daniel Fairman   ⟵ **Contact Person and Phone Number**
Daniel Fairman
312-567-1234

Funding seekers request RFPs from funding agencies based on information contained in FBO synopses.

Federal procurement contract RFPs are organized according to a *Uniform Contract Format*. This format divides procurement contract solicitations into parts and sections and prescribes the content for each according to the FAR. Procurement contract sections C, L, and M provide specific information about the solicitation and should be carefully reviewed prior to examining other RFP sections. Section C presents the statement of work, section L presents instructions, conditions, and notices, and section M presents evaluation criteria. **See Exhibit 1-6**.

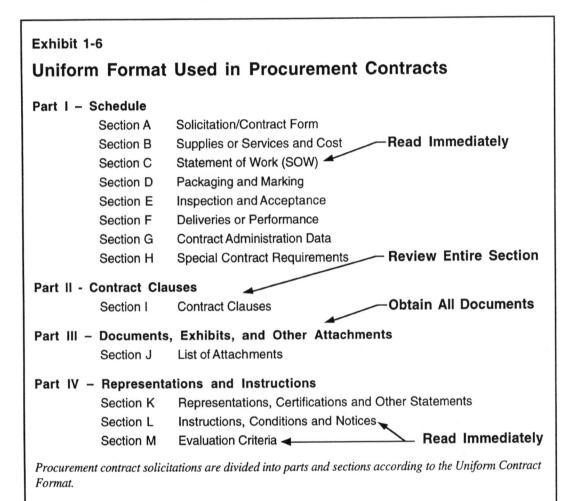

Exhibit 1-6

Uniform Format Used in Procurement Contracts

Part I – Schedule

Section A	Solicitation/Contract Form
Section B	Supplies or Services and Cost
Section C	Statement of Work (SOW)
Section D	Packaging and Marking
Section E	Inspection and Acceptance
Section F	Deliveries or Performance
Section G	Contract Administration Data
Section H	Special Contract Requirements

Read Immediately

Review Entire Section

Part II - Contract Clauses

Section I	Contract Clauses

Obtain All Documents

Part III – Documents, Exhibits, and Other Attachments

Section J	List of Attachments

Part IV – Representations and Instructions

Section K	Representations, Certifications and Other Statements
Section L	Instructions, Conditions and Notices
Section M	Evaluation Criteria

Read Immediately

Procurement contract solicitations are divided into parts and sections according to the Uniform Contract Format.

A comprehensive comparison between grants and procurement contracts indicates many similarities and differences. In general, grants provide financial assistance for a public purpose (such as providing funds to assist underrepresented students to succeed in college). In contrast, procurement contracts are awarded to secure goods or services to meet government needs. For example, the government may issue an RFP to acquire 10,000 widgets for the Department of Defense. Or, another agency may issue a procurement contract to obtain information regarding effective treatment for drug offenders.

Grants allow funding seekers the opportunity to indicate what will be done and how funds will be spent in response to specific criteria established by the funding agency. However, in procurement contracts, funding seekers indicate how specific tasks will be accomplished to provide products or services to the government. Grants offer multiple awards and upfront payments. Procurement contracts usually make only one award and payments are made after expenditures. **See Exhibit 1-7.**

Exhibit 1-7

Grant and Procurement Contract Differences

Grants	Procurement Contracts
• Found in the Federal Register (FR)	• Found in the FedBizOpps (FBO)
• Project announcements	• Competitive bidding announcements
• Multiple awards	• One award
• Respond to criteria	• Respond to tasks
• Initiated by funding seeker	• Initiated by Contracting Officer (CO)
• Funding seeker determines direction	• CO determines direction
• Publications	• Deliverables
• Limited oversight	• Substantial oversight
• Funding seeker keeps equipment	• Government may keep equipment
• Up-front payments	• Payments made after expenditures
• Major sections	• Major sections
• Abstract	• Executive Summary
• Introduction (optional)	• Introduction
• Problem/Need	• Statement of Work (SOW)
• Goals/Objectives	• Management/Organization/Staffing
• Methods/Activities	• Corporate Experience
• Evaluation Plans	• Facilities and Equipment
• Budget	• Budget (as a separate document)
• Appendices	• Appendices

Grants provide financial assistance to recipients to accomplish a proposed project. Procurement contracts are used to acquire services or products to be used by the government.

Funding seekers can spend numerous hours searching government documents looking for potential funding sources that match their needs. Several organizations provide customized searches of the FR, FBO, and other funding documents based on key word descriptors. See *Community of Science, Inc.* (www.cos.com) or *American Association of State Colleges and Universities Grants Resource Center* (www.aascu.org/ofpopen/ofpopen.htm).

Although this book is primarily written for grant seekers, many of the same proposal development principles apply to cooperative agreements and procurement contracts. Depending on your organization's needs, funding seekers may also want to consider cooperative agreements and procurement contracts as viable funding opportunities. These strategies may also be useful to those seeking private funds.

Chapter 1 Review

(Chapter 1 Review answers are found on page 211)

Directions: For statements 1 through 15, circle T for True or F for False.

T F   1. The main purpose of most grants is to provide financial support to accomplish a proposed project where there is no substantial involvement between funding agencies and recipients during performance.

T F   2. A comprehensive listing of grant programs is found in the *Catalog of Federal Domestic Assistance* (CFDA).

T F   3. A new edition of the *Federal Register* (FR) is issued 52 times per year.

T F   4. Grant applications are published in the FR.

T F   5. Discretionary grants are non-competitive.

T F   6. Discretionary grants are governed by the *Federal Acquisition Regulations* (FAR).

T F   7. Discretionary grant awards (over $250,000) are usually for one year.

T F   8. Entitlement grants are allocated by state agencies to institutions based on a pre-determined formula.

T F   9. Funding agencies can refuse to award funds under entitlement grants if and when grantees fail to comply with requirements under which the program was established.

T F   10. Cooperative agreements involve agency collaboration or participation in the management of projects and tend to be used in large clinical research trials.

T F   11. Procurement contracts acquire services or products for the direct benefit or use by the federal government.

T F   12. Procurement contract solicitation synopses are published in the FAR.

T F   13. The FAR is a primary document used by federal agencies that contains uniform policies and procedures governing federal procurement contract acquisition activity.

T F   14. The Uniform Contract Format organizes procurement contract solicitations into parts and sections.

T F   15. Grants provide payments after expenditures.

Exercise 1-1

Locating and Reviewing Solicitations

(Exercise 1-1 answers are found on page 215)

Funding seekers must be able locate what government agencies have funded in the past as well as what they intend to fund in the future. Experienced funding seekers are efficient and relentless solicitation hunters that are acquainted with traditional resource publications as well as electronic searching tools to prevent potential solicitations from being overlooked. Funding seekers must locate solicitations that match the grant seeking institution's needs with government wants.

Directions: Locate a recent (within the last three years) grant solicitation from the Federal Register (FR) that promotes the use of technology (e.g., distance learning) in education. Review the solicitation and identify the following information:

1. CFDA#/Title:

2. Sponsoring agency:

3. Publication date:

4. Eligible applicants:

5. Funding allocations:

6. Selection criteria:

7. Solicitation summary:

Directions: Locate a recent (within the last 3 years) procurement contract solicitation synopsis from the FedBizOpps (FBO) (www.fedbizopps.gov) that provides treatment services for drug abuse offenders. Review the synopsis and provide the following information:

1. Title:

2. Solicitation number:

3. Sponsoring agency:

4. POC/Phone #/e-mail:

5. Publication date

6. Solicitation summary:

Exercise 1-1 continues on the next page

Exercise 1-1 (Continued)

Locating and Reviewing Solicitations

(This part of Exercise 1-1 is based on individual interest and no answers are provided in the appendix)

Directions: Visit the Federal Register Online Web site at http://www.access.gpo.gov/ su_docs/aces/aces140.html and locate potential grant solicitations that are related to your area of interest. Choose one solicitation and identify the following information:

1. CFDA#/Title:

2. Sponsoring agency:

3. Publication date:

4. Eligible applicants:

5. Funding allocations:

6. Selection criteria:

7. Solicitation summary:

Directions: Locate the Catalog of Federal Domestic Assistance (CFDA) at the library (information is available in hardcopy, high-density floppy diskettes, or CD-ROM). Review the CFDA categories and subcategories and identify a program that might provide funding related to your area of interest. Review the program announcement and identify the following information:

1. Name of federal agency:

2. Goals/Objectives of the program:

3. Eligibility requirements:

4. Total funding/Number of awards:

5. Solicitation summary:

Exercise 1-2

Analyzing Grant Solicitations
(Use Solicitation *CFDA* #278G to complete this exercise)
(Exercise 1-2 answers are found on pages 216 - 218)

Directions: Read the School-To-Work (S-T-W) Opportunities Solicitation for Grant Application (SGA) from the Department of Labor and Department of Education (pages 15 through 22). Using this SGA, answer the following questions. Along with each answer, provide the location (page and column) in the SGA where you found the information.

1. Identify the contact person and telephone number to obtain further information about this solicitation.

2. Where should the application be hand delivered?

3. Where will the bidders' conferences be held? Please provide dates, times, and locations.

4. How many days do states have to review applications?

5. How long is the period of performance? How many years may the grant be extended?

6. What is the total amount of money available for this competition?

7. Approximately how many awards will be made?

8. What is the range of first-year awards? The amount of an award depends on what criteria?

9. What are the six distinct parts of the application?

10. What items should be included in Part II: "Budget and Certification" of the application?

11. What are the five selection criteria and point values for Part V: "Program Narrative" of the application?

12. Explain what "administrative costs" may include.

Exercise 1-2 continues on the next page

Monday
April 14, 1997

Part III

Department of Labor
Employment and Training Administration

Department of Education
Office of Vocational and Adult Education

**School-to-Work Opportunities; Urban/
Rural Opportunities Grants; Application
Procedures; Notice**

Exercise 1-2 continues on the next page

DEPARTMENT OF LABOR

Employment and Training Administration

DEPARTMENT OF EDUCATION

Office of Vocational and Adult Education

School-to-Work Opportunities; Urban/Rural Opportunities Grants; Application Procedures

AGENCIES: Employment and Training Administration, Department of Labor. Office of Vocational and Adult Education, Department of Education.

ACTION: Notice of availability of funds, solicitation for grant application (SGA) and an Empowerment Zone/Enterprise Community EZ/EC invitational priority for School-to-Work Urban/Rural Opportunities Grants.

SUMMARY: This notice announces the 1997 competition for Urban/Rural Opportunities Grants authorized under Title III of the School-to-Work Opportunities Act of 1994 (the Act). This notice contains all of the necessary information and forms to apply for funds appropriated in FY 1996. Urban/Rural Opportunities Grants enable local partnerships serving youth who reside or attend school in high poverty areas to develop and implement School-to-Work Opportunities initiatives in high poverty areas of urban and rural communities. These initiatives offer young Americans in these communities access to School-to-Work Opportunities programs specifically designed to address barriers to their successful participation in such programs and to prepare them for further education and training and first jobs in high-skill, high-wage careers.

DATES: Applications for grant awards will be accepted commencing April 14, 1997. The closing date for receipt of applications is June 30, 1997 at 2 p.m. (Eastern time) at the address below. Telefacsimile (FAX) applications will not be accepted.

ADDRESSES: Applications must be mailed to: U.S. Department of Education, Application Control Center. Attention: CFDA #278G, Washington. DC 20202–4725.

FOR FURTHER INFORMATION CONTACT: Christine Camillo, National School-to-Work Office, Telephone: (202) 401–6222 (this is not a toll-free number). Individuals who use a telecommunications device for the deaf (TDD) may call the Federal Information Relay Service (FIRS) at 1–800–877–8339 between 8 a.m. and 8 p.m., Eastern time, Monday through Friday.

SUPPLEMENTARY INFORMATION:

Section A. Background

The Departments of Labor and Education are reserving funds appropriated for FY 1996 for a competition for Urban/Rural Opportunities Grants authorized under Title III of the Act. Grants under this competition will be awarded to local partnerships that serve high-poverty areas and that are also prepared to develop and implement local School-to-Work Opportunities initiatives in these areas. The Departments recognize that high-poverty areas face particular challenges in implementing School-to-Work initiatives, including: Few large private or public employers; dropout rates that, in many cases, are over 50 percent: poor students who may be much less aware of post-secondary opportunities than students in other areas; strong peer pressure that does not [necessarily] promote achievement among youth; pressure on youth from situations outside of school that may affect their school performance; schools with students of more diverse ethnic and racial backgrounds than schools in other areas; proportionately more out-of-school youth than in other areas; and uneven quality in educational and employment opportunities available to high-poverty area youth.

Due to these particular challenges, a local partnership in a high-poverty area must identify and address a great variety of needs of youth residing, or attending school, in these areas. The Departments encourage applications from only those local partnerships that propose innovative and effective ways to deliver the common features and basic program components as outlined in Title I of the Act and that have the potential to serve large numbers of students who reside or attend school in the targeted area. Further, the Departments wish to emphasize the importance of a local partnership's ability to coordinate its strategies for serving in-school and out-of-school youth; for achieving its planned goals and outcomes; for assessing and addressing the multiple needs of high-poverty area youth, particularly the human service needs; and for linking effectively with both schoolwide reform efforts and with State and community plans for a comprehensive School-to-Work Opportunities system.

In accordance with the authority provided in Section 5 of the Act, the Departments have determined that the administrative provisions contained in the Education Department General Administrative Regulations (EDGAR), at 34 CFR parts 74, 75, 77, 79, 80, 82, 85

and 86, will apply to grants awarded to local partnerships under this Urban/Rural Opportunities Grant competition.

This notice contains the definition of the term "administrative costs," as established by the Departments in a final notice published on November 14, 1995 (60 FR 57276), and a 10 percent cap on administrative costs incurred by local partnerships receiving grants under Title III. This notice also establishes an invitational priority for funding EZ/EC applicants, and contains all of the other necessary information and forms to apply for a grant.

Section B. Purpose

Under this competition, the Departments will award grants to local partnerships serving youth who reside or attend school in high-poverty areas that have built a sound planning and development base for their school-to-work programs, to begin implementation of School-to-Work Opportunities initiatives that will become part of statewide School-to-Work Opportunities systems. These local initiatives offer young Americans access to programs designed to increase their opportunities for further education and training, to prepare them for first jobs in high-skill, high-wage careers, and to address the special needs of youth residing or attending school in high poverty areas.

Section C. Application Process

1. Eligible Applicants

(A) Local Partnership Definition

A local entity that meets the definition of "local partnership" in section 4(11) of the Act is eligible to apply for an Urban/Rural Opportunities Grant. As defined in the Act, an eligible partnership must include employers, representatives of local educational agencies and local postsecondary educational institutions (including representatives of area vocational education schools, where applicable), local educators, representatives of labor organizations or nonmanagerial employee representatives, and students. Other entities appropriate to effective implementation of a local School-to-Work Opportunities initiative should also be included in the partnership. Such partnerships must be in place prior to submitting an application for funding.

Under section 302(b)(2) of the Act, a local partnership is eligible to receive only one (1) Urban/Rural Opportunities Grant.

Exercise 1-2 continues on the next page

(B) High-Poverty Area Definition

In addition to meeting the definition of "local partnership" in section 4(11) of the Act, under section 307 of the Act, applicants seeking funding under this notice are required to meet the definition of "high-poverty area" as stated in that section and to describe the urban or rural high poverty area to be served. The description must include:

• A map indicating the urban census tract, contiguous group of urban census tracts, block number area, contiguous group of block number areas, or Indian reservation to be served by the local partnership. To be considered contiguous, the tracts, areas or reservations to be served must be touching at any point.

• The population of each urban census tract, block number area, or Indian reservation to be served, along with the total population of the entire area to be served; and

• The poverty rate for each urban census tract, block number area, or Indian reservation to be served, among individuals under the age of 22, as determined by the U.S. Bureau of the Census, along with an average poverty rate among this age group for the entire area to be served. Only U.S. Bureau of Census statistics may be submitted for review.

Only those applicants that both provide the required map and population/poverty rate data in their applications in the format outlined in this subsection of this notice and that meet the definition of a high poverty area as described in this subsection will be considered for funding. The Departments intend to pre-screen all applications for high poverty area eligibility prior to the panelists' review and will not consider any applications that do not contain the required map and population/poverty rate data. Information in addition to what is required in this notice with regard to population/poverty rate data is not necessary and will have no influence upon meeting the high poverty area definition. Applicants will not have the opportunity to submit additional or revised information should a determination be made that the identified area does not meet the high poverty definition.

Note: U.S. Bureau of Census information may be obtained through a local college or university, city planning department, State data center, or through the Data User Service Division of the U.S. Bureau of the Census. Applicants are encouraged to utilize local providers of U.S. Bureau of Census data. For those applicants who are unable to locate such data, please contact the Census Bureau State Data Center for your local area. A list

of State and Local Data Center contacts is included in an appendix to this notice. Population/poverty rate data published by the Bureau of the Census is provided in age ranges: 0–5, 6–11, 12–17, 18–24, and 25 and up. The Departments will accept poverty rate data for the age range up to 17 or up to 24, whichever is higher, for the purposes of eligibility. In order to be considered for funding, all census tracts or blocks within the area to be served must be characterized by a poverty rate of 20.0 percent or greater among the age group.

2. State Comments

The local partnership must submit its application to the State for review and comment before submitting the application to the Departments, in accordance with section 303(a) of the Act. The application should be submitted to the State's School-to-Work Contact. A list of State School-to-Work Contacts is included in an appendix to this notice. The Departments expect that the State School-to-Work Contact will provide all members of the State School-to-Work Partnership listed in section 213 (b)(4)(A)–(K) of the Act an opportunity to review and comment on the local partnership's application.

Of particular importance to the Departments are each State's comments on the consistency of the local partnership's planned activities with the State's plan for a comprehensive statewide School-to-Work Opportunities system and the relationship of any proposed activities with other local school-to-work partnerships or plans, especially if the grant applicant is not specifically identified as a local partnership within the State system.

In accordance with section 305 of the Act, if a State has an approved State School-to-Work Opportunities plan, the State must confirm that the plan submitted by the local partnership is in accordance with the State plan. The application from the local partnership must contain this confirmation.

Section 303(b)(1) of the Act requires that each State review and comment on a local partnership's application within 30 days from the date on which the State receives the application from the local partnership. Therefore, even though an applicant has 75 days to apply for a Urban/Rural Opportunties Grant under this notice, it must provide its application to its State in time for the State to have at least 30 days before the due date to review and comment on the application.

Furthermore, under section 303(c)(2) of the Act, the State's comments must be included in the local partnership's application. However, if the State does not provide review and comment within the 30-day time period described above,

the local partnership may submit the application to the Departments without State comment. In such a case, the local partnership should provide proof that the State received a copy of the local partnership's application at least 30 days prior to the application due date.

3. Period of Performance

The period of performance for Urban/Rural Opportunities Grants is sixty (60) months from the beginning of the project period.

4. Option to Extend

Urban/Rural Opportunities Grants may be continued up to 4 additional years, regardless of the State Implementation Grant status of the State in which the partnership is located. Additional funding will be based upon availability of funds and the progress of the local partnership towards its objectives as stated in its performance agreement and will be subject to the annual approval of the Secretaries of Labor and Education (the Secretaries). It is expected that the amount of Federal funds, if any, that are awarded to local partnerships under this notice in subsequent years, will decrease.

5. Available Funds

Approximately $14 million is available for this competition.

6. Estimated Range of Awards

The amount of an award under this competition will depend upon the scope, quality, and comprehensiveness of the proposed initiative and the relative size of the high poverty area to be served by the local partnership. While there is no limitation on the size of a high poverty area, the Departments expect that the resources available for individual grants will effectively serve high poverty areas of no more than a total of 50,000 in population. The Departments further expect that first-year award amounts will range from a minimum award of $200,000 to a maximum award of $500,000. These estimates, which are provided to assist applicants in developing their plans, are not binding.

7. Estimated Number of Awards

The Departments expect to award 30–40 grants under this competition.

Note: The Departments are not bound by any estimates in this notice.

8. Grantee Reporting Requirements/Deliverables

(a) Reporting requirements.
The local partnership grantee will be required, at a minimum, to submit:

Exercise 1-2 continues on the next page

—Quarterly Financial Reports (SF 269 A);
—Quarterly Narrative Progress Reports;
—Performance Agreement or Performance Standards;
—Annual Financial Reports (ED Form 524 B, and SF 269);
Budget Information for Upcoming Years, if necessary;
—An Annual Performance Report providing data on performance measures; and
—A close-out report at the end of the grant.
  (b) Deliverables.
  The local partnership grantee will be required to:
  • Provide information on best practices and innovative school-and work-based curricula suitable for dissemination to States and other stakeholders;
  • Participate in two grantee meetings per year sponsored by the National School-to-Work Office;
  • Act as a host to outside visitors who are interested in developing and implementing School-to-Work Opportunities initiatives in urban or rural areas of high poverty and to other visitors interested in the replication, adaptation and/or impact of successful program elements; and
  • Participate as needed in national evaluation and special data collection activities.

9. Application Transmittal Instructions

An application for an award must be mailed or hand delivered by the closing date.

(A) Applications Delivered by Mail

An application sent by mail must be addressed to the U.S. Department of Education, Application Control Center, Attention CFDA # 278G, 600 Independence Avenue, SW, Washington, DC 20202-4725.

An application must show proof of mailing consisting of one of the following:
  • A legibly dated U.S. Postal Service Postmark;
  • A legible mail receipt with the date of mailing stamped by the U.S. Postal Service;
  • A dated shipping label, invoice, or receipt from a commercial carrier; or
  • Any other proof of mailing acceptable to the U.S. Secretary of Education.

If an application is sent through the U.S. Postal Service, the Secretaries do not accept either of the following as proof of mailing:
  • A private metered postmark; or
  • A mail receipt that is not dated by the U.S. Postal Service.

An applicant should note that the U.S. Postal Service does not uniformly provide a dated postmark. Before relying on this method, an applicant should check with its local post office. An applicant is encouraged to use registered or at least first class mail. Each late applicant will be notified that its application will not be considered.

(B) Applications Delivered by Hand

An application that is hand delivered must be taken to the U.S. Department of Education, Application Control Center, Room 3633, Regional Office Building 3, 7th and D Streets, SW, Washington, DC.

The Application Control Center will accept hand delivered applications between 8:00 a.m. and 4:30 p.m. (Eastern time) daily, except Saturdays, Sundays and Federal Holidays.

Individuals delivering applications must use the D Street Entrance. Proper identification is necessary to enter the building.

In order for an application sent through a courier service to be considered timely, the courier service must be in receipt of the application on or before the closing date.

Section D. Organization and Content of Applications

Applicants are encouraged to submit an original and three (3) copies of their application. The Departments suggest that the application be divided into six distinct parts: detachable description addressing the high poverty area definition, budget and certifications, abstract, State comments, program narrative, and appendices. To ensure a comprehensive and expeditious review, the Departments strongly suggest that applicants submit an application formatted as follows:

Table of Contents

I. Eligibility Requirements

Part I must contain detailed information as described in the Eligible Applicants, High Poverty Area Definition subsection of this notice and, for pre-screening purposes, should be separate and easily detachable from the remainder of the application.

II. Budget and Certifications

Part II should contain the Standard Form (SF) 424, "Application for Federal Assistance," and SF 524, "Budget." One copy of the SF 424 must have original signatures of the designated fiscal agent, who will be the grantee. In addition, the budget should include—on a separate page(s)—a detailed cost break-out of each line item on SF 524. Applicants should list any non-Federal resources within their narrative applications. Any non-Federal resources listed on the applicant's SF 424 or ED Form 524, Section B, will be considered binding. Assurances and Certifications found in an appendix to this notice should also be included in Part II of the application and should include the original signatures of the fiscal agent/grantee.

III. Abstract

Part III should consist of a one-page abstract summarizing the essential components and key features of the local partnership's plan.

IV. State Comments

Part IV should contain the State's comments on the application. Details on this section can be found under the State Comments heading of this notice.

V. Program Narrative

Part V should contain the application narrative that demonstrates the applicant's plan and capabilities in accordance with the selection criteria contained in this notice. In order to facilitate expeditious evaluation by the panels, applicants should describe their proposed plan in light of each of the selection criteria. No cost data or reference to price should be included in this part of the application. The Departments strongly request that applicants limit the program narrative section to no more than 40 one-sided, double-spaced pages.

VI. Appendices

All applicable appendices including letters of support, resumes, and organization charts should be included in this section. The Departments recommend that all appendix entries be cross-referenced back to the applicable sections in the program narrative.

Note: Applicants are advised that the peer review panels evaluate each application solely on the basis of the selection criteria contained in this notice and the School-to-Work Opportunities Act. Appendices may be used to provide supporting information. However, in scoring applications, reviewers are required to take into account only information that is presented in the application narrative, which must address the selection criteria and requirements of the Act. Letters of support are welcome, but applicants should be aware that support letters contained in the application will strengthen the application only if they contain commitments that pertain to the selection criteria.

Based on their experience with past competitions, and in an effort to ensure and confirm the commitment of key partners to their partnership, the Assistant Secretaries may wish to contact the applicants and their key

Exercise 1-2 continues on the next page

partners before making final funding decisions.

Section E. Safeguards

The Departments will apply certain safeguards, as required under Section 601 of the Act, to School-to-Work Opportunities programs funded under this notice. The application must include a brief assurance that the following safeguards will be implemented and maintained throughout all program activities:

(a) No student shall displace any currently employed worker (including a partial displacement, such as a reduction in the hours of non-overtime work, wages, or employment benefits).

(b) No School-to-Work Opportunities program shall impair existing contracts for services or collective bargaining agreements, and no program funded under this notice shall be undertaken without the written concurrence of the labor organization and employer concerned.

(c) No student shall be employed or fill a job—

(1) When any other individual is on temporary layoff, with the clear possibility of recall, from the same or any substantially equivalent job with the participating employer; or

(2) When the employer has terminated the employment of any regular employee or otherwise reduced its workforce with the intention of filling the vacancy so created with the student.

(d) Students shall be provided with adequate and safe equipment and safe and healthful workplaces in conformity with all health and safety requirements of Federal, State, and local laws.

(e) Nothing in the Act shall be construed so as to modify or affect any Federal or State law prohibiting discrimination on the basis of race, religion, color, ethnicity, national origin, gender, age, or disability.

(f) Funds awarded under the Act shall not be expended for wages of students or workplace mentors.

(g) The grantee shall implement and maintain such other safeguards as the Secretaries may deem appropriate in order to ensure that School-to-Work Opportunities participants are afforded adequate supervision by skilled adult workers, or to otherwise further the purposes of the Act.

Section F. Waivers

Under Title V of the Act, the Secretaries may waive certain Federal requirements that impede the ability of a State or local partnership to carry out the purposes of the Act. Only local partnerships in States with approved School-to-Work Opportunities plans

may apply for waivers. A local partnership that seeks a waiver should contact its State School-to-Work Contact to determine what documentation is required and to whom it should be sent.

In May, 1995, the National School-to-Work Opportunities Office issued a document entitled "School-to-Work Opportunities Waiver and Plan Approval Process Questions and Answers." This document was sent to every Governor and State School-to-Work Contact. The document contains answers to many of the questions that localities may have when preparing their waiver requests. Local Partnerships interested in applying for waivers should contact the National School-to-Work Opportunities Office or their State School-to-Work Contact for a copy of the waivers document.

Section G. Bidders' Conferences

Bidders' Conferences for interested School-to-Work Urban/Rural Opportunities representatives are scheduled from 1:00 p.m. to 4:00 p.m., on the dates and locations listed below:

- May 9, 1997, Dallas, Texas.
- May 12, 1997, Chicago, Illinois.

Registration for both conferences will be held from 12–1 p.m. (Central Time). More information on the location of each conference will be provided to applicants at the time of registration.

Participants at each of the Conferences will receive a detailed description of the School-to-Work Opportunities Act, the selection criteria and high poverty area definition and how they will be applied, and will have the opportunity to ask questions of Federal School-to-Work officials.

All partnerships must pre-register by faxing the names and addresses of up to three members of the local partnership planning to attend, the name of the local partnership, and a phone number to: Jeffrey Way, Way and Associates, 7338 Baltimore Avenue, Suite 107, College Park, MD 20740, (301) 277–2050; FAX: (301) 277–2051.

Questions regarding the solicitation may be submitted in advance. If you are unable to attend one of the Bidders' Conferences but would like the conference materials and a conference transcript, submit your request via fax to the fax number listed above. All reservations must be submitted no later than April 25, 1997. You will be sent a confirmation along with hotel accommodation information once your registration has been received.

School-to-Work Local Partnership Grants

Administrative Cost Cap

The Departments are applying the 10 percent cap on administrative costs contained in section 215(b)(6) of the Act to local partnerships receiving grants directly under this competition. As was explained in the notice announcing the FY 1995 competition, section 215(b)(6) of the Act applies the 10 percent administrative cap to subgrants received by local partnerships from a State. Applying the 10 percent cap to Urban/Rural local partnership grants under this competition is consistent with the Act's intent and its broader limitations on administrative costs, as well as with section 305 of Title III, which requires conformity between School-to-Work Opportunities plans of local partnerships and State School-to-Work Opportunities plans.

Definition of Administrative Costs

All definitions in the Act apply to local School-to-Work Opportunities systems funded under this and future Urban/Rural Opportunities Grant competitions. Since the Act does not contain a definition of the term "administrative costs" as used in section 217 of the Act, as was explained in the notice announcing the FY 1995 competition, the Departments will apply the following definition to competitions for Urban/Rural Opportunities Grants.

The term "administrative costs" means the activities of a local partnership that are necessary for the proper and efficient performance of its duties under the Urban/Rural Opportunities Grant pursuant to the School-to-Work Opportunities Act and that are not directly related to the provision of services to participants or otherwise allocable to the program's allowable activities listed in section 215(b)(4) and section 215(c) of the Act. Administrative costs may be either personnel or non-personnel costs, and may be either direct or indirect. Costs of administration include those costs that are related to this grant in such categories as—

A. Costs of salaries, wages, and related costs of the grantee's staff engaged in—

- Overall system management, system coordination, and general administrative functions, except evaluation activities;
- Preparing program plans, budgets, and schedules, as well as applicable amendments;
- Monitoring of local initiatives, pilot projects, subrecipients, and related systems and processes;

Exercise 1-2 continues on the next page

18206   **Federal Register** / Vol. 62, No. 71 / Monday, April 14, 1997 / Notices

• Procurement activities, including the award of specific subgrants, contracts, and purchase orders;

• Developing systems and procedures, including management information systems, for ensuring compliance with the requirements under the Act;

• Preparing reports and other documents related to the Act;

• Coordinating the resolution of audit findings;

B. Costs for goods and services required for administration of the School-to-Work Opportunities system;

C. Costs of system-wide management functions; and

D. Travel costs incurred for official business in carrying out grants management or administrative activities.

EZ/EC Priority

The Departments invite applications from local partnerships proposing to implement a School-to-Work Opportunities initiative for youth residing or attending school in an Empowerment Zone or Enterprise Community (EZ/EC), designated under section 1391 of the Internal Revenue Code (IRC), as amended by Title XIII of the Omnibus Budget Reconciliation Act of 1993. This is an invitational priority, under authority of 34 CFR 75.105(c)(1), whereby the Departments seek to encourage EZ/EC communities to apply for grants in this competition.

Selection Criteria

Under the School-to-Work Urban/ Rural Opportunities Grant competition, the Departments will use the following selection criteria in evaluating applications and will utilize a peer review process in which review teams, including peers, will evaluate applications using the selection criteria and the associated point values. The Departments will base final funding decisions on the ranking of applications as a result of the peer review, and such other factors as replicability, sustainability, innovation, geographic balance, and diversity of system approaches.

Further, as established in section 302(b)(3) of the Act, the Secretaries, in awarding grants under this notice, shall give priority to local partnerships that have demonstrated effectiveness in the delivery of comprehensive vocational preparation programs with successful rates in job placement through cooperative activities among local educational agencies, local businesses, labor organizations, and other organizations.

Selection Criterion 1: Comprehensive Local School-to-Work Opportunities System (40 Points)

Considerations: In applying this criterion, reviewers will consider—

A. *20 Points.* The extent to which the partnership has designed a comprehensive local School-to-Work Opportunities plan that—

• Includes effective strategies for integrating school-based and work-based learning, integrating academic and vocational education, and establishing linkages between secondary and postsecondary education;

• Is likely to produce systemic change that will have substantial impact on the preparation of all students for a first job in a high-skill, high-wage career and in increasing their opportunities for further learning;

• Ensures that all students will have a full range of options, including options for higher education, additional training and employment in high-skill, high-wage jobs;

• Ensures coordination and integration with existing school-to-work programs, and with related programs financed from State and private sources, with funds available from Federal education and training programs (such as the Job Training Partnership Act and the Carl D. Perkins Vocational and Applied Technology Education Act); and where applicable, communities designated as Empowerment Zones or Enterprise Communities (EZ/EC);

• Serves a geographical area that reflects the needs of the local labor market (i.e., considers the needs of the local labor market that encompasses the high poverty area), and is able to adjust to regional structures that the State School-to-Work Opportunities plan may identify;

• Targets occupational clusters that represent growing industries in the partnership's geographic area; and, where applicable, demonstrates that the clusters are included among the occupational clusters being targeted by the State School-to-Work Opportunities system; and

• Consistent with section 301(2) of the Act, includes an effective strategy for assessing and addressing the academic and human service needs of students and dropouts within the high poverty area, making improvements or adjustments as necessary, with particular emphasis on the coordination of various human services provided within the community.

B. *20 Points.* The extent to which the partnership's plan demonstrates its capability to achieve the statutory requirements and to effectively put in place the system components in Title I of the School-to-Work Opportunities Act, including—

• A work-based learning component that includes the statutory "mandatory activities" and that contributes to the transformation of workplaces into active learning components of the education system through an array of learning experiences such as mentoring, job-shadowing, unpaid work experiences, school-sponsored enterprises, and paid work experiences;

• A school-based learning component that provides students with high-level academic and technical skills consistent with academic standards that the State establishes for all students, including, where applicable, standards established under the Goals 2000: Educate America Act;

• A connecting activities component to provide a functional link between students' school and work activities, and between workplace partners, educators, community organizations, and other appropriate entities;

• Effective processes for assessing skills and knowledge required in career majors, and issuing portable skill certificates that are benchmarked to high-quality standards such as those States will establish under the Goals 2000: Educate America Act, and for periodically assessing and collecting information on student outcomes, as well as a realistic strategy and timetable for implementing the process in concert with the State;

• A flexible School-to-Work Opportunities system that allows students participating in the local system to develop new career goals over time, and to change career majors; and

• Effective strategies for: providing staff development for teachers, worksite mentors and other key personnel; developing model curricula and innovative instructional methodologies; expanding career and academic counseling in elementary and secondary schools; and utilizing innovative technology-based instructional techniques.

Selection Criterion 2: Quality and Effectiveness of the Local Partnership (20 Points)

Considerations: In applying this criterion, reviewers will refer to section 4(11) of the Act and consider—

• Whether the partnership's plan demonstrates an effective and convincing strategy for continuing the commitment of required partners and other interested parties in the local School-to-Work Opportunities system. As defined by the Act, partners must include employers, representatives of

Exercise 1-2 continues on the next page

local educational agencies and local postsecondary educational institutions (including representatives of area vocational education schools, where applicable), local educators (such as teachers, counselors, or administrators), representatives of labor organizations or nonmanagerial employee representatives, and students, and may include other relevant stakeholders such as those listed in section 4(11)(B) of the Act, including employer organizations; community-based organizations; national trade associations working at the local levels; industrial extension centers; rehabilitation agencies and organizations; registered apprenticeship agencies; local vocational education entities; proprietary institutions of higher education; local government agencies; parent organizations; teacher organizations; vocational student organizations; private industry councils under JTPA; Federally recognized Indian tribes, Indian organizations, and Alaska Native villages; and Native Hawaiian entities;
• Whether the partnership's plan demonstrates an effective and convincing strategy for continuing the commitment of workplace partners and other interested parties in the local School-to-Work Opportunities system;
• The effectiveness of the partnership's plan to include private sector representatives as joint partners with educators in both the design and the implementation of the local School-to-Work Opportunities system;
• The extent to which the local partnership has developed strategies to provide a range of opportunities for workplace partners to participate in the design and implementation of the local School-to-Work Opportunities system, including membership on councils and partnerships; assistance in setting standards, designing curricula, and determining outcomes; providing worksite experiences for teachers; helping to recruit other employers; and providing worksite learning activities for students such as mentoring, job shadowing, unpaid work experiences, and paid work experiences;
• The extent to which the roles and responsibilities of the key parties and any other relevant stakeholders are clearly defined and are likely to produce the desired changes in the way students are prepared for the future;
• The extent to which the partnership demonstrates the capacity to build a quality local School-to-Work Opportunities system; and
• Whether the partnership has included methods for sustaining and expanding the partnership as the program expands in scope and size.

Note: As indicated in the Background section of this notice, in accordance with section 301(2) of the Act, the Departments recognize the significance of a local partnership's capability to provide for a broad range of services that sufficiently address the various needs of high poverty area youth. Applicants are, therefore, reminded that local partnerships should include members that are appropriate to the effective implementation of the local initiative, particularly community-based organizations and others experienced in dealing with the distinctive needs of youth residing or attending schools in high poverty areas.

Selection Criterion 3: Participation of All Students (15 Points)

Considerations: In applying this criterion, reviewers will refer to the definition of the term "all students" in section 4(2) of the Act, and consider—
• The extent to which the partnership will implement effective strategies and systems to provide all students with equal access to the full range of program components specified in sections 102 through 104 of the Act and related activities such as recruitment, enrollment, and placement activities, and to ensure that all students have meaningful opportunities to participate in School-to-Work Opportunities programs;
• Whether the partnership has identified potential barriers to the participation of any students, and the degree to which it proposes effective ways of overcoming these barriers;
• The degree to which the partnership has developed realistic goals and methods for assisting young women to participate in School-to-Work Opportunities programs leading to employment in high-performance, high-paying jobs, including non-traditional jobs;
• The partnership's methods for ensuring safe and healthy work environments for students, including strategies for encouraging schools to provide students with general awareness training in occupational safety and health as part of the school-based learning component, and for encouraging workplace partners to provide risk-specific training as part of the work-based learning component, as well the extent to which the partnership has developed realistic goals to ensure environments free from racial and sexual harassment; and
• The extent to which the partnership's plan provides for the participation of a significant number or percentage of students in School-to-Work Opportunities activities listed under Title I of the Act.

Selection Criterion 4: Collaboration With State (15 Points)

Considerations: In applying this criterion, reviewers will consider—
• The extent to which the local partnership has effectively consulted with its State School-to-Work Opportunities Partnership, and has established realistic methods for ensuring consistency of its local strategies with the statewide School-to-Work Opportunities system being developed by that State Partnership;
• Whether the local partnership has developed a sound strategy for integrating its plan, as necessary, with the State plan for a statewide School-to-Work Opportunities system;
• The extent to which the local partnership has developed effective processes through which it is able to assist and collaborate with the State in establishing the statewide School-to-Work Opportunities system, and is able to provide feedback to the state on their system-building process; and
• Whether the plan includes a feasible workplan which describes the steps that will be taken in order to make the local system part of the State School-to-Work Opportunities System, including a timeline that includes major planned objectives during the grant period.

Selection Criterion 5: Management Plan (10 Points)

Considerations: In applying this criterion, reviewers will consider—
• The feasibility and effectiveness of the partnership's strategy for using other resources, including private sector resources, to maintain the system when Federal resources under the School-to-Work Opportunities Act are no longer available;
• The extent to which the partnership's management plan anticipates barriers to implementation and proposes effective methods for addressing barriers as they arise;
• Whether the plan includes feasible, measurable goals for the School-to-Work Opportunities system, based on performance outcomes established under section 402 of the Act, and an effective method for collecting information relevant to the local partnership's progress in meeting its goals;
• Whether the plan includes a regularly scheduled process for improving or redesigning the School-to-Work Opportunities system based on performance outcomes established under section 402 of the Act;
• The extent to which the resources requested will be used to develop

Exercise 1-2 continues on the next page

18208   **Federal Register** / Vol. 62, No. 71 / Monday, April 14, 1997 / Notices

information, products, and ideas that will assist other States and local partnerships as they design and implement local systems; and

• The extent to which the partnership will limit equipment and other purchases in order to maximize the amounts spent on delivery of services to students.

Note: Experience with the 1994 and 1995 Urban/Rural Opportunities Grant competitions provided the Departments with a greater awareness with regard to a local partnership's responsibilty for understanding and coordinating an array of programs and services available to high poverty area youth. In considering this criterion, applicants should address the partnership's capacity to manage the implementation of the local School-to-Work Opportunities initiative.

Dated: April 7, 1997.

Raymond Uhalde,

Acting Assistant Secretary for Employment and Training, Department of Labor.

Patricia McNeil,

Assistant Secretary for Vocational and Adult Education Department of Education.

BILLING CODE 4000–01–P

Chapter 2

Proposal Development Process—An Overview

The federal government awards more than $200 billion in grants on an annual basis and competition for these grants is becoming more rigorous. It is not how many grant applications you write, but how many you win that is important. "Winning isn't everything, it's the only thing" (Red Sanders, Vanderbilt University, 1953).

RFPs and RFAs are announced on a wide variety of topics every business day through the FR and other publications. Solicitations (RFPs/RFAs) are documents that seek proposals that explain how problems can be solved. In essence, proposals provide strategies for solving problems related to a funding agency's needs.

Proposals prepared in response to solicitations create competitive situations where only the most knowledgeable funding seekers and the best-of-the-best proposal solutions win. Being successful in a highly competitive environment requires that funding seekers use extensive planning before developing grant applications. Developing winning grant proposals is based on: (1) obtaining accurate and reliable information about upcoming solicitations, (2) analyzing RFPs/RFAs, (3) making intelligent bid/no-bid decisions, (4) writing strong and convincing narrative, (5) developing realistic and cost efficient budgets, (6) organizing material in a logical, readable, and attractive package, and (7) delivering the appropriate number of proposals to the funding agency on or before the due date.

All proposal submissions are reviewed by funding agency readers according to criteria published in the RFP/RFA. Funding agency representatives may hold discussion and/or negotiation sessions with funding seekers before a final award decision is determined. Grant winners receive a notice of award and/or contract that must be signed before the project begins. **See Exhibit 2-1.**

Exhibit 2-1

Grant Process: From Acquisition to Award

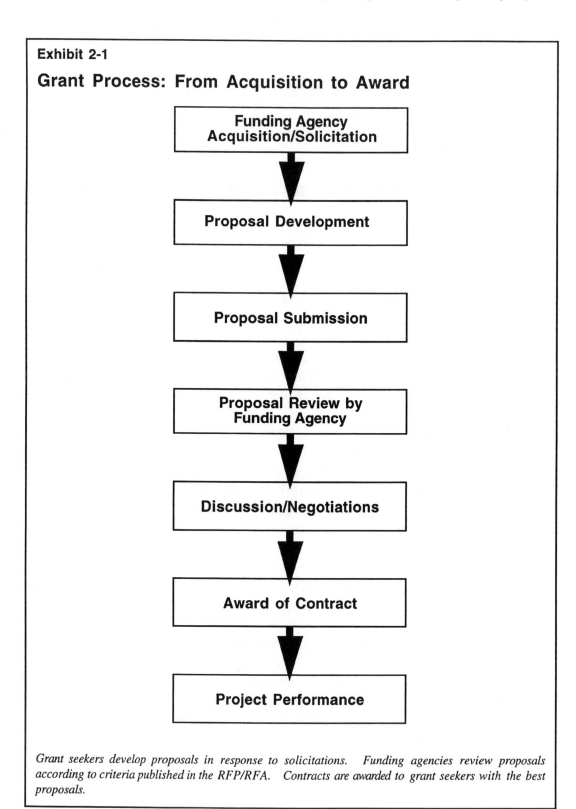

Grant seekers develop proposals in response to solicitations.   Funding agencies review proposals according to criteria published in the RFP/RFA.   Contracts are awarded to grant seekers with the best proposals.

The proposal development process consists of a series of comprehensive activities, each of which must be completed if funding seekers plan to win consistently. Most winning grant proposals require the completion of six distinct development phases:

- activities *before* the RFP/RFA is released;

- prewriting activities *after* the RFP/RFA is released;

- writing, reviewing, rewriting, and editing narrative;

- preparing budgets;

- producing, reproducing, packaging, and delivering proposals; and

- postsubmission activities. **See Exhibit 2-2.**

The proposal development process is further complicated by time constraints– proposals are commonly due 30 days after the release of RFPs/RFAs. Experienced funding seekers understand that conducting activities before the solicitation is released is critical to winning. Proposal directors must carefully schedule writing and reviewing activities after the solicitation is released to ensure that grant applications are prepared within the limited time allotted by funding agencies. **See Exhibit 2-3**.

Activities Before the RFP/RFA Is Released

Many grant seekers fail to receive funding because they wait until the RFP/RFA is published in the FR before developing a proposal. Waiting until the RFP/RFA is publicly announced is a common and critical mistake made by inexperienced funding seekers. Key activities that should be completed prior to the release of the RFP/RFA include:

- gathering intelligence about the solicitation;

- making a preliminary bid/no bid decision;

- identifying the proposal director and team members;

- identifying partners, subcontractors, and consultants;

- developing a "model" solicitation;

- establishing a preliminary budget;

- creating "boilerplate" materials; and

- writing a preliminary proposal draft.

Details about activities that should take place *before* the RFP/RFA is released are covered in Chapter 3.

Exhibit 2-2

Proposal Development Process

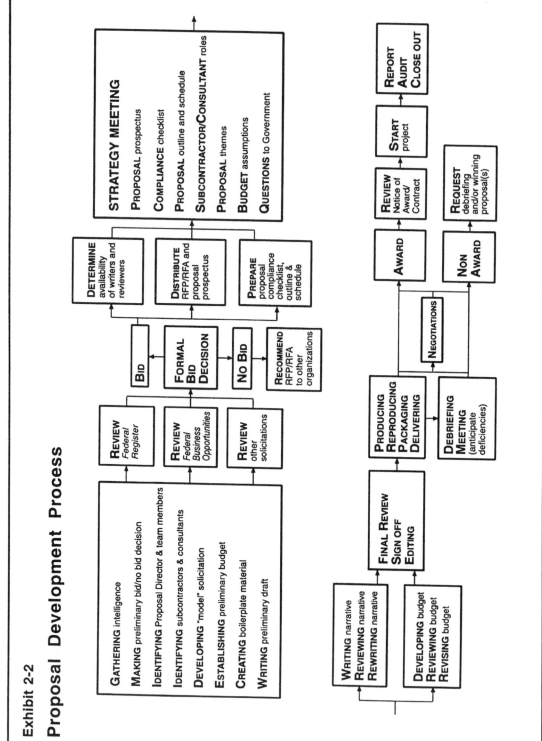

The proposal development process involves a series of comprehensive activities that must be completed if funding seekers plan to win consistently.

Exhibit 2-3

Proposal Development Schedule

Day-to-Day Schedule

Activities Before RFP/RFA Is Released

- Gathering intelligence
- Making preliminary bid/no bid decision
- Identifying Proposal Director and team members
- Identifying partners, subcontractors, and consultants
- Developing "model" solicitation
- Establishing preliminary budget
- Creating boilerplate materials
- Writing preliminary draft

Activities After RFP/RFA Is Released

Activity	1	2	3	4	5	6	7	8	9	10	11	12	13	14	15	16	17	18	19	20	21	22	23	24	25	26	27	28	29
Review RFP/RFA and make formal bid/no bid decision	X	X	X																										
Determine availability of writers and reviewers	X	X																											
Distribute prospectus and RFP to writers and reviewers		X																											
Develop compliance checklist		X	X																										
Prepare proposal outline and schedule		X	X																										
Hold strategy meeting			X																										
Discuss writing assignments and schedule			X																										
Discuss writing strategies/themes			X																										
Establish budget assumptions			X																										
Formulate questions for funding agency			X																										
Assemble appendix materials				X	X	X	X	X	X	X	X	X	X	X	X	X	X	X	X	X	X	X							
First draft of proposal narrative and budget due								X																					
Reviewers' meeting										X																			
Second draft of proposal narrative and budget due															X														
Reviewers' meeting																	X												
Final draft of proposal narrative and budget due																							X						
Final review																								X	X	X			
Administrative/management sign off																										X			
Editing																									X	X	X	X	
Production and reproduction																												X	
Packaging and delivery																													X
Postsubmission Debriefing Meeting																													X

The proposal development process includes activities before and after the release of the RFP/RFA. After solicitations are released, funding seekers have 30 days to develop and deliver grant applications.

Grant application formats vary from agency to agency; however, there are several common components found in most grant proposals. Funding seekers should use these components as a starting point to develop a preliminary proposal draft prior to release of the RFP/RFA. The preliminary proposal draft is compared with specific RFP/RFA requirements after the solicitation is released. Even if the draft meets only some of the RFP/RFA requirements, the funding seeker is ahead of others who are trying to write a complete proposal from scratch in the post RFP/RFA 30-day timeframe. After carefully reading the RFP/RFA, funding seekers make appropriate changes in the preliminary draft to ensure compliance with specific solicitation requirements and guidelines. **See Exhibit 2-4.**

Prewriting Activities After the RFP/RFA Is Released

Many funding seekers lose grants because they fail to plan winning strategies before developing proposals in response to RFPs/RFAs. Prewriting activities *after* solicitations are released involve three days of preparation and planning before attempting to develop a proposal.

Day 1

The first day after release of a solicitation should be spent reviewing the RFP/RFA and obtaining information to clear up any ambiguities in solicitation requirements. During this first day, the estimated probability of winning is calculated and upper management makes a decision to bid or not bid.

Day 2

The second day after release of the RFP/RFA should be spent developing organizational and planning tools necessary to prepare the grant proposal narrative and budget. The proposal director and team members should prepare a *proposal prospectus, compliance checklist, proposal outline,* and *proposal schedule* as tools to guide writers and reviewers.

Day 3

The third day after release of the RFP/RFA, the proposal director should hold a *strategy (kickoff) meeting* with all proposal writers and reviewers. Discussion should focus on assigning writing tasks, adhering to a proposal schedule, developing questions about unclear segments of the RFP/RFA, and formulating budget assumptions.

Details about how grant seekers can prepare planning and organizational tools prior to developing the proposal narrative and budget are covered in Chapter 4.

Exhibit 2-4

Common Grant Application Components

Proposal Components*	Description/Guidelines
Application Cover Sheet (See pages 96-97)	Standard Form 424 serves as the cover sheet for most grant applications. Follow directions carefully and provide appropriate information in the blank spaces.
Abstract (See page 77)	Cogent summary of the proposed project. Most abstracts are brief statements of 500 words or less that emphasize major proposal components.
Table of Contents (TOC) (See page 99)	Listing of major sections and subsections of the proposal with specific page numbers. The TOC should also list documents in the appendix.
Project Narrative (See Chapter 5)	Persuasive essay of proposed project. Common narrative components include problem/need statement, goals/objectives, methods/activities, and evaluation plans.
Budget (See Chapter 6)	Costs to complete the project. Includes a proposed narrative description that details how funds will be spent. Usually includes a financial commitment by the grantee.
Assurances/Certifications (See page 95)	Various requirements (e.g., drug free workplace) imposed on applicants as conditions for receiving an award. Read and follow instructions and have all forms signed by the organization's upper administration.
Appendices (See page 92)	Information peripheral to the grant application. Used especially when funding agencies impose page limitations. Usually includes résumés, letters of support, etc.

* Proposal components vary from agency to agency. Read the RFP/RFA to ensure compliance.

Most funding agencies require similar proposal components. Funding seekers should develop preliminary proposal drafts prior to the release of solicitations.

Writing, Reviewing, Rewriting, and Editing Narrative

Armed with the necessary planning and organizational tools (proposal prospectus, compliance checklist, and proposal outline and schedule), writers prepare two to three drafts of the proposal narrative. Narrative components in most grant proposals include the following:

- Introduction – Optional component that introduces readers to the organization, programs, target population, and community to be served.

- Problem/Need – Persuasively written statement that convinces readers that there is a problem that needs to be resolved and demonstrates a need for funding. Use facts, statistical data, and research results to support the claims made in this section.

- Goals/Objectives – Direction statements that identify project outcomes. Goals are broad outcomes and objectives are smaller stepping-stones to each goal. Goals and objectives should be measurable in terms of participant behaviors and project activities. State what will be done and under what conditions and how the target population will be affected as a result of the proposed activities.

- Methods/Activities – Specific activities and events that will be completed to meet each objective. Activities should describe the who, what, when, and how of the project. A proposal activity/time chart or table is often used to present a schedule of activities for the project duration.

- Evaluation Plans – Evaluation procedures and criteria used to determine project success. This section identifies what information will be measured and how data will be collected and analyzed. Plans should also describe what would be included in reports to the funding agency.

After each proposal draft, reviewers should provide detailed feedback to writers about the strengths and weaknesses of each narrative section. The final proposal draft (including all tables and figures) should be checked for compliance by team leaders and edited for content and style. All grant application assurance and certification forms must be carefully completed and signed by an appropriate administrator as part of the proposal submission package. Details about writing proposal narrative components and completing assurance and certification forms are covered in Chapter 5.

Preparing Budgets

Based on RFP/RFA specifications, prior budget assumptions, and actual cost figures, several budget drafts are prepared, reviewed, and revised to account for all cost items in the proposed project narrative. Proposal budgets should include a breakdown of all direct and indirect costs (unless indirect costs are not allowed).

Direct costs normally include:

- personnel and fringe benefits,

- purchased services,

- supplies and equipment, and

- travel and per diem.

Indirect costs include subtle expenditures such as telephone, utility, and facility maintenance costs. Indirect cost rates are calculated as a percentage of the total direct costs.

Budgets should also show cost sharing contributions (if any) by the grantee to indicate project commitment. Budgets are often presented in a three-column format with the first column presenting the amount requested from the funding agency; the second column presenting cost sharing contributions; and the third column presenting total amounts.

Budget detail and narrative should be included to provide a thorough explanation of cost expenditures. Final budgets must reflect realistic costs sufficient to complete proposed projects within the funding ranges specified in solicitations. Details about preparing proposal budgets are covered in Chapter 6.

Producing, Reproducing, Packaging, and Delivering Proposals

The best written proposal is a winner only if it is produced, reproduced, packaged, and delivered to the funding agency on or before the deadline. Grant application production involves verifying that all proposal sections (e.g., abstract, narrative, budget, assurance and certification forms) and all narrative components (e.g., introduction, problem/need, goals/objectives) identified in the RFP/RFA are included in the grant application. Proposals with missing or out-of-order components may be considered non-compliant. Proposal reproducing involves making the necessary copies for both the funding agency and proposal team members. Quality control checks before and after the grant proposal has been reproduced are vital to ensure a complete and error-free submission. Proposal packaging and delivery must follow exact specifications indicated in the solicitation guidelines. Transmittal letters should accompany grant submissions to funding agencies. Details about producing, reproducing, packaging, and delivering proposals are covered in Chapter 7.

Postsubmission Activities

Immediately after proposal submission, a debriefing meeting should be scheduled with writers and reviewers to discuss the proposal's strengths and weaknesses. In anticipation of questions from the funding agency, proposal team members should determine proposal deficiencies and correct errors.

If the grant is awarded, the proposal director and upper administration should carefully review the notice of award (or contract) before signing and returning it to the funding agency. If funding is not awarded, the proposal director should contact the funding agency representative to ascertain why the proposal was not funded. More details about postsubmission activities are covered in Chapter 8.

Chapter 2 Review

(Chapter 2 Review answers are found on page 211)

Directions: For statements 1 through 10, circle T for True or F for False.

T F   1. Normal time allocated to respond to a solicitation is 60 days.

T F   2. Many organizations fail to receive awards from funding agencies because they wait until RFPs/RFAs are released before starting to develop proposals.

T F   3. A proposal prospectus, compliance checklist, proposal schedule and outline are planning and organizational tools developed prior to writing proposal narrative.

T F   4. Proposal organizational and planning tools should be developed the first day after the RFP/RFA is released.

T F   5. A kickoff meeting is a strategy session where all proposal writers and reviewers meet and discuss writing assignments, budget assumptions, and proposal scheduling.

T F   6. Experienced proposal teams prepare two or three drafts of proposal narrative before the final grant application is edited for content and style.

T F   7. Final budgets should reflect the cost to complete the proposed project within the government agency's funding range.

T F   8. Grant applications with missing components will still be considered compliant by most funding agencies.

T F   9. Quality control checks before and after grant applications have been reproduced are vital to ensure complete and error-free submissions.

T F   10. Debriefing meetings allow writers and reviewers the opportunity to discuss grant proposal strengths and weaknesses and correct deficiencies in anticipation of questions from funding agencies.

Exercise 2-1

Determining Winning Grant Proposal Characteristics

(Exercise 2-1 answers are found on pages 219 - 220)

*Directions: Most winning grant proposals share common attributes. Develop a list of ten winning proposal characteristics based on your background in preparing grant applications. Rank order the importance of each characteristic from most important (1) to least important (10). ***

    1.

    2.

    3.

    4.

    5.

    6.

    7.

    8.

    9.

    10.

* Note: Exercise 2-1 was intentionally placed here to cause readers to think about the characteristics of winning proposals in preparation for what will be discussed in the next chapters. This exercise is most effective as a group discussion activity with three to four participants per group. After 20 to 30 minutes of discussion, one member of each group should provide a brief summary of their group's responses.

Chapter 3

Activities Before the RFP/RFA Is Released

Most institutions are neither prepared nor organized to write grant applications. Seeing a solicitation in the FR for the first time is generally too late to prepare a winning grant application in the time allotted by funding agencies. Therefore, preknowledge about the funding agency, solicitation, competition, and funding available is a requirement. Proposal planning and writing must be done before RFPs or RFAs are released if winning grant submissions are going to be prepared. Winning grant proposals are developed by individuals who understand both the funding agency's *needs* (basic requirements included in the RFP/RFA) and *wants* (what the funding agency would ideally like to see mentioned in a winning proposal). Understanding the needs and wants of funding agencies goes beyond the information included in RFPs/RFAs.

Funding Agency's Needs:
- Include proposal requirements that may not be disclosed until release of the RFP/RFA or may be readily available in previous solicitations or reports.
- Include requirements the funding agency believes most grant seekers will fulfill.
- Reflect the funding agency's mission, goals, and institutional environment.

Funding Agency's Wants:
- Include subtle (read between-the-lines) RFP/RFA elements that could make the difference between a winning or losing proposal.
- Reflect funding agency staff members' interpretation of RFP/RFA guidelines and requirements.

Six months to one year prior to release of the RFP/RFA, funding seekers should: (1) gather intelligence, (2) make a *preliminary bid/no bid decision*, (3) identify a proposal director and team members, (4) identify partners, subcontractors, and/or consultants, (5) develop a "model" solicitation, (6) establish a preliminary budget, (7) create "boilerplate" materials, and (8) write a preliminary proposal draft. **See Exhibit 3-1**.

Exhibit 3-1

Activities Before the RFP/RFA Is Released

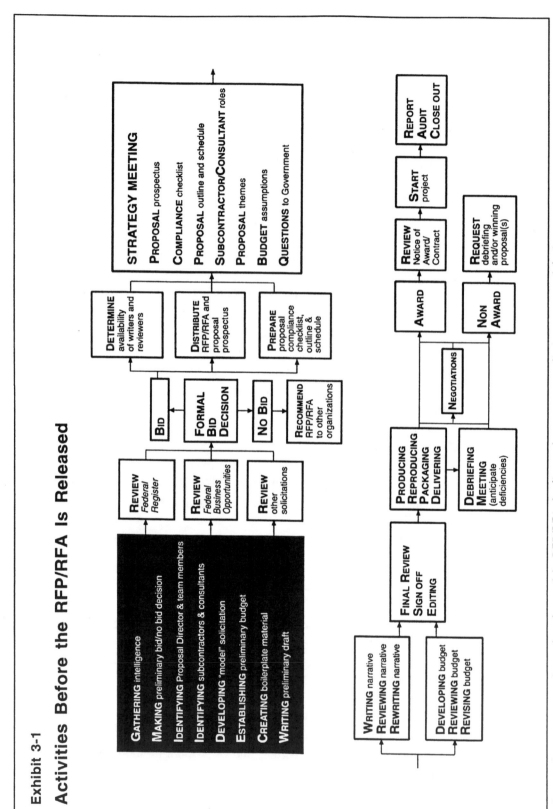

Six months to one year prior to the release of the RFP/RFA, funding seekers prepare preliminary proposal drafts.

Gathering Intelligence

Intelligence-gathering activities conducted prior to release of solicitations are vital to preparing winning grant proposals and help to verify information, build bridges, and establish credibility. Whether you are an individual or part of a large organization, information-gathering activities are essential to successful grant seeking. These pre-solicitation activities include cultivating outside contacts and obtaining relevant information from the: (1) point of contact (POC), (2) past award winners, and (3) funding agency proposal readers.

Point of Contact (POC)

Preknowledge about grant competition is imperative to winning. It is estimated that chances for success go up 300% when proposal directors contact funding sources before the proposal is written (Bauer, 1999). Funding seekers must understand the:

- funding agency's priorities and agenda,
- proposal guidelines and application materials,
- proposal themes to be emphasized (as well as points to be avoided), and
- proposal review process and procedures.

Funding seekers should direct all inquiries about RFPs/RFAs to the POC identified in FR announcements. The POC is the single most important contact you can cultivate in seeking grant funds. POCs are an excellent resource to provide you with recent grant information and guidance. If the RFP/RFA has not been released, the proposal director should contact the funding agency and ask for the name, address and phone number of the POC for upcoming grant competitions.

Before making a face-to-face visit or calling POCs, funding seekers should formulate questions to direct the conversation. Write specific questions that require specific answers; vague questions will invite vague answers. Conversation with POCs should be well prepared, brief, and concise. **See Exhibit 3-2**. Stress your project objectives and ask the following questions:

- Does the proposed project fall within funding priorities?
- What is the total funding available? What is the average award?
- Will awards be made on the basis of special criteria (e.g., geographic region)?
- What is the anticipated application/award ratio?
- What common mistakes have prevented funding seekers from winning?
- What should be in a proposal that other applicants may have overlooked?
- Should the proposal be written for reviewers with nontechnical backgrounds?
- How are proposals reviewed?
- What is the agency's preference for proposal submission?
- Would you review a 2 to 3 page prospectus and/or proposal draft?
- Are there any unsolicited funds to support project ideas?

According to the *Government Performance and Results Act* (GPRA), all federal agencies are required to manage their activities with attention to the consequences of those activities. Each federal agency interprets this statute in different ways to reflect accountability. Consequently, funding seekers should contact the POC to determine what information to include in their grant application in order to comply with the agency's interpretation of the GPRA.

Exhibit 3-2

Telephone Interviews With the Point of Contact

Direct inquiry is one of the most effective ways of acquiring information from funding agencies. Since time is a precious commodity, POCs seldom give face-to-face interviews with potential applicants. If a personal meeting is not possible, try to talk with a POC about your project over the phone. (Note: Some funding agencies may not allow their POCs to conduct one-on-one meetings with prospective applicants.)

Before the Call
- Prepare a list of questions.
- Know the name of the POC with whom you would like to speak.

The Interview
- Introduce yourself, describe succinctly what your responsibilities are within your organization, and state the reason(s) for calling. If you contacted the agency previously, ask for the same individual when calling back.
- Ask the POC for at least ten minutes of their time to ask specific questions about your project plan.
- Do not ask vague questions about the fundability of a project or use the interview time for brainstorming. Rather, briefly outline the benefits of your project and cite statistics to support it. State how project methods will address current needs.
- While you should have conducted research in advance to determine whether or not the project falls within the activities of the funding source, confirm whether the project coincides with the funding source's priorities. If needed, ask for further clarification about the criteria used to evaluate proposals.
- Be sure to take notes of recommended changes to your plan and/or issues clarified by the POC during your discussion.

Follow up
- Make follow-up calls for any future questions. Ask for the same contact. Keep follow-up calls to a minimum as POCs have duties other than answering questions about RFPs/RFAs and proposal submissions.
- Upon contacting a prospective funding source, you may receive a negative response regarding a project concept. React positively. A "no" can lead to as much useful information as a "yes." If the response is negative, ask the POC to explain how or why the project does not meet funding priorities; whether there are any recommended proposal changes to increase the fundability of the proposed project; and whether other areas within the organization might be more appropriate for your project.

The United States Conference of Mayors · Technical Assistance Reports · October, 1996

Grant seekers should formulate questions before contacting funding agency representatives.

At the conclusion of your conversation with the POC, request a list of past award winners and ask for copies of winning grant proposals from prior years. You may be required to pay for postage, duplication cost, and clerical time to reproduce proposal copies; however, these documents may prove invaluable in preparing your grant application. Send a letter that references the *Freedom of Information Act* (FOIA) when requesting copies of winning proposals from non-responsive agency representatives. FOIA is part of the *Administrative Procedures Act* that allows the public to have access to agency records maintained by government agencies. **See Exhibit 3-3.**

Exhibit 3-3

Sample Letter to Request Winning Proposal(s)

April 3, 20XX

Mr. Todd Henson
National School-To-Employment Office
600 Ohio Avenue
Suite 210
Washington, DC 20024   — **Include CFDA Number and Grant Title**

Subject: CFDA #278G – School-To-Work

Dear Mr. Henson: — **Cite FOIA**

In compliance with the Freedom of Information Act, John W. Jones and Associates requests examples of winning proposals for the above-referenced grant. Please invoice John W. Jones and Associates for any costs incurred and send copies to:

   Evelyn Lesniak   —**Where to Send Proposals**
   John W. Jones and Associates
   596 W. Jackson Blvd.
   Chicago, IL 60606

Thank you for your assistance in this matter.

Sincerely,

Evelyn Lesniak   — **Contact Person and Phone Number**
Evelyn Lesniak
Director of Grants and Contracts
312-567-1234

Funding seekers should reference the Freedom of Information Act (FOIA) when requesting copies of winning grant proposals from non-responsive agencies.

Past Award Winners

In addition to contacting the POC, funding seekers should contact several past grant award winners to gather relevant information that may not be available elsewhere. A list of award winners is public information and is available from funding agencies. Before contacting past winners, prepare questions relevant to the proposed development process and grant submission criteria. Specific questions for past award winners might include:

- Did you contact the POC before writing the proposal?
- Who did you find most helpful on the funding agency's staff?
- Did the funding agency's POC review a concept paper or proposal draft prior to final submission?
- What materials did you find most helpful in developing your grant proposal?
- How close was your initial budget to the awarded amount? What budget items, if any, were cut?
- What would you do differently next time?

Funding Agency Proposal Readers

Names and phone numbers of proposal readers are not always available to the general public. If a list of readers is not available, ask the POC to provide general information about the readers (e.g., background, training, and selection process) and describe the proposal review process (e.g., how points were allocated to proposals). Prepare specific questions before contacting readers, such as:

- How did you become a proposal reader?
- Did you follow a particular scoring system?
- What were you told to look for in proposals?
- How many grant proposals were you given to read? How much time were you given to read each proposal?
- What were the most common mistakes you saw in proposal submissions?
- How would you write a grant proposal differently now that you have been a proposal reader?

Making Preliminary Bid/No Bid Decisions

After gathering intelligence from various sources, upper administration/management should make a preliminary decision to submit a grant proposal or to terminate all activity. *Bid/no bid decisions* should be based on whether proposal development team members are able to prepare a winning grant application within the limited time allotted by the funding agency. To make the best decision, funding seekers should consider the following questions:

- Is there time to do data gathering activities prior to release of the solicitation?
- Is there time to formulate a quality project design?
- Is there time for internal proposal reviews?
- Is there time to complete internal and external draft revisions?

A decision to not proceed is correct if you: (1) are not prepared to write a winning proposal, (2) do not have adequate support from administration, or (3) cannot carry out the proposed grant activities. A decision should be based on first-hand information obtained from intelligence gathering activities. Preparing a winning grant proposal demands time and energy. Making a decision to proceed should be based on answers to the following questions:

- Is your organization eligible to apply for this funding? Can your organization meet or exceed the proposed requirements?

- Why is this proposed project important to your organization? Does the proposed project fit within your organization's strategic plan? What will change as a result of receiving funding for this project? How does the project represent an improvement over current practices? What is innovative about this project?

- What will it cost to develop a winning grant proposal? Does your organization have the necessary intellectual workforce available to prepare a proposal within the time limits?

- What are your chances of winning? How many applications are expected from peer institutions and how many awards will be made by the funding agency? Why should the funding agency award your organization the funding?

- Can your organization do the work within the budget range? Are adequate staff members available to complete the proposed grant activities and submit reports to the funding agency in a timely fashion? Can the project sustain itself after the grant funding period?

Ultimately, the decision to go forward with developing a grant proposal is based on knowledge about: (1) the funding agency and their needs and wants, (2) your organization's odds against the competition, and (3) your proposed project's strengths and weaknesses. A bid/no bid decision should be based on whether your organization has a competitive advantage. If the competition can do similar grant work for the same cost, your organization has no competitive advantage. Competitive advantage is determined by identifying features that distinguish you from the competition, identifying benefits derived from these features, and using these benefits in themes throughout the grant proposal.

Identifying the Proposal Director and Team Members

Proposal directors should be identified by upper administration/management as soon as a decision to prepare a grant proposal has been made. Proposal directors must have the experience and time available to guide the grant proposal development effort. In addition, proposal directors should be emerging or demonstrated leaders, who are committed to–and believe in–the proposed topic.

After the proposal director is identified, key team members must be selected to work on the grant proposal. Roles assigned to these team members include writing the narrative, preparing a budget, and/or reviewing the proposal at various stages of development. Proposal writers and reviewers should be content experts who are innovators in their discipline. Financial/budget staff members must be cognizant of contemporary costs associated with the proposed project. Other proposal support members may include an editor, graphic designer, and word-processing and reproduction/mailing staff. The proposal director should brief all team members on major points of the RFP/RFA and provide a rationale about the importance of the proposed project. A cohesive team with a common mission and support from upper administration will lead to a well-developed proposal. **See Exhibit 3-4.**

Using External Grant Writers

When developing grant applications, upper administration must decide if there are internal staff members who have the knowledge and time to develop a proposal or if they need to hire outside grant writers to do the multi-task activities associated with developing a grant submission. There are several pros and cons for using internal staff members versus hiring outside grant writers. Hired grant writers are usually expensive, but will often bring fresh ideas to the proposal development process. Using internal staff members is less expensive, but they may not have the expertise concerning the proposal development process. Upper administration must carefully weigh the pros and cons before making a decision whether to use internal staff members or hire grant writers to develop grant applications. **See Exhibit 3-5.**

Identifying Partners, Subcontractors, and Consultants

Upper administration/management must understand their organization's capabilities and deficiencies when responding to funding agency solicitations. If you are planning to respond to a solicitation and your organization has specific *deficiencies,* you should immediately identify partners, subcontractors, and/or consultants who can fill those voids. *Partners, subcontractors,* and *consultants* should be included only when it enhances your project. Outside subcontractors and consultants must be able to demonstrate successful past performance with similar work and be able to meet deadlines. Formal written teaming agreements should be established with subcontractors and consultants before grant applications are submitted to funding agencies. Within the teaming agreements you should identify the work to be completed, paying attention to roles, expected performance levels, timelines, and financial compensation. At this pre-RFP/RFA stage, subcontractors should submit capability statements, examples of similar past work, and résumés of key staff members who will participate in the proposed grant project. Consultants should submit résumés and brief biographical sketches that highlight past experience with similar projects. Federal and state grants are often looking for applications that include local partners in support of proposed projects. Letters of commitment from these partners should be included in proposal appendices.

Exhibit 3-4

Proposal Development Team Members

Members *	Responsibilities
Upper Administration/ Management	• Read RFP/RFA and make formal bid decision with proposal director • Provide release time for staff members to work on the proposal. • Provide necessary resources for proposal development • Serve as a final reviewer of the proposal • Sign cover letter, cover sheet, and assurance and certification forms
Proposal Director (PD)	• Read RFP/RFA and make formal bid decision with administration • Develop proposal prospectus and compliance checklist • Develop proposal outline and schedule • Chair strategy (kickoff) meeting • Serve as the contact with government agency representatives • Serve as the contact with subcontractors, partners, and consultants • Chair proposal review meetings with writers and reviewers • Serve as a final reviewer of the proposal • Oversee quality control for reproduction, packing, and delivery • Chair debriefing meeting after proposal submission • Respond to questions from the funding agency about the proposal
Writer(s)	• Read RFP/RFA • Write proposal narrative • Rewrite proposal narrative based on feedback from reviewers
Financial/Budget Staff Member(s)	• Read RFP/RFA • Prepare budget based on proposal narrative and RFP/RFA • Redo budget based on feedback from reviewers
Reviewer(s)	• Read RFP/RFA • Review proposal narrative and budget • Provide feedback to writers and budget staff members
Editor(s)	• Read RFP/RFA • Develop proposal style sheet • Review proposal narrative for style and consistency • Edit/rewrite proposal narrative • Serve as a final reviewer of the proposal
Graphic Designer(s)	• Develop proposal tables, figures, charts, and illustrations • Review overall design and layout of proposal
Partner(s), Consultant(s), and Subcontractor(s)	• Provide proposal narrative and budget expenditures • Provide support documents (e.g., résumés)
Word Processing Staff Member(s)	• Assemble proposal narrative and budget • Type cover sheet, assurance and certification forms • Prepare shipping label(s) for proposal package(s)
Reproduction/Mailing Staff Member(s)	• Reproduce sufficient copies of proposal • Package proposal copies • Ship proposal copies to funding agency

* Teams often have members who play multiple roles. In some cases, only a few people develop a proposal.

Proposal development team members must have expertise and time to prepare winning proposals.

Exhibit 3-5

Using Internal Staff Members Versus External Grant Writers

Pros / Cons	Internal Staff Members	External Grant Writers
Pros	Using internal staff members is an inexpensive way to develop grant applications.	External grant writers bring a fresh perspective to the proposed project and usually have a thorough understanding of the grant development process and what it takes to win.
	Internal staff members will be responsible for completing the daily activities identified in the proposed project, if the grant is awarded.	External grant writers develop proposals without interrupting the daily duties of staff members.
Cons	Internal staff members may have a limited understanding about the grant development process and are often naive about what it takes to win.	External grant writers are usually expensive. Some grant writers charge a flat fee while others charge a percentage of the total award.
	Grant development activities take time away from staff members to perform their daily duties.	External grant writers will not be responsible for completing the daily activities identified in the proposed project, if the grant is awarded.

Upper administration must weigh the pros and cons before hiring external grant writers.

Developing "Model" Solicitations

Information obtained during the intelligence gathering activities coupled with an analysis of similar RFPs/RFAs from the same agency usually yield sufficient information to develop a *model grant solicitation*. Depending on annual changes, the model solicitation may include 60% or more of the same information included in RFPs/RFAs yet to be released. In some instances, very few changes are made to RFPs/RFAs from year-to-year. If this is the case, last year's grant solicitation announcement will serve as an accurate guide to developing a proposal draft prior to the RFP/RFA release. Never wait until RFPs/RFAs are released to prepare proposal drafts. Sound intelligence gathering practices usually provide sufficient information to prepare preliminary grant proposal drafts.

Creating Boilerplate Materials

Boilerplate materials include well-written narrative and budget materials that are used and reused to prepare grant proposals. Boilerplate materials often provide writers with an excellent starting point, however, these materials must not be thought of as final proposal documents. Rather, these materials must be customized to meet the funding agency's needs and wants (specified in the RFP/RFA) in order to be effective. Well-developed boilerplate files must be organized and categorized. Examples of organized proposal boilerplate materials are presented below.

Introduction
- Mission and purpose statements
- Organization's strategic plan with implications for the proposed project
- Organizational fact sheet that includes current demographic data
- Biographical information about the organization's board of directors/trustees
- Annual reports (financial report, etc.)
- Organization's prior experience with grant-funded projects

Problem/Need
- Reports from surveys, community forums, and case studies that document current problems that will be addressed as a result of grant funding
- Supportive data from state and federal legislators, universities, community agencies, professional organizations, crisis centers, chambers of commerce, and planning commissions

Goals/Objectives
- Goals/Objectives from approved proposals completed by your organization
- Goals/Objectives from approved proposals completed by other organizations

Methodology/Activities
- Various time/task and project organizational charts
- Description of data-gathering instruments used in similar projects
- List of organizational resources that support your project

Evaluation Plans
- Successful evaluation strategies used in similar winning grant proposals
- Names and résumés of project evaluators
- Examples of projects successfully evaluated in the past

Budget
- List of components included in your institution's fringe benefits package
- Indirect cost rate used with similar grant applications (including the cost rate agreement)
- Overall operating budget for the organization
- Similar grant budgets developed at your institution

Appendices
- Assurance and certification forms from similar grant submissions
- Model letters of support from partners, subcontractors, and consultants
- Résumés of key staff members who worked on prior grant projects
- List of similar grant projects
- Organizational charts of upper administration/management and where the proposed project would fit within the organization
- Membership list of the organization's board of directors/trustees
- Annual reports

Writing Preliminary Proposal Drafts

Preliminary proposal drafts are developed prior to the release of RFPs/RFAs using "model" solicitations and information obtained from intelligence gathering activities. Most grant proposals include the following narrative requirements: (1) abstract, (2) problem/need, (3) goals/objectives, (4) methodology/activities, and (5) evaluation plans. Preliminary proposal drafts should follow model solicitation guidelines, address proposal evaluation criteria, and provide information that is easy for the reader to locate. Simple language that communicates clearly to the intended audience is the best. Write to express, not impress.

Grant writers should submit proposals that inform funding agencies about their organization and the services it will provide in response to RFPs/RFAs. Evidence of past experiences demonstrating similar work done well and on time should be included. In addition, the proposal's tone should emphasize a commitment to the project by all involved. Proposals should persuade funding agency readers that your organization could address the needs (requirements) and wants of funding agencies. Remember, proposal competition is fundamentally an essay contest through which you must show that your project is better than those of other funding seekers. As such, proposals must describe the benefits of awarding funding to you rather than the competition.

Preparing Preliminary Budgets

Once previous RFPs/RFAs from the funding agency and proposals from past award recipients have been obtained, *preliminary budgets* should be developed. Budgets should provide an estimate of costs associated with proposed activities to be completed during the performance period. It is helpful to consider the following advice for getting started: "If you have a difficult time writing a grant proposal, one should start with the budget. Assume that the funding agency just sent your organization a check to complete the proposed grant project. Now, think about how you are going to spend the money." Preliminary budgets can be determined after direct expenditures are categorized into common cost areas such as personnel, fringe benefits, purchased services, supplies and equipment, and travel. Indirect costs and cost sharing (institutional commitment) contributions are also tentatively determined at this preliminary stage. See Chapter 6 for more information on preparing budgets.

Chapter 3 Review

(Chapter 3 Review answers are found on page 211)

Directions: For statements 1 through 10, circle T for True or F for False.

T F 1. Most institutions are neither prepared nor organized to write grant proposals due to lack of planning.

T F 2. Proposal planning and writing should be done before RFPs/RFAs are released.

T F 3. Funding agency "wants" are basic requirements found in the RFP/RFA.

T F 4. Intelligence-gathering activities involve obtaining information from past grant award winners.

T F 5. Questions should be formulated before talking with prospective funding agency representatives, past award winners, and funding agency proposal readers so discussions are well directed.

T F 6. Before making a preliminary decision to submit a grant application, a key consideration should take into account "if the proposal development team has sufficient time to develop a winning proposal."

T F 7. Teaming agreements should be established with subcontractors, partners, and/or consultants after the grant application is submitted for funding.

T F 8. Model solicitations are prepared by funding agencies prior to release of RFPs/RFAs.

T F 9. Preliminary proposal drafts should be developed before RFPs/RFAs are released.

T F 10. A preliminary budget should be developed before RFPs/RFAs are released using information from previous solicitations and proposals from past award recipients.

Exercise 3-1

Planning Activities Before the Solicitation's Release

(Exercise 3-1 answers are found on page 221 - 222)

Directions: Describe the planning activities you would complete to identify and prepare for appropriate grant funding opportunities.

Chapter 4

Prewriting Activities After the RFP/RFA Is Released

With increasing competition for grant funds, prewriting activities are an essential prerequisite if funding seekers plan to be successful. Novice funding seekers often do not take the time to plan before responding to government solicitations, typically resulting in mediocre proposals with little chance of winning.

Prewriting activities after the RFP/RFA is released involve: (1) reviewing the solicitation and obtaining necessary clarification, (2) making a formal bid/no bid decision, (3) developing a proposal prospectus, (4) developing a compliance checklist, (5) preparing a proposal outline and schedule, and (6) holding a strategy meeting with proposal development team members. **See Exhibit 4-1**.

Prewriting activities must be completed prior to writing proposal narrative and preparing budgets. The adage "plan your work and work your plan" accurately describes this critical phase of the proposal development process.

Typically, prewriting activities involve three days of preparation and planning before development of grant proposals. **See Exhibit 4-2**. Day one involves analyzing the RFP/RFA and making a formal bid/no bid decision. Day two is focused on developing planning tools (e.g., outline, schedule) necessary to guide writers and reviewers in preparing grant applications. During this period, the proposal director, in conjunction with institutional administrators, establishes proposal directives that provide guidance regarding how the project would fit within the institution's mission. Day three involves holding a strategy session with writers and reviewers. During this meeting, the proposal director describes the overall purpose of the RFP/RFA with potential impact for the institution. In addition, the proposal director assigns writing tasks, discusses budget assumptions, and presents a schedule for writing, reviewing, editing, and delivering the proposal.

Exhibit 4-1

Prewriting Activities After the RFP/RFA Is Released

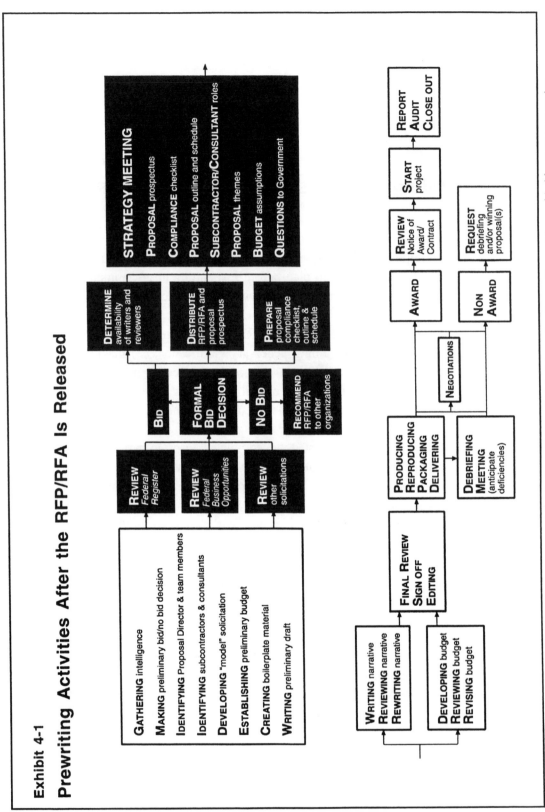

GATHERING intelligence

MAKING preliminary bid/no bid decision

IDENTIFYING Proposal Director & team members

IDENTIFYING subcontractors & consultants

DEVELOPING "model" solicitation

ESTABLISHING preliminary budget

CREATING boilerplate material

WRITING preliminary draft

REVIEW Federal Register

REVIEW Federal Business Opportunities

REVIEW other solicitations

BID

FORMAL BID DECISION

NO BID

RECOMMEND RFP/RFA to other organizations

DETERMINE availability of writers and reviewers

DISTRIBUTE RFP/RFA and proposal prospectus

PREPARE proposal compliance checklist, outline & schedule

STRATEGY MEETING

PROPOSAL prospectus

COMPLIANCE checklist

PROPOSAL outline and schedule

SUBCONTRACTOR/CONSULTANT roles

PROPOSAL themes

BUDGET assumptions

QUESTIONS to Government

WRITING narrative
REVIEWING narrative
REWRITING narrative

DEVELOPING budget
REVIEWING budget
REVISING budget

FINAL REVIEW SIGN OFF EDITING

PRODUCING REPRODUCING PACKAGING DELIVERING

DEBRIEFING MEETING (anticipate deficiencies)

NEGOTIATIONS

AWARD

NON AWARD

REVIEW Notice of Award/Contract

REQUEST debriefing and/or winning proposal(s)

START project

REPORT AUDIT CLOSE OUT

After the release of the RFP/RFA, funding seekers should make formal bid/no bid decisions, develop writing guides and hold a strategy meeting.

Exhibit 4-2

Three Days After Release of the RFP/RFA

Day 1
- Analyze RFP/RFA immediately (e.g., eligibility, criteria, due date)
- Identify ambiguities and request clarification
- Adjust/re-evaluate estimated probability of winning
- Make formal bid/no bid decision

Day 2
- Prepare a compliance checklist
- Prepare a proposal prospectus
- Prepare a proposal outline with specific writing assignments
- Adjust/redefine budget
- Adjust/redefine proposal schedule

Day 3
- Hold proposal strategy meeting with writers and reviewers
- Present compliance checklist and proposal prospectus
- Assign writing tasks
- Discuss budget assumptions
- Schedule proposal review dates
- Schedule editing, reproduction, and delivery of proposal

Typically, prewriting activities involve three days of decision making, preparation, and planning before proposal writing and budget development.

Reviewing Solicitations and Obtaining Necessary Clarification

A careful review of major RFP/RFA sections should be completed before a formal bid decision is made. The first issue to consider before spending time developing a grant proposal is whether your organization is eligible to apply for funding. Some government agencies limit eligibility to selected organizations (e.g., state education agencies), organizations that serve only a particular population or group (e.g., K-12 students), or organizations that meet other criteria.

Proposal directors should analyze the entire grant solicitation and determine whether key information is different from what was anticipated. Careful review of RFPs/RFAs will often lead to questions that must be answered before formal bid/no bid decisions are made. Proposal directors should ask the POC to clarify any incomplete or unclear information found in solicitations. Since time is a precious commodity, face-to-face meetings are often difficult to arrange with POCs. If personal meetings are not possible, try to obtain RFP/RFA clarification from the POC over the telephone or send written questions by fax or e-mail.

As in the pre-proposal interview, questions should be formulated before placing calls to funding agencies. Always identify the solicitation by the RFP/RFA number and title when requesting to speak to funding agency POCs.

Provide your name, position, and organization. Then ask your questions, referencing specific pages from the solicitation when applicable. Take thorough notes and communicate the information gained from conversations with the POC to all proposal writers and reviewers. Use follow-up calls to resolve future questions and always speak with the same POC. In addition, funding seekers should always attend *pre-proposal conferences* held by funding agencies to discuss RFP/RFA requirements.

Making Formal Bid/No Bid Decisions

Based on the RFP/RFA and information provided by the POC, formal bid/no bid decisions should be made in conjunction with administration/management. Bid/no bid decisions are usually based on answers to the following questions:

- Is this project consistent with the organization's mission statement and goals?
- Is the organization qualified to complete the proposed project in a timely manner?
- Are cost sharing funds available to support this project?
- Is there commitment by the organization beyond the funding period?

Bid decisions should be based on the: (1) estimated value of the proposed work, (2) estimated effort in terms of *person hours* and cost to develop the proposal, (3) probable competition, (4) major strengths and weaknesses of the institution in response to this funding opportunity, (5) arguments for and against bidding, and (6) estimated probability of winning. This information, coupled with the organization's readiness and support from upper administration, forms the basis for a smart bid decision. Institutions not in a good position to write a winning grant proposal might be better off waiting for later competitions or looking for teaming (consortium) partners who are in a better position to win. **See Exhibit 4-3**.

Determining Availability of Proposal Writers and Reviewers

If an organization decides to develop a grant proposal in response to an RFP/RFA, the first activity is to reaffirm the availability of staff members to serve as writers and reviewers. Upper administration must support this effort by providing time and support services to complete the proposal development process. Grant proposals should not be developed without administrative support. Ideal proposal teams include a *proposal director*, *writers*, *reviewers*, and *support staff members* (see Exhibit 3-4 in Chapter 3). Proposal directors provide leadership and guidance in completing proposals. Writers and reviewers must be interested in the proposed topic, have a proven record of delivering quality written documents, and be able to meet deadlines. Grant proposal success demands committed leadership, creative staff members, clear assignments, persuasive writing, realistic budgeting, quality and schedule controls, and upper administrative support.

Exhibit 4-3

Bid Decision Form

Estimated $ Value of Grant:

Estimated Effort (Person Hours/$ to Develop the Proposal):

Probable Competition:

Major Strengths of Institution/Organization:

Major Weaknesses of Institution/Organization:

Arguments Pro:

Arguments Con:

Estimated Win Probability:

Funding seekers use bid decision forms to make go/no go proposal development decisions.

Developing a Proposal Prospectus

A proposal prospectus, used to develop basic ideas before writing begins, is an organizational writing tool that requires prospective applicants to think about questions associated with most proposal components: (1) problem/need, (2) goals/objectives, (3) methods/activities, (4) evaluation plans, and (5) estimated costs. **See Exhibit 4-4**.

Exhibit 4-4

Proposal Prospectus

Directions: A proposal prospectus is a brief summary of project ideas. It is an important tool in designing the project before you begin to write. The prospectus communicates project plans to administrators, staff, and/or funding agency representatives in an effort to locate appropriate funding sources. Answer the questions below as they relate to the proposed project. Use this prospectus as a guide in writing the proposal.

Project Title (What is a brief descriptive title of the proposed project?)

Problem/Need (Why does this project need to be done? What problems will this project attempt to eradicate? What evidence (data, reports, or trends) is available to support the need for this project?)

Goals/Objectives (What are the overall goals of this project? Are the objectives specific and measurable? Can the objectives be evaluated at the end of the project?)

Exhibit 4-4 continues on the next page

Exhibit 4-4 (Continued)

Proposal Prospectus

Methods/Activities   (How will objectives be accomplished?   What is the plan of action for the proposed project? What resources will be used?)

Evaluation Plans (How will project accomplishments be evaluated?)

Estimated Cost (Approximately how much will this project cost? Where will most of the cost be incurred – personnel, instructional materials, equipment?)

A proposal prospectus provides an overview of the proposed project.

Developing Compliance Checklists and/or Work Breakdown Structures

Based on a thorough analysis of grant solicitations, proposal directors should develop compliance checklists as a basis for generating proposal content and organization. *Compliance checklists* identify every "shall" and "must" requirement in RFPs/RFAs. Identifying grant RFP/RFA requirements involves a careful reading of each RFP/RFA sentence. Compliance checklist requirements should be written as action statements (e.g., develop a plan of action) and identify the page location within the RFP/RFA. Compliance checklists should specifically address proposal requirements, format, and limitations.

Work breakdown structures (WBS) are a hierarchical analysis of RFP/RFA requirements into basic components. Work breakdown structures provide an understanding of the underlying nature of the funding agency's needs as well as the relationships among RFP/RFA parts.

Preparing Proposal Outlines

Proposal outlines correspond with RFP/RFA requirements and identify proposal authors. Outlines should always include the RFP/RFA number, title, distribution date, annotated RFP/RFA sections, and list of appendix materials. A good outline serves as a road map for developing proposals. It should: (1) use clear, concise, and descriptive headings, (2) be numbered sequentially, (3) follow a logical order, and (4) progress from simple to complex. Three levels of headings are generally used to develop proposal outlines:

- level 1 headings are major content areas,
- level 2 headings are subdivisions of level 1 headings, and
- level 3 headings are subdivisions of level 2 headings. **See Exhibit 4-5**.

If a proposal outline is provided in the RFP/RFA, follow it exactly. Do not leave anything up to the funding agency reader's imagination. However, do not include extraneous information. Also note what the RFP/RFA prohibits from being included in the grant application.

Preparing Proposal Schedules

A carefully planned schedule is an essential element in developing proposals. Poor scheduling is a common mistake by beginning funding seekers. Proposal schedules must allow sufficient time for writing and rewriting as well as budgeting and rebudgeting. Schedules must also allow time to obtain materials from partners, subcontractors, and/or consultants, as well as time for editing, producing, reproducing, and delivering the proposal to the funding agency. Proposal schedules should identify proposal activities to be accomplished within a specific timeframe and include a list of all writers, reviewers, and support staff members involved in the proposal development process. A good technique to develop proposal schedules is to determine the proposal due date and work backward to estimate the time needed to complete writing and reviewing of each draft. **See Exhibit 4-6**.

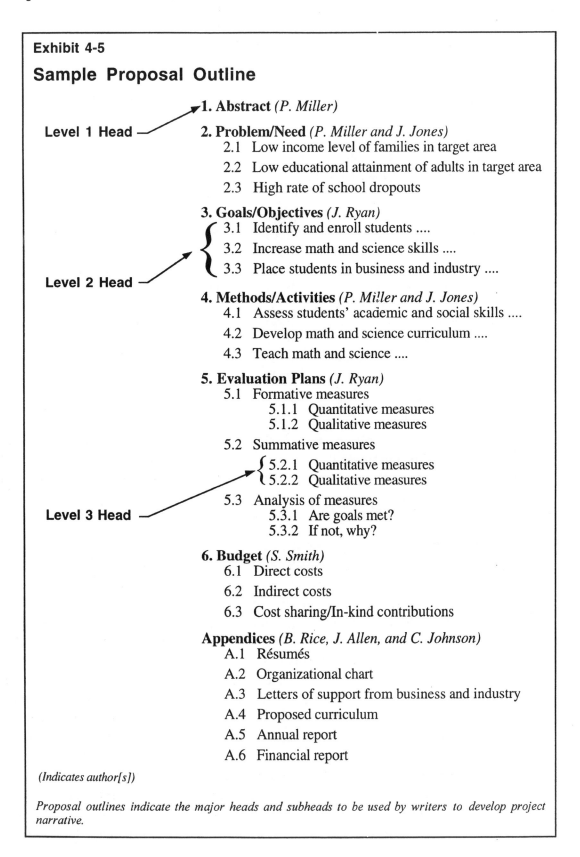

Exhibit 4-5

Sample Proposal Outline

1. Abstract *(P. Miller)*

Level 1 Head ⟶

2. Problem/Need *(P. Miller and J. Jones)*
  2.1 Low income level of families in target area
  2.2 Low educational attainment of adults in target area
  2.3 High rate of school dropouts

3. Goals/Objectives *(J. Ryan)*
  3.1 Identify and enroll students ....
  3.2 Increase math and science skills ....
  3.3 Place students in business and industry ....

Level 2 Head ⟶

4. Methods/Activities *(P. Miller and J. Jones)*
  4.1 Assess students' academic and social skills ....
  4.2 Develop math and science curriculum ....
  4.3 Teach math and science ....

5. Evaluation Plans *(J. Ryan)*
  5.1 Formative measures
        5.1.1 Quantitative measures
        5.1.2 Qualitative measures
  5.2 Summative measures
        5.2.1 Quantitative measures
        5.2.2 Qualitative measures
  5.3 Analysis of measures
        5.3.1 Are goals met?
        5.3.2 If not, why?

Level 3 Head ⟶

6. Budget *(S. Smith)*
  6.1 Direct costs
  6.2 Indirect costs
  6.3 Cost sharing/In-kind contributions

Appendices *(B. Rice, J. Allen, and C. Johnson)*
  A.1 Résumés
  A.2 Organizational chart
  A.3 Letters of support from business and industry
  A.4 Proposed curriculum
  A.5 Annual report
  A.6 Financial report

(Indicates author[s])

Proposal outlines indicate the major heads and subheads to be used by writers to develop project narrative.

Exhibit 4-6

Sample Proposal Schedule

Distribution: September 16, 20XX
Agency: U.S. Department of Education
CFDA #:   84.024A
Issue date: September 15, 20XX
Due date: October 15, 20XX

Tentative Schedule

Activity	Date	Time	Place or Person
Strategy (kickoff) meeting	9/18	10:00 a.m.	Conference room 210 *
1st draft to reviewers	9/24	5:00 p.m.	Johnson
Reviewers' meeting	9/26	11:00 a.m.	Conference room 210 *
2nd draft to reviewers	10/5	5:00 p.m.	Johnson
Reviewers' meeting	10/8	1:00 p.m.	Conference room 210 *
Final draft to edit/production	10/11	flow basis	Johnson
Final draft to reproduction	10/13	1:00 p.m.	Johnson and Rice
To Department of Education	10/13	5:00 p.m.	Miller and Johnson
Proposal due	10/15	4:00 p.m.	

Writers
Jones, Miller,[1] Ryan, Smith

* All writers and reviewers must attend.

Reviewers
Baker,[2] Kraft, Miller,[2] Peters, Ryan,[2] White

Support Staff Members
Rice, Allen, Johnson

[1] Proposal director
[2] Final proposal review member

Proposal schedules identify activities to be accomplished within a specific timeframe.

Holding Strategy (Kickoff) Meetings

Three days after receipt of the RFP/RFA a strategy meeting should be held with all writers and reviewers. Strategy meetings serve as both a serious working session and pep rally. Proposal directors should distribute relevant materials (RFP/RFA, outline, schedule, etc.) prior to the strategy meeting so team members have sufficient time to review them and come to the meeting with questions and comments. During this meeting, proposal directors provide an overview of the strategies/themes to be used in the proposal narrative and lead a discussion concerning budget assumptions associated with the proposed project based on the prospectus and compliance checklist. Proposal directors also use this meeting time to discuss specific proposal writing assignments and due dates for proposal drafts identified in the schedule.

During the strategy meeting, proposal directors should provide information about partners, subcontractors, and/or consultants (if used), and their roles and responsibilities. Questions about the RFP/RFA are collected by the proposal director and submitted to the funding agency for answers. Grant writing and budget development must start immediately after the strategy meeting. Appendix materials such as résumés, letters of commitment, and other support documents should be collected and assembled by support staff members.

Proposal writers usually have writing styles that vary and thus the final proposal will have numerous stylistic inconsistencies. All writers, reviewers, and editors should follow a style sheet in preparing proposal sections. *Style sheets* present guidelines for document formatting, naming conventions, headings, tables, and other style information. If no format is recommended in the RFP/RFA, a style sheet developed in the early phases of the proposal will save considerable time and effort in the final stages of proposal preparation. **See Exhibit 4-7**.

Exhibit 4-7

Sample Style Sheet

Title: Early Childhood Longitudinal Study–Kindergarten Cohort
Use this style sheet in conjunction with the proposal outline. Writers must use Microsoft Word for all narrative to eliminate formatting differences when sections are combined.

Naming Conventions
The official name of the proposal is indicated above; it is abbreviated "ECLS-K." The federal sponsor is the Department of Education, National Center for Education Statistics. Use the abbreviation "NCES/ED" for the sponsor.

Specific Jargon
In referring to school grades, please use "grade 1... grade 5," but "first grader" or "first grade students" (no hyphen). Note that "kindergarten" is not capitalized; use "kindergarten student" rather than "kindergartner;" "preschool student" rather than "preschooler." Note that Head Start is two words, both capitalized. State and local education agencies may be referred to as "SEAs" and "LEAs."

Headings
Section heads should be centered (e.g., "3. Methodology"). All other heads should be "flush-left heads." Three levels of flush-left heads may be used in addition to the section head. Additional heads should be treated as "run-in heads." See below.

3. Methodology
[centered section head—14 pt. Helvetica Bold]

3.1 Project Initiation and Planning
[flush left, first-level head—12 pt. Helvetica Bold]

3.1.1 Meeting with NCES/ED
[flush left, second-level head—11 pt. Helvetica Bold]

3.1.1.1 Provide Agenda
[flush left, third-level head—11 pt. Helvetica Bold Italic]

Proposal style sheets present guidelines that writers and editors follow in developing proposal narrative.

Chapter 4 Review

(Chapter 4 Review answers are found on page 211)

Directions: For statements 1 through 10, circle T for True or F for False.

T F   1. Prewriting activities are essential prerequisites to winning grant funding.

T F   2. Formal bid decisions should be made before RFPs/RFAs are released.

T F   3. Typically, prewriting activities involve ten days of preparation and planning.

T F   4. The first issue to consider before spending time developing a proposal is whether your organization is eligible to apply for funding.

T F   5. A proposal prospectus is a planning tool used to develop basic ideas before project writing.

T F   6. Compliance checklists involve developing a list of requirements from grant solicitations that are used as guides in developing proposals.

T F   7. Proposal outlines correspond with RFP/RFA requirements and identify proposal authors.

T F   8. Carefully planned schedules are essential to developing proposals.

T F   9. Strategy (kickoff) meetings are held with writers and reviewers to discuss proposal development activities.

T F   10. Style sheets provide formatting guidelines that writers, reviewers, and editors follow in preparing proposals.

Exercise 4-1

Preparing Compliance Checklists

(Exercise 4-1 answers are found on pages 223 - 225)

Directions: Read solicitation OJP-92-R-008 Drug Use Forecasting Program found on pages 62 to 65 and complete the compliance checklist form found on page 66.

Situation: You are serving as a proposal director. One of your responsibilities is to review the following solicitation excerpts and create a comprehensive compliance checklist to guide writers in completing the proposal narrative.

To create a compliance checklist, you must read "Section L: Special Information for Developing Proposals."   Look for "shall" and "must" statements to identify requirements.

On the "Compliance Checklist" form (page 66) list every task the writers must address. In the left-hand column, under the heading "Requirements," describe each task briefly, from the writer's perspective.   Use an action statement, such as "List management personnel by name, title, and projected percentage of time" (not simply "personnel list"). Be as specific as possible. In the right-hand column, under the heading "RFP Location," indicate the section in which you found each requirement.

Be sure to include all requirements identified in the solicitation. Remember that missing requirements may make the difference between a winning or losing proposal.

Exercise 4-1 continues on the next page

Exercise 4-1

Preparing Compliance Checklists

Solicitation OJP-92-R-008: Drug Use Forecasting Program Synopsis

The National Institute of Justice (NIJ) requests proposals in response to three tasks required by the Drug Use Forecasting (DUF) Program:

Task 1 – Rapid and high quality editing, entry, preparation, and maintenance of data from DUF interviews and urine specimens available from 24 cities.

Task 2 – Publication of scheduled reports and special-purpose analytical monographs, which are accurate and timely and meet high editorial and graphic standards.

Task 3 – Consistent and attentive procedural training at all local DUF sites as well as technical assistance to local criminal justice agencies interested in DUF methodology.

Section L: Special Information for Developing Proposals

L-12. Technical Proposal Preparation

A. The term of the contract will comprise one base year and three one-year options.

B. The proposal should be structured to accommodate all requirements and the evaluation criteria.

C. In the proposal, the offeror shall describe how work set forth in this proposal will be carried out.

D. The offeror shall submit a background statement stating its experience and qualifications to perform the resultant contract. The offeror shall include résumés of all principal staff and consultants involved in data entry, data analysis, data preparation, editing of text, technical editing, and graphic design under this RFP as well as the primary contact for inquiries relating to contract compliance issues. The offeror shall include technical qualifications, such as current duties, education, and experience.

E. The offeror shall list private and government clients with whom they recently (within the last three years) have had contracts. The references will be contacted as part of the evaluation of offerors. The offeror shall provide the following information: name and number of contract, name of client, address, telephone number, and contact person.

F. The offeror shall describe in detail the quality control procedures that will be followed in accomplishing the work set forth in this RFP, including data entry, data preparation, data editing, site training, technical editing, and graphics.

G. With the technical proposal, the offeror shall include a detailed management and staffing plan, including the hours or percentage of time for each individual and/or position identified.

H. The offeror shall list all equipment that will be used in accomplishing the work set forth in the RFP.

Exercise 4-1 continues on the next page

I. Suggestions for Preparation
  1. After a thorough analysis of Section C: Statement of Work, to assure a complete understanding of the background and the scope of work to be performed, the offeror shall present a plan to accomplish the objectives. This section should demonstrate an understanding of the pertinent problems involved and methods of overcoming them. The technical proposal should be presented in a clear and concise manner to assist in the evaluation effort.
  2. The offeror should address each of the specific tasks contained in Section C, specifying methodology/approach for accomplishing and indicating number of person hours estimated for each task. (Note: person hours for each task should also be indicated in the cost proposal). Offerors should provide their approach to each task, including the necessary procedures, formats, and designs to indicate how they will meet the requirements of and manage the tasks listed in Section C.

L-13 Special Requirements
  A. Task 1: Data Editing, Entry, Preparation, and Maintenance

  1. Offerors should know that the DUF interview instrument will change over time.

  2. Offerors are required to show their expertise in using SPSS or SPSSPC and show their ability to modify data entry programs and log programs, which will be provided by the National Institute of Justice (NIJ) as needed.

  3. Offerors shall describe procedures to ensure quality and shall demonstrate experience in maintaining data integrity during data entry of interviews, multi-source data merging, and data reporting. Offerors are encouraged to identify other problems which may occur in completing tasks specified in this RFP and to recommend procedures to prevent or resolve them.

  a. The DUF program involves data collection in booking facilities from diverse sites with changing local staff. Data are continually being generated and submitted to the contractor. Given the realities of urban booking center operations, instructions provided to DUF site personnel regarding data collection and editing may not always be followed exactly. The offeror must show an understanding and mastery of the complex practical issues involved in organizing, tracking, processing, and reporting results from a national multi-site data collection program.

  b. Offerors must demonstrate successful implementation of quality control measures and availability of personnel to respond to diverse quality control issues. Offerors shall propose procedures for attaining the following goals and cite recent experience in successfully accomplishing similar goals on projects involving collection of data from multiple independent sites:

  (1) ensure that the total number of interviews per gender/age group received from a site is processed;

  (2) ensure that all interview data are reported;

  (3) ensure that the total number of specimen results received from the laboratory is processed;

  (4) ensure that the total number of specimen results received from the laboratory is reported;

  (5) ensure that data are reported separately for each site and each quarter;

  (6) ensure that data are reported separately for each gender/age group;

  (7) ensure that all data are entered accurately;

Exercise 4-1 continues on the next page

(8) ensure contract compliance with schedules outlined in this RFP;

(9) ensure confidentiality of site results;

(10) ensure confidentiality of DUF data, e.g., DUF data can not be released without written approval;

(11) ensure accuracy in matching interview data and urine data when merging files; and

(12) ensure that data sets are free from errors for all files, e.g., data files, system files and merged files.

B. Task 2: Publication of Special Reports

1. Quality control issues

Offerors are required to respond to the quality control issues described in this RFP concerning editing, graphics, and layouts of DUF publications. Offerors may suggest other layouts, which may improve the publication. Offerors may also suggest problems, which may occur in the publication tasks specified in this RFP and propose solutions or procedures to prevent them.

2. Graphics and presentation of data

a. Offerors should propose new graphics in their proposals for NIJ review.

b. Offerors shall propose procedures to ensure a high-quality presentation of data. Also, offerors shall demonstrate experience in accurately representing quantitative data and shall provide points of contact for substantiation.

3. Publication

a. DUF data are published annually and quarterly in the National Institute of Health's *Research In Brief* series (RIB). Special analyses of DUF research findings are also published in monographs. For purposes of this RFP, offerors should assume two monograph publications per year, averaging 16 pages each. (Copies of the RIBs and monographs may be viewed in the Office of Justice Programs (OJP) reading room or may be ordered from the Contracting Officer.) The offerors must demonstrate an understanding of the issues involved in publishing results from a national program under tight time schedules.

b. Offerors must demonstrate experience in graphic design, editing, and report development. Offerors must further demonstrate that sufficient quality control measures are in place and that personnel are available to respond to diverse quality control issues. Offerors shall propose procedures for attaining the following goals and cite recent experience in successfully accomplishing similar goals on projects involving quantitative information for publication:

(1) ensure that the data received from NIJ are accurately transposed into graphic layouts;

(2) ensure that all materials are presented according to NIJ specifications;

(3) ensure that data presented in tables, graphs, or charts are consistent with corresponding text;

(4) ensure that a final review of the entire publication is conducted with emphasis on accuracy within the publication;

(5) ensure compliance with respect to timelines set out in this RFP; and

(6) ensure confidentiality of data until publication is released.

Exercise 4-1 continues on the next page

   C. Task 3: Procedural Training

      1. For purposes of this proposal, offerors should assume four trips per year to provide technical assistance. Trips dedicated to technical assistance are in addition to the 12 DUF site visits.

      2. Offerors are encouraged to submit samples of weekly reports and monthly reports with their technical proposals. Also, offerors should provide a modified sample of the quarterly report along with their technical proposals. A sample financial report should be submitted with the technical proposal.

      3. Offerors are required to demonstrate their capability to accomplish subitems A (meet with the Contracting Office Technical Representative in Washington on regular basis and sometimes at short notice) and B (identify and enter into an agreement with a pool of consultants to provide a number of diverse tasks) of the Special Requirements.

L-14 Management Portion of Technical Proposal

   A. The management proposal should set forth all relevant information concerning the offeror's ability to run and effectively manage a project of this type, including a detailed discussion of its experience and familiarity in this subject area. Description of the offeror's managerial staff, along with résumés of each of the staff members shall also be submitted. It should also demonstrate the degree of importance that offerors attach to projects of this nature.

   B. Organizational Structure proposed should be included as part of the Management Proposal.

   C. Résumés of key personnel to be employed on this contract must be included.

Exercise 4-1 continues on the next page

Exercise 4-1 (Continued)

Preparing Compliance Checklists

Compliance Checklist Form

Requirements	RFP Location

Note: Reproduce this compliance checklist form if more space is needed.

Exercise 4-2

Developing Proposal Outlines and Schedules

(Exercise 4-2 answers are found on pages 226 - 227)

Directions: Read the memorandum and RFP from the State Community College Board (pages 68 through 72) and develop a proposal outline and schedule. Assume that you have 30 days to prepare the proposal.

Proposal Outline

Develop a proposal outline that:

- corresponds with solicitation requirements,
- includes major proposal sections and proposed authors, and
- lists appendix materials.

Proposal Schedule *

Develop a proposal schedule that:

- allows sufficient time for proposal writing and budget preparation;
- identifies writers, reviewers, and support staff members; and
- allows time for reviewing, editing, producing, reproducing, and delivering the proposal to the funding agency.

---

* *Note: A good way to develop a schedule is to determine the due date and work backwards, estimating the time needed to complete the writing and reviewing of each proposal draft.*

Exercise 4-2 continues on the next page

State Community College Board
401 East Highway Road
Capital City, IN 58765-1234

Memorandum

Date: March 15, 20XX

To: Community College Presidents

From: Dr. Jean E. Thomas, Chief Financial Officer

Subject: State Community College Board Special Initiatives Grants

The State Community College Board (SCCB) received an appropriation for a new special initiative grant program. Since the State will be facing a critical shortage of qualified workers in the field of Information Technology (IT), $300,000 in grant funds will be dedicated to support innovative programs designed to increase the number of Information Technology (IT) professionals graduating or receiving certification from community colleges. To address this need, SCCB is conducting a competitive Request for Proposal (RFP) to fund 8 to 10 projects with budgets of $25,000 to $50,000. Attached is the RFP for the special initiative. Proposals are due April 15, 20XX. Grant awards will be made in June. The period of performance is July 1 through June 30. If you have questions, please do not hesitate to contact me at jthomas@sccb.org.

Exercise 4-2 continues on the next page

Innovative Programs to Increase Information Technology Graduates
Request for Proposal (RFP)

Background/Purpose

In the next fiscal year, the State Community College Board (SCCB) will support innovative programs designed to increase the number of Information Technology (IT) professionals graduating or receiving certification from state community colleges. Funds will be awarded to support the development and implementation of programs to: (1) increase high school students' awareness of career opportunities in IT, and (2) increase the number of high school graduates who enroll in IT programs at the postsecondary level.

Proposed high school/college linkages should be designed to support the development and implementation of new programs or enhance and expand existing programs in the IT field that: (1) begin with the junior year of high school and move through a certificate or AAS degree, and (2) provide students with connections to workplace experiences. Proposals must include at least one high school partner and at least one business partner. The following article may contain several helpful suggestions concerning IT:

> Meares, C.A. & Sargent, Jr., J.F. (20XX). *The Digital Work Force:*
> *Building Infotech Skills at the Speed of Innovation.* Washington, DC:
> U.S. Department of Commerce Office of Technology Policy.

Each college applicant is required to contribute a cash match of 25% of the amount requested from SCCB. For example, if an application is for a $40,000 grant, the college must contribute a cash match of $10,000. Consortia of two or more colleges are encouraged to apply.

Application Requirements

Grant applications should include a detailed description of project activities and costs. Include the following information in the application package (note the weighted value of each component in brackets):
- Application and Project Abstract (5 points)
- Problem/Need (25 points)
- Project Leadership and Partners (25 points)
- Goals/Objectives, Project Activities, and Timeline (35 points)
- Budget (10 points)

Exercise 4-2 continues on the next page

Selection Criteria
- Strategies and activities designed to accomplish the proposed objectives
- Replicability of outcomes at other community colleges
- Broad impact on the information technology area
- Financial viability of the budget

Application Submittal

Proposal narrative should be no more than five typewritten pages. A complete grant application must include a proposed budget. Narrative may be developed to supplement and detail budget items.

Each community college district is eligible to submit one grant application. Colleges are encouraged to work together to assist in achieving the broadest impact of the proposed program.

Please mail six copies of the application to:
State Community College Board
Attn: Dr. Jean E. Thomas, CFO
401 East Highway Road
Capital City, IN 58765-1234

Applications must be received no later than 4:00 p.m. CST on April 15, 20XX. Questions should be directed to Dr. Jean E. Thomas at jthomas@sccb.org.

Exercise 4-2 continues on the next page

Special Initiative Grant
Application and Project Abstract

Name of college:

Contact person:

Office address:

Telephone:

Fax:

e-mail:

Descriptive title of application:

Abstract (no more than 200 words):

Exercise 4-2 continues on the next page

Special Initiative Grant
Budget

Name of college:

CEO name:

CEO signature:

Line Item and Description	Grant Funds	Matching Funds	Total Amount
Salaries:			
_____	___	___	___
_____	___	___	___
_____	___	___	___
_____	___	___	___
Employee benefits:			
_____	___	___	___
_____	___	___	___
_____	___	___	___
_____	___	___	___
Contractual services:			
_____	___	___	___
_____	___	___	___
_____	___	___	___
Supplies and materials:			
_____	___	___	___
_____	___	___	___
_____	___	___	___
Conference and meetings:			
_____	___	___	___
_____	___	___	___
_____	___	___	___
Capital outlay:			
_____	___	___	___
_____	___	___	___
_____	___	___	___
Total:	___	___	___

Chapter 5

Writing, Reviewing, Rewriting, and Editing Narrative

Writing, reviewing, rewriting, and editing several drafts of the narrative before a final proposal is submitted to a funding agency is key to having a winning grant proposal. Grant proposals are only as good as the effort invested. Government agencies receive far more good proposals than they can fund. A well thought out and succinct grant proposal will always have the best chance to win.

Writing Narrative

Winning grant writers must possess subject-matter knowledge, writing skills, analytical and creative expertise, and marketing savvy. If one (or more) of these attributes is missing, it will be evident in the final grant submission.

In addition to skills, grant writers must have a place to write, tools for writing, and time to write. The place to write must be a comfortable atmosphere that is away from distractions. Disruptions from the telephone, co-workers, and sales people will hinder grant proposal writing. Grant writers must get away from daily activities and focus on writing tasks. Tools for writing include the RFP/RFA, winning grant proposals from similar competitions, the proposal prospectus, and the proposal outline. Other necessary aids include a dictionary and thesaurus, computer, tape recorder, calculator, paper, pencils, sticky notes, and highlighters. Finally, grant writers must have reasonable goals. Grant authors should not expect to write a proposal in one sitting. Authors should block out specific time for writing. Reasonable expectations for each writing session will ensure a well-written proposal. The key is to not procrastinate, but to keep a consistent writing schedule until the grant application is finished. **See Exhibit 5-1**.

Experienced grant writers: (1) follow RFP/RFA guidelines, (2) read examples of past winning grant proposals prior to writing, and (3) use an outline that organizes thoughts and captures the RFP/RFA evaluation criteria. When developing the first proposal draft, grant writers should write ideas quickly without worrying about style. Grammar and syntax can be improved later. **See Exhibit 5-2**.

Exhibit 5-1

Writing, Reviewing, Rewriting, and Editing Narrative

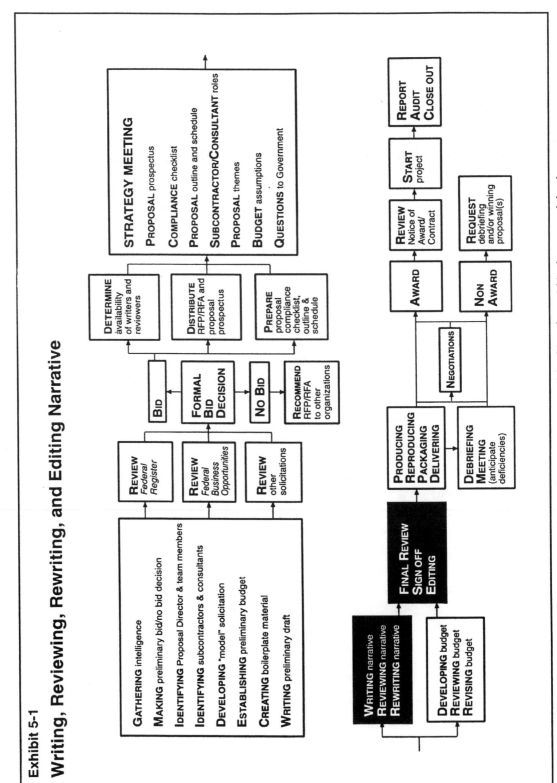

Writing, reviewing, rewriting, and editing proposal narrative consumes most of the thirty days within the proposal development process.

Exhibit 5-2

Guidelines for Writing Proposals

Follow RFP/RFA Guidelines/Read Other Proposals
- Read the complete RFP/RFA and provide exactly what is required
- Read and reread all grant application forms–follow directions
- Read the proposal evaluation criteria to be used by funding agency readers
- Read examples of prior winning grant proposals

Develop Proposal Organizational Tools
- Develop a proposal compliance checklist
- Develop a proposal prospectus
- Develop an annotated proposal outline with organizational heads and subheads

Write Proposal Narrative
- Write text that follows an outline and proposal prospectus
- In case of writer's block, insert "??" in the text and keep on writing–use the computer search command to locate missing ideas and write text at a later time
- Use place holders for graphics, tables, and figures
- Write to inform, not to impress–use concise and accurate language
- Use lists when appropriate
  - Steps in sequence
  - Materials or parts needed
  - Items to remember
  - Criteria for evaluation
  - Conclusions and recommendations

Ask for Feedback from Colleagues
- Content expert
- Style expert

Experienced grant writers follow RFP/RFA guidelines, develop organizational tools, write several proposal drafts, and seek feedback from content and style experts.

When completing proposal drafts, grant writers should strive to develop a project idea that presents proposal themes and benefits in an easy-to-read format. All grant writers should adhere to the four "Cs" of proposal writing: content, communication, commitment, and consistency. Specifically, grant writers should:

- have a thorough understanding of the proposed project *content*,
- *communicate* information to the reading audience,
- *commit* to completing the grant writing tasks within a specified time, and
- be *consistent* with format and presentation of information.

Proposal writers must: (1) aim for clarity of thought and expression, (2) specify clear objectives, and (3) provide a detailed description of project activities. Grant seekers always have burden of proof and must *demonstrate* how the solicitation criteria will be met. It is essential to follow RFP/RFA directions and provide exactly what is required. Experienced grant seekers keep their writing clear, factual, supportable, and professional. Well-written grant proposals include concise writing with short words, short sentences, and short paragraphs to avoid unnecessary verbiage and reduce reader fatigue. In addition, graphics should be used to illustrate key proposal concepts.

Writing must be as specific as possible and substantiate all claims with measurable data (e.g., "the proposal director has 23 years of experience overseeing 55 projects" rather than "the proposal director has overseen numerous projects"). Grant writers should avoid subjective adjectives (e.g., "unique," "state-of-the-art"), since they usually do not communicate new information. Finally, grant writers must always write for the audience (funding agency readers). **See Exhibit 5-3**.

Exhibit 5-3

Tips to Improve Writing

Know what you want to say. Plan your message carefully and state it as succinctly as possible.

Outline. Start with an outline that includes major and minor points to be addressed in the proposal.

Be clear and concise. Don't use more words than necessary. Good writing means using words your audience will understand.

Use the active voice. Say, "We serve 350 people..." not, "A total of some 350 people were served..." The active voice is more forceful and easier to follow.

Be specific and vivid. The most effective writing paints a picture of the situation. It's better to show a particular family struggling to find safe, affordable childcare than to use vague language and figures. Statistics are important, but it's also important to "put faces on the numbers."

Know your audience. Funding agency readers almost never know as much about your subject as you do. Modify your message to fit the specific audience.

Experienced proposal writers plan their message for a specific audience.

All proposals require persuasive writing to produce convincing narrative that will positively influence funding agency readers. Proposal narrative sections must always consider the reading audience and thoroughly describe the who, what, where, and how of the proposed project.

Some narrative sections can be adapted from boilerplate materials while other sections must be written fresh for each proposal. In either case, all narrative sections must adapt the message to meet the needs and wants of the funding agency.

Although each proposal will be unique, there are basic sections that are standard to most grant proposals. Most funding agencies require some form of grant narrative sections listed below:

- Abstract
- Introduction (optional)
- Problem/Need
- Goals/Objectives
- Methods/Activities
- Evaluation plans
- Appendices (optional)

Abstract

Abstracts represent the first impression of your organization and as such must educate agency readers about you, your organization, and your proposed ideas. Abstracts are cogent summaries of proposed projects. Most abstracts are brief statements of 500 words or less that highlight the features and benefit of major proposal components (e.g., problem/need, goals/objectives, methods/activities, evaluation plans, and costs) and cause agency reviewers to want to read further. Abstracts are usually the proposal opening but often the last section written by funding seekers. Proposal abstracts must be carefully checked and rechecked by a style editor to ensure that every sentence has meaning.

Introduction (Optional)

Grant *introductions* are used to introduce agency readers to your organization, programs, target population, and community to be served. Funding agencies may require introduction information as a separate section or may require this information in problem/need statements. In either case, the introduction should clearly describe the local or regional area and how the institution's professional and organizational qualifications relate to the proposed grant project.

Grant application introductions should use up-to-date information that provides descriptive detail about the community to be served. Illustrations should be used whenever possible to make information stand out and break up the monotony of straight text. Regional areas to be served are often presented in map-form supplemented by demographic information. **See Exhibit 5-4**. Introductions also identify the institution's mission and goals, establish institutional eligibility, provide evidence of previous accomplishments, set the context for the proposed project, and lead logically to the problem/need statement.

Exhibit 5-4

Sample Community/Region Map

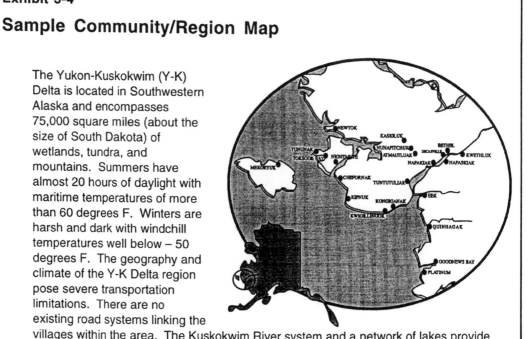

The Yukon-Kuskokwim (Y-K) Delta is located in Southwestern Alaska and encompasses 75,000 square miles (about the size of South Dakota) of wetlands, tundra, and mountains. Summers have almost 20 hours of daylight with maritime temperatures of more than 60 degrees F. Winters are harsh and dark with windchill temperatures well below – 50 degrees F. The geography and climate of the Y-K Delta region pose severe transportation limitations. There are no existing road systems linking the villages within the area. The Kuskokwim River system and a network of lakes provide links between villages by boat in summer and by snow machines, trucks, or all-terrain vehicles along rivers and their tributaries after freezing.

Experienced funding seekers use regional or community maps to identify the area to be served.

Proposal introductions should paint vivid pictures about the target population in the minds of agency readers. Textboxes are often used in proposal introductions to present brief snapshots of the community, organization, and/or target population. Textboxes should include up-to-date information supported by relevant statistics to grab the funding agency reader's attention. **See Exhibit 5-5**.

Exhibit 5-5

Sample Textbox Used to Describe Target Population

Anytown State College (ASC) was established in 1960 and the Nursing Department began instruction in 1966. ASC's student population is culturally diverse with 45 percent African American or Hispanic. The nursing program is also culturally diverse with 46 percent African American or Hispanic. The college's

Anytown State College Fall, 20XX	
ASC Students	**ASC Nursing Students**
• 4,792 total students	• 112 nursing students
• Mean age 29; Median age 24	• Mean age 30; Median age 30
• 60% female; 40% male	• 93% female; 7% male
• 55% Caucasian	• 54% Caucasian
• 34% African American	• 38% African American
• 11% Hispanic	• 8% Hispanic

economic strata is equally diverse. ASC's district spans from the impoverished community of City Heights (one of the poorest communities in the United States) to fairly affluent communities of Wright Fields and Richville. Twelve percent of students receive PELL grants.

Textboxes are used in proposal introductions to highlight key points about the population to be served.

Problem/Need

Problem/need statements are persuasively written essays that convince readers a problem exists that must be solved. Problem/need statements must establish the significance (importance) of the problem and identify the population to be affected by the proposed project. Specifically, problem/need statements should:

- document a need that relates directly to the funding agency's interest,
- identify a problem of reasonable size that can be solved,
- describe a problem/need within a context, and
- provide a vision for solving the problem.

Problem/need statements should avoid the use of "lack of" or the "need for" in the problem/need description. Because there is a "lack of" or "need for" goods or services does not necessarily provide a justification for them. **See Exhibit 5-6**.

Problem/need statements should be supported by recent (within the last three years) and relevant information (e.g., census, local, and community data). Facts, statistical data, and research results are often used to demonstrate need for funding a project that will correct or reduce a problem in a reasonable period of time. Collect contemporary comparative information from local, state, and federal documents to support problem/need statements. **See Exhibit 5-7**.

Exhibit 5-6

Bad and Good Problem/Need Statements

Bad Problem/Need
Lack of adequate equipment and facilities to support students in mathematics classes.

Good Problem/Need
Thirty percent of students fail key mathematics courses.

Avoid problem/need statements that only declare the problem as "the lack of" or "the need for."

Exhibit 5-7

Problem/Need Supported by Recent Information

Low-Income Families in Northern Plains Below Poverty Level			
Target Area	Families	Number of Low-Income Families	% of Low-Income Families
Banks County	13,928	5,181	37.2%
Franklin County	10,514	4,825	45.9%
Henry County	16,953	6,577	38.8%
Lake County	5,814	2,674	46.0%
Martin County	18,218	7,287	40.0%
Pitts County	12,931	5,883	45.5%
Russ County	4,025	1,720	42.7%
Totals/%	**82,383**	**34,147**	**42.3%**
State	**1,847,796**	**537,708**	**29.1%**

Source: U.S. Census Bureau, 20XX

Recent and relevant information should be used to support the problem/need statement.

Graphics (pie charts, bar charts, etc.) should be used to illustrate statistical comparison information and drive home key points to funding agency readers. Remember that the major purpose of problem/need statements is to convince readers that a problem exists and grant funds are necessary to provide a solution. Finally, problem/need statements should serve as a foundation for the project's goals/objectives, methods/activities, and evaluation plans. **See Exhibit 5-8.**

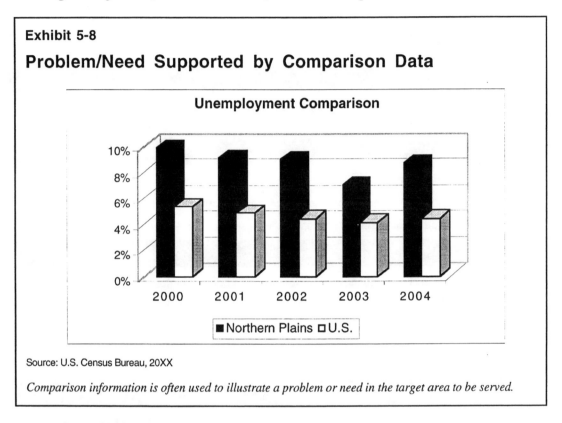

Exhibit 5-8

Problem/Need Supported by Comparison Data

Unemployment Comparison

■ Northern Plains □ U.S.

Source: U.S. Census Bureau, 20XX

Comparison information is often used to illustrate a problem or need in the target area to be served.

Goals/Objectives

Goals/objectives are the intellectual heart of grant applications and provide direction for proposed projects. Goals/objectives should directly relate to the funding agency's wants and needs. Goals (ultimate) are broad outcomes and objectives (intermediate) are smaller stepping-stones to each goal. Each goal should have several objectives and flow logically from the problem/need statement. Note that some agencies do not make a distinction between goals and objectives and use the same term to refer to both.

Goals/objectives form a basis for sequencing project activities and identify project outcomes within a timeframe. Goals/objectives indicate what will be done, under what conditions, and how the target population will be affected as a result of the proposed activities. In addition, goals/objectives provide a premise for evaluating project success. **See Exhibit 5-9.**

Exhibit 5-9

Sample Goal/Objectives Stemming From Problem/Need

Problem/Need

According to the Information Technology Association of America, more than 840,000 Information Technology (IT) jobs have gone unfilled this past year. There is a virtual explosion of IT job opportunities; however many local high school students are not prepared for these jobs (Roberts, 20XX).

Goal

Increase high school students' awareness of IT career opportunities throughout the district.

Objectives

- Recruit 150 high school students to enroll in IT programs.

- Provide 100 high school students with a core curriculum in computer networking.

- Provide 50 high school students with workplace experiences.

Activities

- Develop IT marketing program to inform and recruit high school students.

- Develop IT courses for high school students that articulate with college-level courses.

- Send instructors to training workshops in preparation for IT courses.

- Schedule workplace visitations and job shadowing for high school students at local businesses.

Evaluation Plans

- Assess the IT marketing program to inform and recruit students. For example:
  - 500 brochures, 10 press releases, and 4 newspaper ads were developed.
  - Three IT informational meetings were held for students and parents at local schools.

- Assess the IT courses developed for high school students. For example:
  - Objectives and daily activities were developed for each course.
  - Textbooks and lab manuals for courses were purchased.

- Determine the number of instructors who attended IT training workshops.

- Determine the number of high school students enrolled in IT courses and the number of students who were provided IT workplace experiences at local businesses.

Timeframe

- January 1, 20XX to December 31, 20XX.

Goals/objectives form a basis for sequencing project activities and identify project outcomes within a timeframe.

Good project objectives are:

- clear and concise statements listed in chronological order of achievement,
- measurable in quantitative terms,
- manageable, ambitious, but attainable (i.e., do you have time and needed resources to accomplish the objectives?), and
- practical and cost effective. **See Exhibit 5-10**.

Do not include extra objectives in the RFP/RFA. If you receive the grant, you will be held accountable for these extra objectives, which will create additional work and make your overall objectives more difficult to achieve.

Exhibit 5-10

Sample Project Objective

Objective	Relates to Problem/Need	Measurable	Ambitious, but Attainable
Assist target area participants so that 60% of all high school graduates will undertake a program of post-secondary education.	Only 45% percent of high school graduates in the target area currently undertake a program of postsecondary education, and only 34% of these graduate with a four-year degree. This objective seeks to improve the situation by encouraging more students to undertake a program of postsecondary education.	Specific number of target area adults undertaking a program of postsecondary education is quantifiable and can be measured by graduates self-reporting as well as college registrar reports.	The objective is ambitious because is seeks to increase the number of high school graduates undertaking a program of postsecondary education by 15%, which represents a substantial increase. The objective is attainable because the program will use a variety of proven workshops, informational videos, and speakers, as well as experienced college counselors to encourage students to undertake a program of postsecondary education.

Objectives must tie directly to the problem/need and be measurable and ambitious, but attainable.

Methods/Activities

Proposal *methods/activities* describe specific tasks required to meet project goals and objectives. Methods/activities are *project means* to meet the objectives/goals (*project ends*). Proposal methods/activities should provide a clear, logical, and detailed description of project activities and events to be completed within the performance period. **See Exhibit 5-11**.

Exhibit 5-11

Sample Project Methods/Activities Chart

Anytown State College's Project Implementation Activities

<u>Objective</u>: To identify and serve at least 1,000 participants each year of the project

Activities/Methods	Staff Member(s)	Time Schedule	Resources
Recruit prospective participants by implementing a comprehensive marketing campaign.	Project Director Coordinator	Monthly	<u>Community</u> • Community agencies • Local businesses • Local civic organizations • Local church groups • Recreation centers • Secondary schools • Postsecondary schools • Veteran groups • Employment services <u>College</u> • Public relations office • Communications group • Foundations office • Mailing/duplication center • College newspaper <u>Local Public Relations</u> • Radio and television • Local newspapers
Distribute audio and video public service message via television and radio stations in the target area.	Project Director	Monthly	
Distribute brochures to businesses and community groups throughout the target area with contact information about outreach activities.	Project Director Coordinator	On-going	
Contact postsecondary institutions in the target area to promote services and request referrals.	Project Director	Monthly	
Contact secondary schools in the target area to promote services and request referrals.	Project Director Coordinator	Monthly	
Contact community agencies in the target area to promote services and request referrals.	Project Director Coordinator	On-going	

Proposed project activities should be directly tied to objectives and identify staff members responsible for completing tasks.

Time and task charts, flow charts, and diagrams are often used to summarize, illustrate, and sequence the "who," "what," "when," and "how" of activities within the workplan. These charts are also used to help readers visualize full implementation of the proposed project. Activities should be reasonable so that they can be completed with available project resources and within the funding agency's deadline. **See Exhibit 5-12**.

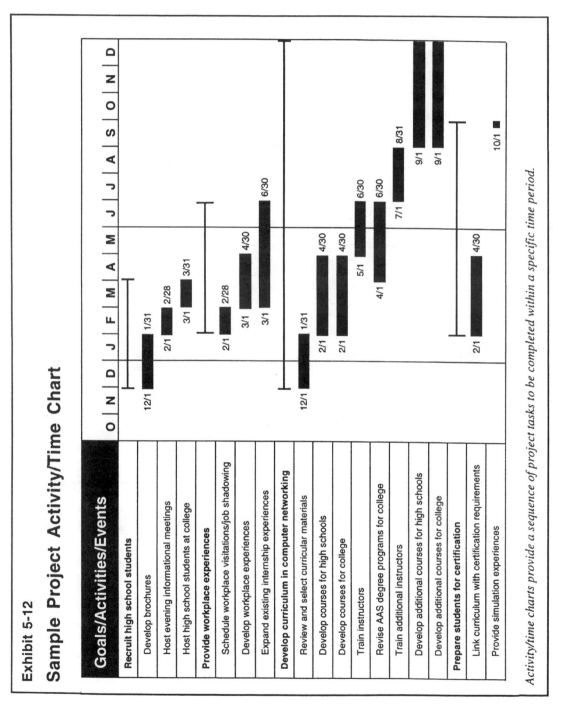

Exhibit 5-12

Sample Project Activity/Time Chart

Goals/Activities/Events	O	N	D	J	F	M	A	M	J	J	A	S	O	N	D
Recruit high school students															
Develop brochures		12/1		1/31											
Host evening informational meetings				2/1	2/28										
Host high school students at college					3/1	3/31									
Provide workplace experiences															
Schedule workplace visitations/job shadowing				2/1	2/28										
Develop workplace experiences					3/1		4/30								
Expand existing internship experiences					3/1				6/30						
Develop curriculum in computer networking															
Review and select curricular materials		12/1		1/31											
Develop courses for high schools				2/1			4/30								
Develop courses for college				2/1			4/30								
Train instructors						5/1		6/30							
Revise AAS degree programs for college						4/1		6/30							
Train additional instructors									7/1	8/31					
Develop additional courses for high schools										9/1					
Develop additional courses for college										9/1					
Prepare students for certification															
Link curriculum with certification requirements				2/1			4/30								
Provide simulation experiences										10/1					

Activity/time charts provide a sequence of project tasks to be completed within a specific time period.

Methods/activities should describe key personnel to be used in the project as well as indicating their reporting lines of authority within the organization. Funding agencies prefer to see project directors with prior grant management experience and close ties to upper management in the organizational chart. **See Exhibit 5-13**. It is also helpful to include an organizational chart that describes the project team's organization as well as the specific name, role, and time commitments of all key personnel who will be involved in the project. This grant application section must demonstrate that the proposed project team has the skills and experience necessary to deliver a successful project. **See Exhibit 5-14**.

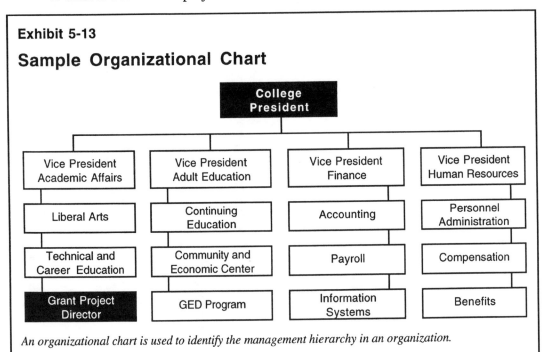

Exhibit 5-13
Sample Organizational Chart

An organizational chart is used to identify the management hierarchy in an organization.

Exhibit 5-14

Sample Time Commitments of Key Project Personnel

Name	Project Position	Time Commitment
John Schmidt	Project Director	100%
Bruce Wilson	Education Specialist	100%
Sharon Shields	Counseling Director	100%
Linda Black	Site Coordinator for Area 1	50%
Joyce Weather	Site Coordinator for Area 2	50%
Gregory Steinz	Financial Manager	25%

Charts should be used to indicate the name, position, and time commitments of all key personnel in the proposed project.

Specific information about the duties and responsibilities of the *Project Director* (PD) or *Principal Investigator* (PI) (the person who will manage the project) and other key personnel should be discussed in detail. Since a large portion of the budget is often used to support personnel, the applicant should present an overview of the qualifications, prior grant experience, and education of key personnel in the project narrative and provide résumés of all personnel in the appendix. **See Exhibit 5-15**. *Job descriptions* should include a comprehensive presentation of duties and responsibilities required of key personnel to be hired for the proposed project. All job descriptions should include minimum and preferred qualifications concerning education and experience. To save space, job description summaries are included in the narrative and complete descriptions are placed in the appendix. All job descriptions should reference the *American Disabilities Act* (ADA) and *Equal Opportunity Employer* (EOE) compliance statements. Remember that funding agency readers want to support carefully planned projects led by experienced project directors and personnel who will expend grant funds in an appropriate manner to ensure a successful project. **See Exhibit 5-16**.

Exhibit 5-15

Sample Qualifications of Proposed Project Staff

Position	Education		Relevant Experience
Project Director (or Principal Investigator)	M.S. M.S. B.S.	Administration Counseling Counseling	14 years as an administrator 7 years as a counselor 8 years as a grant director
Education Director	M.S. B.S.	Education Education	4 years as an administrator 10 years as a teacher 5 years as a counselor
Counseling Director	M.A. B.A.	Counseling Liberal Arts	6 years as a counseling director 5 years as a site coordinator 6 years as a counselor
Site Coordinator #1	M.A. B.A.	Divinity Liberal Arts	10 years as a site coordinator 12 years as a social worker 5 years as a high school teacher
Site Coordinator #2	M.A. B.A.	Counseling Psychology	5 years as a site coordinator 16 years as a counselor 3 years as a high school teacher
Site Coordinator #3	M.A. B.A.	Education Sociology	4 years as a site coordinator 2 years as a state social worker 3 years as a high school teacher

Education and experience of key personnel should be presented in the methods section of proposals.

Exhibit 5-16

Sample Job Description Used to Hire Personnel

Title: Systems Analyst

Classification: Administrative Staff

Supervisor: Director of Administrative Computing

Position Summary

The Systems Analyst is responsible for assisting the Director of Administrative Computing in the design and implementation of the digital achievement portfolio.

Duties and Responsibilities

- Develop interface between digital achievement portfolio and local area network.
- Work with college committees and the Director of Administrative Computing to identify and select software for the achievement portfolio development project.
- Develop a digital achievement portfolio model for implementation.
- Develop, test, and implement a fully operational digital achievement portfolio with digitized data and audio elements.
- Identify, purchase, develop, and test a prototype system for digitized video storage and retrieval that can become part of the achievement portfolio.
- Maintain the security and reliability of all data in the achievement portfolio.
- Perform system administration tasks, provide technical assistance to users, monitor system security, and conduct other duties as assigned.

Required Qualifications

Bachelor's degree in computer systems analysis or related field, minimum of three years experience in a client/server network environment, and knowledge in database/multimedia application development.

Job descriptions should present specific duties and responsibilities required of personnel to be hired for proposed projects.

Evaluation Plans

Evaluation plans describe procedures to measure success of grant projects. These plans must: (1) identify qualifications of individuals or organizations responsible for evaluation, (2) demonstrate appropriate evaluation procedures for project objectives, (3) describe data gathering instruments and methods used to collect and analyze information, and (4) describe information to be supplied in funding agency reports. Strong evaluation plans use quantifiable methods to measure project success. Organizations may choose to conduct internal or external project evaluations. If you use an external evaluator, be sure to check the individual's prior experiences and establish a clear agreement about responsibilities and project deadlines. Also make sure the cost for the external evaluator's services are in line with the overall budget.
See Exhibit 5-17.

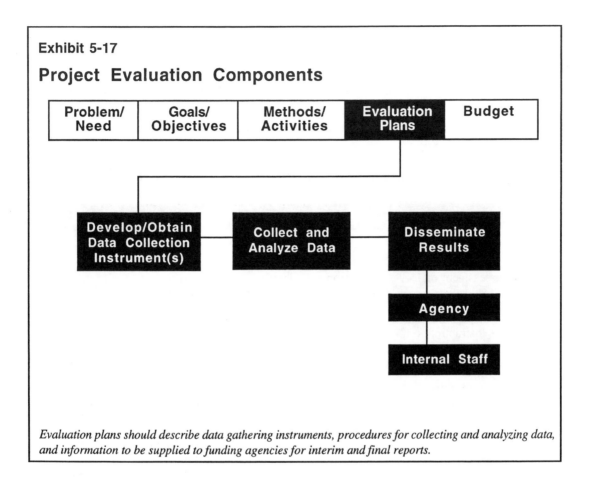

Exhibit 5-17

Project Evaluation Components

Problem/ Need	Goals/ Objectives	Methods/ Activities	Evaluation Plans	Budget

Develop/Obtain Data Collection Instrument(s)	Collect and Analyze Data	Disseminate Results

Agency

Internal Staff

Evaluation plans should describe data gathering instruments, procedures for collecting and analyzing data, and information to be supplied to funding agencies for interim and final reports.

Evaluation plans make decisions about the quality, effectiveness, and value of grant projects. The two forms of evaluation used in most grant applications are formative and summative. *Formative* evaluation is concerned with monitoring the ongoing progress of grant projects. Formative evaluations provide monthly or quarterly reports about: (1) meeting project objectives, (2) completing project activities, (3) measuring participants' progress, and (4) assessing project staff members' performance. Through these formative evaluations, modifications to project activities are made to ensure that project outcomes will be met. *Summative* evaluation is concerned with judging the impact (overall quality or worth) of a grant program at end of the project. Summative evaluation activities should provide qualitative and quantitative information that is directly tied to project goals and objectives. Summative evaluation reports are prepared using formative information (e.g., monthly reports) and follow-up data from project participants. Quantifiable data obtained from evaluation plans are used to describe project success in reports sent to funding agencies.

Proposed project overviews are often summarized in textboxes to provide a "snapshot" of the major narrative grant proposal components (problem/need, goals/objectives, methods/activities, and evaluation plans).   Textboxes should especially be used when proposals are limited to a specific number of pages. **See Exhibits 5-18 and 5-19**.

Exhibit 5-18

Major Narrative Components in Most Grant Proposals

Problem/Need	Goals/Objectives	Methods/Activities	Evaluation Plans
Provide a needs assessment of: • students, • faculty, • institution, and • instruction. Use information from: • test results, • questionnaires, • records/reports, • observations, • literature, and • experts. Describe the need and how the project will correct or reduce the problem. Provide a rationale for the project. Number all problem/need statements.	Provide project direction and detail how problems will be resolved. Must be: • specific, • measurable, • sequential, and • quantifiable. Must show knowledge, skills, or attitudes to be acquired. Must be responsive to the funding agency's wants and needs. Multiple objectives must be written for each goal. Number goals/ objectives to correspond with problem/need statements.	Represent the means to achieve project objectives. Indicate the who, what, where, when, and how of the project. Describe what will be done and provide detailed information about: • staff/consultants, • equipment/supplies, • facilities, and • travel. Include a timetable and indicate what is done and by whom. Indicate staff time to be spent on the project. Number methods/ activities to correspond with problem/need statements and goals/objectives.	Present performance evaluation measures. Show extent of progress made in meeting objectives. Use data to demonstrate what has been achieved. Assessment is: • formative, • summative, • process, or • product. Indicate how the project will continue after grant funds end. Number evaluation plans to correspond with problem/need statements, goals/ objectives, and methods/activities.

Project overviews are used in proposals to provide a "snapshot" of major grant components.

Exhibit 5-19

Sample Grant Proposal Narrative Components

Year	Problem/Need	Goals/Objectives	Methods/Activities	Evaluation Plans
1	1 Limited community based knowledge and experience of faculty	1 Enhance faculty's community based knowledge and experience	1a Host workshops for college faculty and others 1b Attend regional/ national conferences 1c Visit community based clinical sites	1a Evaluate workshops through participants' feedback 1b Present reports of conferences by faculty 1c Present reports of visits by faculty
	2 Limited community based curriculum	2 Establish a strong thread of community based nursing	2 Revise curriculum and instructional materials	2 Reflect strong community based nursing tread across the curriculum in syllabus
	3 Incomplete knowledge of needed services	3 Identify health/ wellness needs of the college community	3 Conduct needs analysis of desired services	3 Prioritize needed services
2	4 No hands-on community based experiences for students	4 Provide students with hands-on experiences in community based nursing	4 Develop student/ faculty rotation plan	4 Assess implementation of student/faculty rotation
	5 No on-campus source of wellness/ health promotion	5 Provide wellness services for college and community	5a Establish and equip wellness center 5b Develop record keeping and documentation 5c Establish collaborative relationships 5d Implement wellness center project	5a Complete renovation and receive equipment 5b Evaluate records and documentation protocols 5c Analyze feedback from collaborative projects 5d Evaluate client satisfaction survey results, monthly report of clients served, and student clinical competencies

Textboxes summarize the problem/need, goals/objectives, methods/activities, and evaluation plans in a two-year grant application.

Appendices (optional)

Appendices contain supplemental information too detailed to include in the proposal narrative. Proposal appendices are often used when funding agencies impose page limitations. Generally, this supplemental information is considered valuable, but is too bulky to include in the main body of the proposal. A table of contents with specific page numbers should precede appendix items. Typical proposal appendices include:

- Organizational mission statements

- Résumés or job descriptions of key personnel

- Partners'/subcontractors'/consultants' letters of support and commitment (Note: letters should be on institutional letterhead, dated, and signed). **See Exhibits 5-20 and 5-21**.

- Financial reports

- Lengthy charts and tables

- Multi-page reports or papers

Exhibit 5-20

Sample Institutional Letter of Support and Commitment

September 1, 20XX   ⟋ **Support**

I am pleased to provide this letter of enthusiastic support and to affirm our commitment for the proposed project. This grant application represents the results of a team effort by our staff to address the problems associated with low college attendance in the eastern part of the State. The Anytown Eastern Educational Center will provide a proactive approach to the comprehensive educational and information counseling and technical assistance for adults who are interested in pursuing postsecondary educational opportunities. Anytown Community College will commit 2,000 square feet of classroom and office space within the main campus building, computer hardware and software, and office furniture and equipment as well as telephones and service.

↖ **Commitment**

We are excited about the opportunity of having this project in our community and the advantages it will bring to our citizens.

Sincerely,   ⟋ **Administrator's Signature**

Jose Ortiz
Jose Ortiz, President

Letters of support and commitment are often included in proposal appendices.

Exhibit 5-21

Sample Partner Commitment Letter

August 15, 20XX

Community School District 555 is pleased to join in partnership with Anytown College and area businesses in developing opportunities for students to become familiar with careers in the field of Information Technology (IT). To promote these opportunities for students, District 555 is committed to supporting the IT program in the following ways:

- disseminate materials aimed at recruiting students into IT careers,
- provide transportation for students from home school to and from Anytown,
- identify teachers who could become qualified to teach within the IT field, and
- explore the future possibilities of teaching shared and dual credit courses on the high school campuses.

Sincerely,

Administrator's Signature ⟵ ⟶ **Commitment**

John Lebowski

John Lebowski, Superintendent of District 555

Commitment letters detail partners' contributions to the proposed project.

Reviewing and Rewriting Narrative

Most winning grant applications require at least two proposal drafts be reviewed by subject-area experts before submission to funding agencies. Reviewers must read each proposal draft to ensure that writers have addressed the evaluation criteria in the RFP/RFA and presented a comprehensive, coherent, and persuasive essay. The primary job of a reviewer is to make sure that grant proposals are compliant and that all information requested by funding agencies is included in the narrative.

Proposal review meetings should be held after reviewers have had sufficient time to read each proposal draft. The primary purpose of proposal review meetings is to ensure that writers and reviewers have an open forum to discuss ways of improving grant applications. Reviewers should discuss general comments about the proposal as a whole followed by specific comments about each proposal section. Stylistic comments should not be the focus of this meeting, but rather handled by a style editor after the narrative has been completely written. Reviewers should return written comments to writers with specific suggestions for improvement. Reviewers should also discuss issues of consistency between the narrative and budget. Proposal narrative that has cost implications must be included in the budget. Proposal team leaders who have ultimate authority over the grant application should review the final proposal. An administrator who has sign-off authority should be a final review team member and view the final proposal in relation to the primary mission of the institution. Proposals should be complementary rather than be tangential to the institution's primary goals.

Editing Narrative

Proposal editors should have adequate time to read and edit the final proposal prior to submission. Generally there are two types of editing: (1) content editing and (2) style editing. Content editing focuses on accuracy and completeness of the proposal topic. Content editors understand the proposal subject matter and closely compare the narrative sections with the compliance checklist and RFP/RFA guidelines. Style editing focuses on clarity and readability of ideas. Style editors understand consistency of writing and closely check manuscripts for grammar and punctuation, internal consistency (checking claims, facts, names, terms, titles, format, etc.), appropriate and sufficient citations, and appropriate use of diagrams, charts, and figures. Style editors review manuscripts according to a style sheet that was distributed at the strategy meeting. The following questions serve as a guide for editors to answer in proofreading manuscripts.

- Can revising, reducing, rearranging, and/or rewriting improve the proposal?
- Are all the major proposal sections in proper order?
- Does the proposal use language that communicates to nonspecialists?
- Would shorter words express the same thought better?
- Is the proposal readable and attractive in terms of typography, layout, and graphic design?

Common tips to use in proofreading proposals include:
- limit sentences to 15 words or less on average,
- check for subject-verb agreement,
- use nonsexist language,
- use the computer to spell check narrative (but don't totally rely on this!), and
- check spelling of proper names and accuracy of numbers. **See Exhibit 5-22**.

Exhibit 5-22

Proposal Editing Guidelines

Desirable	Undesirable
• Active voice	• Passive voice
• Fewest words	• Wordy
• Variety	• Repetitious
• Understandable terms	• Jargon
• Lively phrasing	• Flat, dull language
• Clear syntax	• Misinterpretation
• Complete sentences	• Choppy sentences
• Key points visible	• Key points hidden
• Facts, examples	• Vague, too general

Editors follow guidelines to rework narrative in an effort to present clear messages to readers.

There is no shortcut to good writing. The only way to become a good writer is to write a lot, and the best way to learn how to write a grant proposal is to write one. The only way to win funding often is to submit quality proposals. Be prepared to spend numerous hours writing, rewriting, and editing.

Completing Funding Agency Forms

Various requirements are imposed on applicants as conditions for receiving grant awards. Application packages include forms that funding seekers must agree to sign concerning federal laws, regulations, and/or executive orders. Examples of conditions include *certifications* that the recipient maintains a drug-free workplace or *assurances* related to civil rights or environmental laws. Some funding agencies require only a few assurance and/or certification forms, while other agencies require that several forms be submitted with grant applications. **See Exhibit 5-23**.

Exhibit 5-23

Selected Government-Wide Requirements

- Anti-Discrimination Requirements – The Civil Rights Act of 1964 prohibits discrimination on the basis of race, color, or national origin in any program receiving federal assistance.
- Drug-Free Workplace Requirements – The Drug-Free Workplace Act of 1988 requires each grantee to certify that it will maintain a drug-free workplace. Funding seekers must also establish drug-free awareness programs that meet certain requirements.
- Lobbying Restrictions – The Anti-Lobbying Amendment applies to recipients of grants over $100,000, prohibiting use of appropriated funds for lobbying the Executive or Legislative branches of the federal government. Funding seekers are required to disclose lobbying activities financed with non-federal funds.
- Others
  - Environmental Protection
  - Health, Safety and Welfare of Human Subjects
  - Public Employee Standards
  - Etc.

Grant proposals require that applicants complete and sign certification and/or assurance forms.

Funding agencies require a cover sheet (Standard Form 424) as the first page of grant applications. Funding seekers should carefully follow instructions for completing all information on the form. SF 424 requires information about you and your organization, the proposed project, estimated project funding, and the authorized representative. The form should be checked for completeness and accuracy and the original signed in blue ink to distinguish it from copies. Many required funding agency forms can be obtained from www.ed.gov/offices/OCFO/grants/appforms.html. **See Exhibits 5-24**.

Exhibit 5-24

Grant Application Cover Sheet (SF 424) and Instructions

APPLICATION FOR FEDERAL ASSISTANCE			OMB Approval No. 0348-0043

1. TYPE OF SUBMISSION:		2. DATE SUBMITTED	Applicant Identifier
Application ☐ Construction ☐ Non-Construction	Preapplication ☐ Construction ☐ Non-Construction	3. DATE RECEIVED BY STATE	State Application Identifier
		4. DATE RECEIVED BY FEDERAL AGENCY	Federal Identifier

5. APPLICANT INFORMATION

Legal Name:	Organizational Unit:
Address *(give city, county, State, and zip code)*:	Name and telephone number of person to be contacted on matters involving this application *(give area code)*

6. EMPLOYER IDENTIFICATION NUMBER *(EIN)*:

☐☐ – ☐☐☐☐☐☐☐

7. TYPE OF APPLICANT: *(enter appropriate letter in box)* ☐

A. State	H. Independent School Dist.
B. County	I. State Controlled Institution of Higher Learning
C. Municipal	J. Private University
D. Township	K. Indian Tribe
E. Interstate	L. Individual
F. Intermunicipal	M. Profit Organization
G. Special District	N. Other (Specify) _____

8. TYPE OF APPLICATION:

☐ New   ☐ Continuation   ☐ Revision

If Revision, enter appropriate letter(s) in box(es) ☐ ☐

A. Increase Award   B. Decrease Award   C. Increase Duration
D. Decrease Duration   Other*(specify)*:

_____

9. NAME OF FEDERAL AGENCY:

10. CATALOG OF FEDERAL DOMESTIC ASSISTANCE NUMBER: ☐☐ – ☐☐☐

TITLE:

11. DESCRIPTIVE TITLE OF APPLICANT'S PROJECT:

12. AREAS AFFECTED BY PROJECT *(Cities, Counties, States, etc.)*:

13. PROPOSED PROJECT		14. CONGRESSIONAL DISTRICTS OF:	
Start Date	Ending Date	a. Applicant	b. Project

15. ESTIMATED FUNDING:

			16. IS APPLICATION SUBJECT TO REVIEW BY STATE EXECUTIVE ORDER 12372 PROCESS?
a. Federal	$	.00	a. YES. THIS PREAPPLICATION/APPLICATION WAS MADE AVAILABLE TO THE STATE EXECUTIVE ORDER 12372 PROCESS FOR REVIEW ON:
b. Applicant	$	.00	
c. State	$	.00	DATE _____
d. Local	$	.00	b. No. ☐ PROGRAM IS NOT COVERED BY E. O. 12372
e. Other	$	.00	☐ OR PROGRAM HAS NOT BEEN SELECTED BY STATE FOR REVIEW
f. Program Income	$	.00	**17. IS THE APPLICANT DELINQUENT ON ANY FEDERAL DEBT?**
g. TOTAL	$	.00	☐ Yes If "Yes," attach an explanation. ☐ No

18. TO THE BEST OF MY KNOWLEDGE AND BELIEF, ALL DATA IN THIS APPLICATION/PREAPPLICATION ARE TRUE AND CORRECT, THE DOCUMENT HAS BEEN DULY AUTHORIZED BY THE GOVERNING BODY OF THE APPLICANT AND THE APPLICANT WILL COMPLY WITH THE ATTACHED ASSURANCES IF THE ASSISTANCE IS AWARDED.

a. Type Name of Authorized Representative	b. Title	c. Telephone Number
d. Signature of Authorized Representative		e. Date Signed

Previous Edition Usable
Authorized for Local Reproduction

Standard Form 424 (Rev. 7-97)
Prescribed by OMB Circular A-102

Standard Form 424 is used as a cover sheet for most grant applications submitted to funding agencies.

Exhibit 5-24 (Continued)

Grant Application Cover Sheet (SF 424) and Instructions

INSTRUCTIONS FOR THE SF-424

Public reporting burden for this collection of information is estimated to average 45 minutes per response, including time for reviewing instructions, searching existing data sources, gathering and maintaining the data needed, and completing and reviewing the collection of information. Send comments regarding the burden estimate or any other aspect of this collection of information, including suggestions for reducing this burden, to the Office of Management and Budget, Paperwork Reduction Project (0348-0043), Washington, DC 20503.

PLEASE DO NOT RETURN YOUR COMPLETED FORM TO THE OFFICE OF MANAGEMENT AND BUDGET. SEND IT TO THE ADDRESS PROVIDED BY THE SPONSORING AGENCY.

This is a standard form used by applicants as a required facesheet for preapplications and applications submitted for Federal assistance. It will be used by Federal agencies to obtain applicant certification that States which have established a review and comment procedure in response to Executive Order 12372 and have selected the program to be included in their process, have been given an opportunity to review the applicant's submission.

Item:	Entry:
1.	Self-explanatory.
2.	Date application submitted to Federal agency (or State if applicable) and applicant's control number (if applicable).
3.	State use only (if applicable).
4.	If this application is to continue or revise an existing award, enter present Federal identifier number. If for a new project, leave blank.
5.	Legal name of applicant, name of primary organizational unit which will undertake the assistance activity, complete address of the applicant, and name and telephone number of the person to contact on matters related to this application.
6.	Enter Employer Identification Number (EIN) as assigned by the Internal Revenue Service.
7.	Enter the appropriate letter in the space provided.
8.	Check appropriate box and enter appropriate letter(s) in the space(s) provided:

-- "New" means a new assistance award.

-- "Continuation" means an extension for an additional funding/budget period for a project with a projected completion date.

-- "Revision" means any change in the Federal Government's financial obligation or contingent liability from an existing obligation.

Item:	Entry:
9.	Name of Federal agency from which assistance is being requested with this application.
10.	Use the Catalog of Federal Domestic Assistance number and title of the program under which assistance is requested.
11.	Enter a brief descriptive title of the project. If more than one program is involved, you should append an explanation on a separate sheet. If appropriate (e.g., construction or real property projects), attach a map showing project location. For preapplications, use a separate sheet to provide a summary description of this project.
12.	List only the largest political entities affected (e.g., State, counties, cities).
13.	Self-explanatory.
14.	List the applicant's Congressional District and any District(s) affected by the program or project.
15.	Amount requested or to be contributed during the first funding/budget period by each contributor. Value of in-kind contributions should be included on appropriate lines as applicable. If the action will result in a dollar change to an existing award, indicate *only* the amount of the change. For decreases, enclose the amounts in parentheses. If both basic and supplemental amounts are included, show breakdown on an attached sheet. For multiple program funding, use totals and show breakdown using same categories as item 15.
16.	Applicants should contact the State Single Point of Contact (SPOC) for Federal Executive Order 12372 to determine whether the application is subject to the State intergovernmental review process.
17.	This question applies to the applicant organization, not the person who signs as the authorized representative. Categories of debt include delinquent audit disallowances, loans and taxes.
18.	To be signed by the authorized representative of the applicant. A copy of the governing body's authorization for you to sign this application as official representative must be on file in the applicant's office. (Certain Federal agencies may require that this authorization be submitted as part of the application.)

SF-424 (Rev. 7-97) Back

Grant seekers must follow specific instructions for completing Standard Form 424.

Using Graphics

Experienced grant writers recognize that a picture is worth a thousand words and will often use charts, figures, exhibits, or diagrams to illustrate important content and breakup the narrative. Proposal graphics are used to supplement narrative and provide readers with an illustration of key points. Graphics should be numbered (e.g., Figure 1) and include a descriptive *caption* immediately below the illustration. *Callouts* are used to identify specific parts, components or processes in illustrations. Callouts may be one word or a brief descriptive sentence. References (e.g., See Figure 1) refer readers to a specific illustration. **See Exhibit 5-25**.

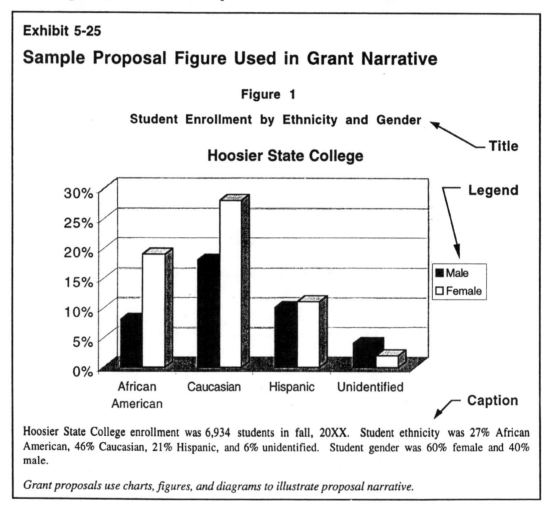

Exhibit 5-25

Sample Proposal Figure Used in Grant Narrative

Figure 1

Student Enrollment by Ethnicity and Gender — Title

Hoosier State College

Legend

Male
Female

African American   Caucasian   Hispanic   Unidentified

Caption

Hoosier State College enrollment was 6,934 students in fall, 20XX. Student ethnicity was 27% African American, 46% Caucasian, 21% Hispanic, and 6% unidentified. Student gender was 60% female and 40% male.

Grant proposals use charts, figures, and diagrams to illustrate proposal narrative.

Tables present a comprehensive and attractive way of providing related information to grant readers. Inaccuracy in tables–especially budget tables–can be very detrimental to grant applications. Tables should be checked and rechecked for missing or incorrect information prior to submitting proposals to funding agencies. **See Exhibit 5-26**.

Exhibit 5-26

Sample Table Used in Grant Narrative

Anytown State College Fall, 20XX Enrollment			
Academic Programs	**Full-Time Students**	**Part-Time Students**	**Total Enrollment**
Business and Management	297	285	582
Technology	212	54	266
Fine Arts and Humanities	224	123	347
Nursing	132	58	190
Professional Communication	168	102	270
Science and Mathematics	191	45	236
Social Science and Humanities	112	25	137
Total	**1336**	**692**	**2028**

Tables must be checked and rechecked for accuracy.

Developing a Table of Contents

Most grant applications call for a *table of contents* (TOC) as part of the grant application, especially if the narrative is lengthy. TOCs should include major proposal narrative heads and subheads (e.g., problem/need, goals and objectives) along with specific page numbers. TOCs are developed to help readers locate specific material quickly and efficiently. Because grant application requirements vary from agency to agency, funding seekers should read and follow agency guidelines for preparing TOCs. Once proposals are finished, page numbers for all narrative sections identified in TOCs should be checked before applications are reproduced and submitted to funding agencies. TOCs should also identify where required application forms are located in proposals. In addition, it is also a good practice to include a separate TOC (with page numbers) as a preface to support materials in appendices.

Chapter 5 Review

(Chapter 5 Review answers are found on page 211)

Directions: For statements 1 through 15, circle T for True or F for False.

T F   1. When developing the first draft of a proposal, writers should develop ideas quickly without worrying about style.

T F   2. Proposal writers must be knowledgeable about the proposed subject matter in order to develop a winning grant application.

T F   3. Experienced grant writers provide exactly what is requested in the *Federal Acquisition Regulations* (FAR).

T F   4. Proposal writing should be as specific as possible and substantiate all claims with measurable data.

T F   5. Effective proposal writing uses the passive voice.

T F   6. Recent and relevant data should be used to support problem/need statements.

T F   7. Goals and objectives provide direction for the proposed project.

T F   8. Job descriptions should include a comprehensive presentation of duties and responsibilities required of key personnel to be hired for the proposed project.

T F   9. Evaluation plans describe specific procedures to measure grant project success.

T F   10. *Formative* evaluation is concerned with judging the overall quality or worth of grant programs at completion of the project.

T F   11. Grant proposals include four major narrative components: problem/need, goals/objectives, methods/activities, and evaluation plans.

T F   12. Résumés for key personnel are normally placed in the proposal narrative.

T F   13. Proposal reviewers make sure that grant applications are compliant and that all information requested by funding agencies is included in the narrative.

T F   14. Content editing focuses on clarity and readability of proposal ideas.

T F   15. Funding agencies include assurances and/or certifications that are signed by funding seekers and included in grant applications.

Exercise 5-1

Preparing Grant Applications

(Exercise 5-1 answers are found on pages 228 - 236)

Directions: Prepare a grant application in response to the State Community College Board (SCCB) RFP for a new special initiative grant program designed to increase the number of Information Technology (IT) graduates. Use the proposal outline and schedule developed in Exercise 4-2 (page 67), reread the memorandum (found on page 68) and RFP (found on pages 69 through 72), and develop a grant proposal that includes the following components:

1. *Transmittal (cover) letter*
2. *Application and project abstract*
3. *Proposal narrative (maximum 5 pages)*
4. *Appendices*

Exercise 5-2

Editing Narrative

(Exercise 5-2 answers are found on page 237)

Unnecessary Words and Phrases

Directions: Rewrite the following sentences to eliminate unnecessary words.

Sentence 1
The proposed project will afford participants the opportunity to master contemporary computer skills.

Sentence 2
Local colleges are producing highly skilled graduates in light of the fact that community businesses are requiring a stronger technical workforce.

Sentence 3
Outside consultants will conduct an evaluation of the entire project.

Sentence 4
The end-of-the-year annual performance report will be written at the end of each program year.

Sentence 5
Each and every report shall conform to the funding agency's instructions.

Sentence 6
The grantee is directed to submit the necessary project reports.

Sentence 7
It is the duty of the grantee to submit documented financial reports.

Sentence 8
The grantee shall submit project reports for the reason that the funding agency's approval is mandatory.

Sentence 9
Partners will make annual contributions of $1,000 a year.

Sentence 10
A comprehensive job description listing all duties connected with the proposal manager's position is included in the appendix.

Chapter 6

Preparing Budgets

The preparation of sound budgets that identify all necessary and reasonable project expenditures are essential for winning grant applications. Usually, several budget drafts are developed and revised before all project expenditures are identified. Budget drafts must be checked closely against the narrative to ensure that expenditures: (1) are in compliance with the RFP/RFA, (2) correspond to the funding seeker's project needs, and (3) are within the proposed cost range identified by the funding agency. Funding seekers should also check applicable OMB circulars and regulations before preparing grant budgets. **See Exhibit 6-1**.

When developing proposal budgets, funding seekers should: (1) adhere to RFP/RFA specifications, (2) use budget information gained from other grant proposals, and (3) present actual costs for project expenditures. Proposal budgets should include direct and indirect costs, unless the funding agency states that indirect costs are not allowed. Cost sharing may also be a grant application requirement.

Direct Costs

Direct costs are specific expenditures required to complete grant projects. Direct costs include expenditures for: (1) personnel and fringe benefits, (2) purchased services, (3) supplies and equipment, and (4) travel expenses. Most funding agencies provide standard forms for budget preparation. Experienced funding seekers supplement these forms with narrative to provide a comprehensive description of project expenditures. Figures enhanced with narrative are often used to illustrate a summary of project expenditures. **See Exhibit 6-2**.

Personnel and Fringe Benefits

Personnel used in grant projects include professional and support staff members. Personnel working on projects, but not paid from grant funds, should be included as in-kind contributions from your organization. Costs for professional staff members should be identified as either replacement costs or stipends. *Full Time Equivalents* (FTEs) may be required by some funding agencies (e.g., a person working one day a week all year = .2 FTE). For example, James Keys will serve as the full-time (1.0 FTE) project director @ $75,000 annually to provide project oversight. Full-time or part-time support staff members may also be shown in FTEs.

Exhibit 6-1

Preparing Budgets

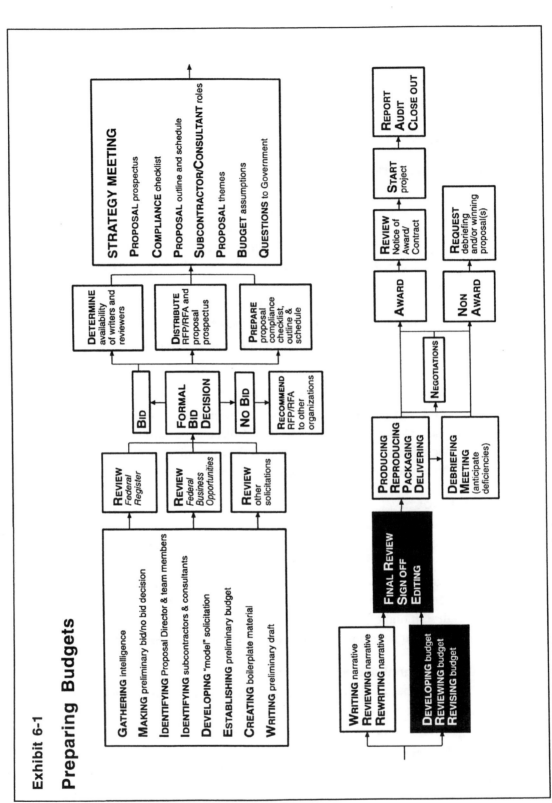

Budgets should be reasonable, cost effective, and adequate.

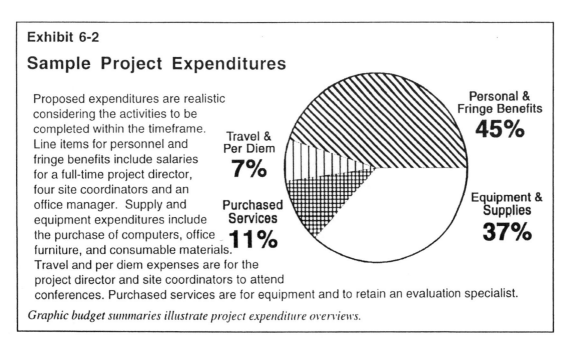

Exhibit 6-2

Sample Project Expenditures

Proposed expenditures are realistic considering the activities to be completed within the timeframe. Line items for personnel and fringe benefits include salaries for a full-time project director, four site coordinators and an office manager. Supply and equipment expenditures include the purchase of computers, office furniture, and consumable materials. Travel and per diem expenses are for the project director and site coordinators to attend conferences. Purchased services are for equipment and to retain an evaluation specialist.

Graphic budget summaries illustrate project expenditure overviews.

Fringe benefits are part of personnel costs and include medical and dental coverage, life insurance, worker's compensation and unemployment, Medicare and retirement pension. Fringe benefits can be broken down or expressed as a percentage of personnel costs. An example of fringe benefits and percentages for personnel is shown in **Exhibit 6-3**.

Exhibit 6-3

Sample Fringe Benefits

Medical and dental insurance	16.57%
Life insurance	1.25%
Worker's compensation and unemployment	.73%
FICA and Medical (Medicare)	1.07%
Retirement pension	8.67%
Total	**28.29%**

Personnel and fringe benefits are direct costs.

Purchased Services

Purchased services may include expenses for consultants, rentals, tuition, service contracts, equipment repairs, and other contractual services (e.g., costs for hiring an outside grant evaluator). When using consultants, indicate the daily consultant fee and the proposed number of days to be worked. Some funding agencies will limit the maximum daily amount that can be charged by consultants. Institutions may also enter into agreements with other institutions as subcontractors. Signed subcontracts between institutions should identify all direct and indirect costs before proposals are submitted to funding agencies.

Supplies and Equipment

Supplies are expendable or consumable items used in proposed projects. Computer software, books, and instructional materials are examples of supplies. When listing supplies, it is advisable to indicate cost detail (e.g., 200 notebooks @ $2.50 = $500). According to the *Office of Management and Budget* (OMB), equipment is any item with a life of more than one year and costs $5,000 or more. Proposed equipment purchases should also show detail. Some funding agencies consider equipment to be unallowable costs. Funding seekers should include budget narrative that indicates the purpose of equipment and supply expenditures.

Travel and Per Diem

Travel costs are used to reimburse personnel working on grant projects for local and out-of-town travel. Travel costs should indicate destinations and include purpose statements. Coach airfare or the latest government per-mile cost for personal ground transportation should be used to calculate travel expenditures. *Per diem costs* are cost per day for lodging, meals, and related incidental expenses. Budget preparation staff should carefully consider per diem costs if project personnel need to travel to locations with higher than average cost-of-living expenses (e.g., New York City). Per diem rates are established annually by the United States General Service Administration (www.policyworks.gov/) for most U.S. cities.

Indirect Costs

Indirect costs are commonly referred to as overhead or *facilities and administrative* (F&A) costs and often include subtle expenditures associated with grant projects (e.g., lighting, heating, and air conditioning of a building, telephone costs, insurance premiums, maintenance costs). Indirect cost rates are calculated as a percentage of the total direct costs. For example, if the direct cost for a proposed project is $100,000 and the allowable indirect cost rate is 25%; the total proposed project cost would be $125,000.

Organizations that develop grant proposals on a regular basis will often negotiate an *indirect cost rate agreement* with one government agency that is used with other funding agencies when applying for grants. Indirect cost rate agreements establish a specific indirect cost percentage ranging from 20% to 60% of the total direct cost. This established indirect cost rate percentage is often honored by other agencies when funding seekers apply for grants.

Some agencies will limit the indirect cost rate percentage that can be charged. In addition, there may also be restrictions on indirect cost rate computation and how indirect rates are applied in proposed grant projects. Indirect costs must follow the government funding agency's guidelines. The OMB *Circular A-21* is designed for educational institutions and *Circular A-133* is designed for state and local governments and non-profit organizations.

Cost Sharing

Some state and federal agencies require funding seekers to provide *cost sharing* contributions when applying for grants. Cost sharing contributions are the difference between actual cost and the amount requested from funding agencies. Cost sharing represents a specific contribution percentage from the funding seeker as matching funds (actual cash) or in-kind contributions. Actual cash can come from the institution's general operating funds, other state or federal grants with similar goals and objectives, or from private sector contributions. In-kind contributions include institution donations from direct costs (e.g., percentage of personnel time, percentage of building space used for the project, purchase or use of supplies and equipment, or use of miscellaneous services such as accounting, security, or cleaning) and indirect costs (e.g., utility costs, telephone expenses). If office space is provided as an in-kind contribution, it is advisable that a floor plan with approximate square footage or room dimensions be included in proposals, even if space is rented. **See Exhibit 6-4**

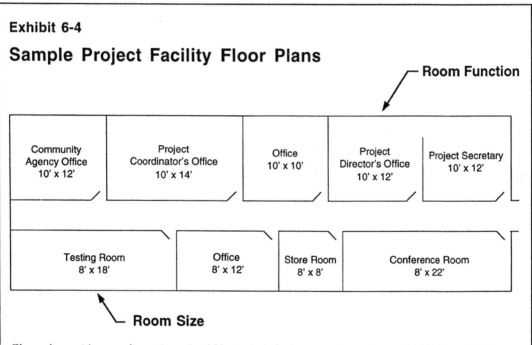

Exhibit 6-4

Sample Project Facility Floor Plans

Room Function

| Community Agency Office 10' x 12' | Project Coordinator's Office 10' x 14' | Office 10' x 10' | Project Director's Office 10' x 12' | Project Secretary 10' x 12' |

| Testing Room 8' x 18' | Office 8' x 12' | Store Room 8' x 8' | Conference Room 8' x 22' |

Room Size

Floor plans with room dimensions should be included when space is used as an in-kind contribution.

Equipment, furniture, supplies, and services that are being provided as in-kind contributions should include detailed information about the quantity of items as well as the name of the institution or partner making the contribution. When indicating in-kind contributions, grant seekers should provide a separate summary table to indicate specific contributions. **See Exhibit 6-5.**

Exhibit 6-5

Sample In-Kind Contributions

In-Kind Contributions by Lincoln College and Partners				
In-Kind Contributions	**Lincoln**		**Partners**	
	#	$ Value	#	$ Value
Computer Equipment and Software				
Desk top computers	20	20,000	5	5,000
Laser printers	5	5,000	3	3,000
Scanners	5	1,000	3	600
Laptop computers	12	18,000	0	0
Software application licenses	20	4,000	5	1,000
Office Furniture and Equipment				
Computer work stations and chairs	25	12,500	0	0
Bookcases	15	7,500	0	0
Office desks	25	12,500	0	0
File cabinets	5	2,000	20	8,000
Credenza	10	5,000	5	2,500
Office Services				
Telephone service	25	3,000	0	0
Internet access	25	3,000	0	0
Photocopying, audio visual/media	25	5,000	0	0
Total Value		$98,500		$20,100

Cost sharing contributions should indicate the item, quantity, and contributor.

When completing proposal budgets that require cost sharing, it is a good practice to establish a three-column budget that includes a separate column for matching funds. The first column indicates grant funds requested from the funding agency, the second column indicates matching funds provided by the funding seeker, and the third column indicates the totals (agency and matching funds) for each line item. **See Exhibit 6-6.**

Cost sharing contributions may include a percentage of indirect costs not claimed. For example, if your institution has an indirect cost rate agreement of 40% and the funding agency will only allow 20% for indirect costs, the remaining 20% may be claimed as a cost sharing contribution.

Exhibit 6-6

Sample Three-Column Budget Including Matching Funds

Line Item and Description	Grant Funds	Matching Funds	Total Amount
Salaries	30,000	9,000	39,000
	30,000	**9,000**	**39,000**
Employee Benefits	3,500	0	3,500
	3,500	**0**	**3,500**
Contractual Services			
Consultant to develop curriculum	4,000	0	4,000
Cabling for classrooms and laboratories	0	3,000	3,000
	4,000	**3,000**	**7,000**
Supplies and Materials			
Instructional	17,000	0	17,000
Outreach	3,000	3,000	6,000
	20,000	**3,000**	**23,000**
Training Workshops			
Training and travel for instructors	12,000	4,000	16,000
	12,000	**4,000**	**16,000**
Capital Outlay			
Equipment	16,000	7,700	23,700
	16,000	**7,700**	**23,700**
Total	**$85,500**	**$26,700**	**$112,200**

Funding seekers should use a three-column budget when agencies require cost sharing contributions.

Budget Detail and Narrative

Grant application *budget detail* is a description of what you propose to do with project funds. These written statements should explain each line item so calculated information is clear to grant reviewers. *Budget narrative* provides a thorough explanation of cost expenditures. Nothing should be in the budget that is not justified in the proposal detail or narrative. **See Exhibits 6-7, 6-8, and 6-9**.

Exhibit 6-7

Sample Budget Detail

Personnel and Fringe Benefits

Project Director (100% of full-time salary)	57,400
Project Coordinator (100% of full-time salary)	54,000
Financial Manager (10% of six months of full-time salary)	3,400
Secretary (10 hours per week for 26 weeks @ $7.50 hourly)	1,950
Total personnel costs	116,750
Fringe benefits ($116,750 x 28.29%)	33,029
	$149,779

Travel and Per Diem

Project Director: $800 airfare x 3 trips	2,400
Project Coordinator: $800 airfare x 2 trips	1,600
Financial Manager: $800 airfare x 1 trip	800
Project Director: $48 per diem x 12 days	576
Project Coordinator: $48 per diem x 8 days	384
Financial Manager: $48 per diem x 4 days	192
	$5,952

Purchased Services

Consultants (2 consultants @ $250 x 5 days)	2,500
Service contracts (2 maintenance contracts @ $250)	500
	$3,000

Equipment and Supplies

Computers (20 computers x $1,250)	25,000
Removable hard drives (60 hard drives @ $150)	9,000
Laser printers (3 printers x $1,500)	4,500
Recruitment materials (flyers and brochures about program)	1,000
Instructional materials (textbooks and workbooks)	6,000
	$45,500

Direct Costs	**$204,231**
Indirect Costs @ 30%	**$61,269**
Total	**$265,500**

Budget detail provides a brief description of proposed project expenditures.

Exhibit 6-8

Sample Budget Narrative

Personnel
The Activity Director is a new permanent full-time employee for the project. This individual will devote 100% time to the project for five years. Funding is requested to support this position 100% in years one and two, 75% in year three, 50% in year four, and 25% in year five. The college will support this position after the grant funding period. The Activity Director's salary is based on current college salaries for faculty members with upper-level experience.

A Network Administrator will be hired as a new permanent full-time employee for the project. This individual will work with the Activity Director to assist with project implementation and will devote 100% time to the project. The college will support this position after the grant-funding period. The salary for the Network Administrator is based on current salaries for personnel in the administrative computing department.

Travel
To keep abreast of national developments in technology, the Activity Director will attend a professional development conference each year of the grant. The information gained from attending these conferences will be used by the Activity Director to train faculty and develop networking programs.

Equipment
In year one, the infrastructure for the campus-wide network will be installed. Funds are requested each year of the project to cover the infrastructure equipment cost of $856,616. Specific equipment needed for the infrastructure includes:

- communications server and expansion port network,
- switching and network access equipment,
- management firewall protector, and
- fiber optic and copper cable.

To complete the network infrastructure, fiber optics and structural wiring will be run to every building on campus. The installation of this equipment will permit access to the intra-campus network, the Internet and voice communication in all buildings on campus including all faculty and staff member offices, residence hall rooms, classrooms, computer labs, and other applicable locations. The college has already secured a tentative agreement with Lucent Technologies to provide the campus infrastructure equipment.

Supplies
The server operating system will integrate a variety of network services needed to run the campus network. The operating system will allow centralized management of the network and will provide a means to automate common tasks and use logon scripts to effectively distribute sofware upgrades, standardize desktops, and enforce security. Licenses will be purchased for 120 users. This will cover the computers in student labs, faculty offices, and administrative offices. Licenses will be purchased as needed for students in residence halls.

Budget narrative provides a thorough explanation of project expenditures.

Exhibit 6-9

Sample Budget With Detail and Narrative

Northern Plains Educational Center	
Federal Funds Requested	
Personnel and Fringe Benefits	**Amount**
Project Director (100%)	57,000
Educational Specialists (100%) 4 @ $30,000 each	120,000
Counselor (100%)	38,000
Project Secretary (100%)	24,000
Subtotal	$239,000
Fringe Benefits @ 30%	$ 71,700
Total Personnel and Fringe Benefits	**$310,700**

The budget includes full-time personnel costs for the project director, four educational specialists to serve seven regions in the target area, a counselor, and project secretary. Salaries are consistent with the State classified compensation plan. The standard college fringe benefits of 30% consist of FICA (7.65%), retirement (11.34%), health insurance (9.38%), group life insurance (.80%), and disability insurance (.83%). Proposed personnel will be able to provide individual attention to the learning needs and academic growth of participants in the target area.

Equipment and Supplies	**Amount**
Computers 30 @ $1,500 each	45,000
Microsoft Office software licenses 30 @ $200 each	6,000
Laser printers 6 @ $3,000 each	18,000
Computer furniture 30 @ $750 each	22,500
Assessment and testing materials	6,700
Instructional materials	3,000
Total Equipment and Supplies	**$101,200**

Equipment and supply expenses include 30 computers and 6 laser printers to equip the main instructional area to be used by project participants. Microsoft Office licenses will be obtained for all computer stations. Thirty computer stations will be purchased with adjustable keyboards and table tops. Assessment and testing materials will be used to screen all participants so proper placement will take place. Instructional materials include computer disks, overhead transparency film, and other consumable items.

Budgets should provide detail and narrative to clarify project costs.

Reviewing and Revising Budgets

At least two grant application budget drafts should be developed and thoroughly checked by proposal reviewers. Reviewers should assess budgets in relationship to project objectives, activities, and RFP/RFA requirements.

Specifically, budget reviewers should ask if proposals:

- conform to RFP/RFA guidelines?
- include all items requested by the funding source?
- provide sufficient resources to complete the project?
- include all costs for personnel mentioned in the proposal?
- contain all budget items necessary to meet the project objectives?
- provide sufficient detail so readers will understand how items were calculated?
- include budget narrative with explanatory notes?
- specify cost sharing contributions, if applicable?
- consider inflation?
- present budget items in a format desired by the agency?
- present a plan for project sustainability (to ensure the project will continue after grant funding)?

Proposal team leaders should review final budgets (direct and indirect costs as well as any cost sharing commitments) in conjunction with the proposal narrative. An editor should review the grant application budget narrative for clarity. An administrator/ manager, who is a member of the *final proposal review team*, should provide final sign-off for grant applications.

Funding agencies operate under different fiscal years and under different budget terms and conditions. For some projects, July 1 through June 30 is a fiscal year, as is the case for many state-funded projects. The federal fiscal year is October 1 through September 30 (note that some federal grants run from September 1 through August 31). Some projects have a combination of funding sources with different deadlines or annual calendars. Grant application budgets are similar to bank accounts where funding is drawn for the life of the grant project. The key is to complete all proposal commitments and spend all available funds within the constraints prescribed by the funding source.

Remember, all project expenditures must be justified. Do not assume that project costs will be obvious to funding agency readers. Always follow specific instructions to complete funding agency budget forms and supplement them with budget narrative to provide detail and explanation. In addition, be prepared to prioritize budget needs if the funding agency provides only partial support for the proposed grant project. **See Exhibit 6-10**.

Exhibit 6-10

Grant Budget Form (SF 524) and Instructions

	U.S. DEPARTMENT OF EDUCATION	OMB Control Number: 1890-0004
	BUDGET INFORMATION	Expiration Date: 02/28/2003
	NON-CONSTRUCTION PROGRAMS	

Name of Institution/Organization

Applicants requesting funding for only one year should complete the column under "Project Year 1." Applicants requesting funding for multi-year grants should complete all applicable columns. Please read all instructions before completing form.

SECTION A - BUDGET SUMMARY
U.S. DEPARTMENT OF EDUCATION FUNDS

Budget Categories	Project Year 1 (a)	Project Year 2 (b)	Project Year 3 (c)	Project Year 4 (d)	Project Year 5 (c)	Total (f)
1. Personnel						
2. Fringe Benefits						
3. Travel						
4. Equipment						
5. Supplies						
6. Contractual						
7. Construction						
8. Other						
9. Total Direct Costs (lines 1-8)						
10. Indirect Costs						
11. Training Stipends						
12. Total Costs (lines 9-11)						

ED Form No. 524

The U.S. Department of Education's budget form 524 (Section A) is used to summarize federal funds.

Exhibit 6-10 (Continued)

Grant Budget Form (SF 524) and Instructions

Name of Institution/Organization

Applicants requesting funding for only one year should complete the column under "Project Year 1." Applicants requesting funding for multi-year grants should complete all applicable columns. Please read all instructions before completing form.

SECTION B - BUDGET SUMMARY
NON-FEDERAL FUNDS

Budget Categories	Project Year 1 (a)	Project Year 2 (b)	Project Year 3 (c)	Project Year 4 (d)	Project Year 5 (e)	Total (f)
1. Personnel						
2. Fringe Benefits						
3. Travel						
4. Equipment						
5. Supplies						
6. Contractual						
7. Construction						
8. Other						
9. Total Direct Costs (lines 1-8)						
10. Indirect Costs						
11. Training Stipends						
12. Total Costs (lines 9-11)						

SECTION C - OTHER BUDGET INFORMATION (see instructions)

ED Form No. 524

The U.S. Department of Education's budget form 524 (Section B) is used to summarize non-federal funds.

Exhibit 6-10 (Continued)

Grant Budget Form (SF 524) and Instructions

Public reporting burden for this collection of information is estimated to vary from 13 to 22 hours per response, with an average of 17.5 hours per response, including the time reviewing instructions, searching existing data sources, gathering and maintaining the data needed, and completing and reviewing the collection of information. Send comments regarding this burden estimate or any other aspect of this collection of information, including suggestions for reducing this burden, to the U.S. Department of Education, Information Management and Compliance Division, Washington, D.C. 20202-4651; and the Office of Management and Budget, Paperwork Reduction Project 1875-0102, Washington DC 20503.

INSTRUCTIONS FOR ED FORM 524

General Instructions

This form is used to apply to individual U.S. Department of Education discretionary grant programs. Unless directed otherwise, provide the same budget information for each year of the multi-year funding request. Pay attention to applicable program specific instructions, if attached.

Section A - Budget Summary
U.S. Department of Education Funds

All applicants must complete Section A and provide a breakdown by the applicable budget categories shown in lines 1-11.

Lines 1-11, columns (a)-(e): For each project year for which funding is requested, show the total amount requested for each applicable budget category.

Lines 1-11, column (f): Show the multi-year total for each budget category. If funding is requested for only one project year, leave this column blank.

Line 12, columns (a)-(e): Show the total budget request for each project year for which funding is requested.

Line 12, column (f): Show the total amount requested for all project years. If funding is requested for only one year, leave this space blank.

Section B - Budget Summary
Non-Federal Funds

If you are required to provide or volunteer to provide matching funds or other non-Federal resources to the project, these should be shown for each applicable budget category on lines 1-11 of Section B.

Lines 1-11, columns (a)-(e): For each project year for which matching funds or other contributions are provided, show the total contribution for each applicable budget category.

Lines 1-11, column (f): Show the multi-year total for each budget category. If non-Federal contributions are provided for only one year, leave this column blank.

Line 12, columns (a)-(e): Show the total matching or other contribution for each project year.

Line 12, column (f): Show the total amount to be contributed for all years of the multi-year project. If non-Federal contributions are provided for only one year, leave this space blank.

Section C - Other Budget Information
Pay attention to applicable program specific
instructions, if attached.

1. Provide an itemized budget breakdown, by project year, for each budget category listed in Sections A and B.

2. If applicable to this program, enter the type of indirect rate (provisional, predetermined, final or fixed) that will be in effect during the funding period. In addition, enter the estimated amount of the base to which the rate is applied, and the total indirect expense.

3. If applicable to this program, provide the rate and base on which fringe benefits are calculated.

4. Provide other explanations or comments you deem necessary.

The U.S. Department of Education provides specific instructions for completing budget form 524.

Common Budget Problems

Budgets are credibility statements. Incomplete budgets signal poor preparation. Inflated budgets indicate waste. Low budgets cast doubt on the applicant's planning ability. Strive to establish realistic budgets. Common problems with grant application budgets are presented below. Funding seekers must carefully check and re-check budgets before submitting grant applications to funding agencies.

Arithmetic Errors in Subtotals and Totals

Arithmetic errors reflect sloppy preparation. Budget totals and subtotals must be checked and re-checked for accuracy. Errors and omissions detract from the overall proposal credibility.

Lack of Budget Detail

Budget detail provides information about how totals and subtotals were determined. For example, 25 computers @ $2,000 = $50,000; 200 books @ $50 = $10,000; 10% time of $50,000 = $5,000. Always include all items requested by funding agencies and provide enough detail so funding agency readers can easily determine budget calculations.

Unrealistic Costs for Budget Items

Budget item must reflect actual costs, not inflated costs. Funding agency readers usually identify budget items that exceed a normal cost range. Never pad a budget. In addition, be prepared to prioritize grant project budget needs.

Budget Items Inconsistent With Proposal Narrative

Proposal narrative and budget items must be carefully reviewed for internal consistency and compliance with the RFP/RFA. Cost items identified in the grant application narrative must always be reflected in the budget. Conversely, budget items must be justified in the proposal narrative.

Little or No Budget Narrative

Budget narrative explains and clarifies cost expenditures. Detailed proposal narrative should always accompany budget items.

Vague and Unexplained Source(s) for Cost Sharing Dollars

Specific detail must be provided for cost sharing contributions. Cost sharing should include information about the contributor, financial amount, and budget categories to be covered by the contribution.

Indirect Costs Are Missing From Budgets

If allowed, funding seekers should always include indirect costs in proposal budgets. Some agencies will only allow a limited percentage of the proposed total funding to count as indirect costs. Other agencies will allow grant seekers to apply the maximum indirect cost percentage established via an indirect cost rate agreement with a government agency.

Chapter 6 Review

(Chapter 6 Review answers are found on page 212)

Directions: For statements 1 through 10, circle T for True or F for False.

T F   1. Direct costs are specific expenditures required to complete grant projects.

T F   2. Fringe benefits are part of indirect costs.

T F   3. Project supplies are classified as cost items under $25.

T F   4. Travel and per diem expenses are part of indirect costs.

T F   5. Indirect costs are commonly called overhead or *facilities and administrative* (F&A) expenses.

T F   6. Cost sharing contributions are the difference between actual cost and the amount requested from funding agencies.

T F   7. Budget narrative provides a thorough explanation of cost expenditures.

T F   8. All funding agencies operate under the same fiscal budget terms and conditions.

T F   9. Proposal budgets are credibility statements.

T F   10. Lack of budget detail is a common problem with grant applications submitted to funding agencies.

Exercise 6-1

Preparing Proposal Budgets (Information Technology)

(Exercise 6-1 answers are found on page 238)

Directions: Prepare a budget for the grant application that you developed for Exercise 5-1 (page 101) in response to the State Community College Board (SCCB) RFP for a new special initiative grant program designed to increase the number of Information Technology (IT) graduates. Use the proposal outline and schedule developed in Exercise 4-2 (page 67) and reread the memorandum (page 68) and RFP (pages 69 through 72) to develop your budget. The budget should follow the format sheet on page 72 and include the following direct cost line items:

1. *Salaries*
2. *Employee benefits*
3. *Contractual services*
4. *Supplies and materials*
5. *Conference and meetings*
6. *Capital outlay*

Exercise 6-2

Preparing Proposal Budgets (School-To-Work)

(Exercise 6-2 answers are found on page 239)

Directions: Read the Proposal Narrative (pages 121 through 123) and identify elements that have budget implications. Use the proposed budget form on page 124 to prepare a line item budget that indicates direct costs for the (1) funding agency and (2) Anytown School District (ASD).

Assume the following information:

1. You are: Dr. John Ling, Superintendent of Schools
                    Anytown School District (Employer # 96-0065765)
                    1311 Northwest Main Street
                    Anytown, USA 98765
                    (555) 435-8400

2. ASD serves a population of 26,000 students.

3. You are submitting a grant application in response to a funding agency solicitation.

4. Proposed project staff members and annual salaries are listed below.

Personnel	Annual Salary
• Project Oversight Manager	$85,010
• Project Administrator	$78,008
• Project Specialist #1	$40,996
• Project Specialist #2	$50,003
• Financial Manager	$85,010
• Document Preparation Specialist	$36,000

5. Other direct expenses associated with the proposed grant project are listed below:

   • 25% Staff Fringe Benefits

   • Airfare and Expenses
      • $100 round trip airfare for teachers, advisory board members, and students
      • $100 round trip airfare for specialists (away from Anytown)
      • $800 round trip airfare for national speaker
      • $400 round trip airfare for each state speaker
      • $140 per diem for teachers, advisory board members, and speakers
      • $ 50 per diem for students
      • $ 35 per diem for specialists (away from Anytown)

   • $1,000 for each curriculum package

   • $1,000 honorarium for national speaker and $500 for each state speaker

   • $1,000 per day rental fee for conference building

   • $50 per square foot per year for the Career Information Center space

Exercise 6-2 continues on the next page

Anytown School District (ASD) Proposal Narrative
Read pages 121 -123 and use the proposed budget form on page 124 to develop a line-item budget

The bulk of federal funding requested for the Anytown School District (ASD) School-To-Work (S-T-W) Implementation Project will be used to hire two project specialists for one year. Each project specialist will be responsible for working with students, parents, teachers, and administrators in 22 ASD local schools for three days. The remaining budget items include a conference for local teachers and area school board members, a student work experience program, travel, and S-T-W curriculum materials. Less than ten percent of costs will be used for administrative overhead. No funds will be used to purchase equipment.

School-To-Work Key Personnel
Successful implementation of the S-T-W program at ASD is directly related to the quality of project staff. Much thought and effort was taken to identify key staff members who would serve in leadership roles to ensure successful implementation of the S-T-W project.

Project Oversight Manager (Dr. John Ling). Under the able leadership of Superintendent John Ling, ASD will take responsibility for ensuring that the S-T-W project complies with federal regulations. *Salary and benefits for Dr. Ling will be provided by ASD.* The Project Oversight Manager responsibilities include:
- Serve as the S-T-W contact for federal officials
- Monitor and evaluate S-T-W implementation in ASD
- Disseminate federal S-T-W information to state and regional representatives

Project Administrator (Mr. James Schmidt). James Schmidt will assume the role of project administrator. Mr. Schmidt, working with the financial manager, will maintain accurate and complete records, which will be reviewed by administrators and auditors. Mr. Schmidt will work closely with the project specialists (Greg Miroski and another project specialist to be hired) to implement S-T-W programs in the ASD area. The Project Administrator responsibilities include:
- Serve as the S-T-W contact for state officials
- Monitor the implementation of S-T-W programs
- Assist in the development of S-T-W curriculum in response to students needs
- Recruit business and industry leaders as S-T-W partners
- Monitor, assist, and evaluate the progress of S-T-W programs at ASD
- Work with ASD Employers' councils and with advisory committees
- Disseminate information regarding current rules and trends in S-T-W
- Work cooperatively with education agencies in ASD
- Evaluate the development of S-T-W curriculum
- Prepare S-T-W quarterly financial and progress reports

Exercise 6-2 continues on the next page

Project Specialists (Mr. Greg Miroski and another project specialist to be hired). Greg Miroski will serve as one of two project specialists who will work in the local ASD area to implement S-T-W. The ASD program will comply fully with all federal, state, and local laws relating to equal employment opportunity and affirmative action when hiring the additional project specialist. In addition, minorities and women, and other under-represented groups, will be encouraged to apply for this position. The Project Specialists' responsibilities include:

- Design and implement S-T-W programs in local schools
- Disseminate S-T-W information to students, parents, and teachers
- Assist students with portfolio development
- Connect students with agencies/businesses
- Recruit outside business representatives for mentoring activities
- Establish work experiences and internships for students
- Coordinate with community agencies and businesses to promote S-T-W employment opportunities for students
- Work with site administrators, counselors, teachers, and students to locate job training placement
- Maintain a systematic set of S-T-W monitoring and enrollment records
- Assist the Project Administrator with other duties as required

Project Financial Manager (Mr. David Black). David Black, Financial Manager for ASD, will be responsible for the management and control of all grant funds. Mr. Black will ensure that all expenditures occur within the regulations of the state and U.S. Departments of Education and Labor. *Salary and benefits for Mr. Black will be provided by ASD.* The Project Financial Manager responsibilities include:

- Maintain accurate financial records for S-T-W activities, which include staff labor and other direct expenses
- Prepare and represent ASD in any S-T-W program audit

S-T-W Document Preparation Specialist (Ms. Sharon Samuels). Sharon Samuels will serve as the document preparation specialist and will handle all word processing and graphic design work for the S-T-W project. *Salary and benefits for Ms. Samuels will be provided by ASD.* The Document Preparation Specialist responsibilities include:

- Prepare all S-T-W documents
- Design final S-T-W reports
- Prepare tables, charts, and graphs for S-T-W presentations
- Schedule S-T-W meetings, conferences, etc.
- Assist the Project Administrator with other duties as required. **See Table 1.**

Exercise 6-2 continues on the next page

Table 1

Time Commitment of S-T-W Project Personnel

Name	Position	Commitment
John Ling *	Project Oversight Manager	15%
James Schmidt	Project Administrator	25%
To be hired	Project Specialist #1	100%
Greg Miroski	Project Specialist #2	100%
David Black *	Financial Manager	10%
Sharon Samuels *	Document Preparation Specialist	25%

* Salary and benefits provided by ASD

S-T-W Conference for Teachers and Area School Board Members

Project specialists will lead a two-day S-T-W conference in Anytown in the Fall. The conference will serve as a public relations meeting for employers and community members, as well as a kickoff/introduction meeting for 22 ASD teachers and 22 ASD Advisory School Board (ASB) members (ASD will provide airfare and per diem for ASB members). The meeting will also serve as an orientation program for local employers and present such topics as the purpose of S-T-W programs, working with youth, job shadowing, and serving as a mentor. One national and two state speakers will be invited to the conference to present innovative S-T-W activities. Speakers will be paid an honorarium, airfare, and per diem to attend this conference.

Student Work Experience Program

The student work experience program is for 20 students for 14 days at Anytown and covers six career pathways. Students learn about technical and management positions; level of education needed for each position; local, state, and national job outlook for careers; and expected wages.

A Career Information Center will be established in Anytown to furnish career and occupational information to students. ASD will provide 400 square feet of office space for the center. ASD will also donate $1,000 per year for student information packets that will be available at the center.

S-T-W Implementation Project in Local Schools

Each project specialist will travel by air to 22 schools in the state (spending three days per visit) and work directly with ASD teachers to implement S-T-W curriculum. Project specialists will introduce S-T-W to all students, parents, administrators, and employers in local schools through the use of ADVANCED curriculum materials to be obtained from ABC Publishers, Inc. One set of curriculum materials will be obtained for each of the 22 schools.

Exercise 6-2 continues on the next page

Proposed Budget Form

Use this form to prepare a line-item budget that indicates direct costs for the Funding Agency and ASD

Funding Agency   ASD

Personnel and Fringe Benefits

Travel and Per Diem

S-T-W Conference

Student Work Experience

S-T-W Implementation Project in Schools

Purchased Services

Equipment and Supplies

Total

Chapter 7

Producing, Reproducing, Packaging, and Delivering Proposals

After the proposal narrative and budget have been developed, proposal directors must make sure the complete grant application is produced and assembled and that adequate copies are reproduced, packaged, and delivered to the funding agency before the deadline. Grant proposal producing, reproducing, packaging, and delivering tasks must not be taken lightly. Poor proposal producing and reproducing can result in missing sections or pages, as well as a host of other problems that can influence funding agency readers' overall rating of grant applications. Packaging in a format other than what is requested in the RFP/RFA can cause funding agencies to reject applications. Grant applications delivered after the due date and time specified in the RFP/RFA are generally not considered for funding. **See Exhibit 7-1**.

Producing Proposals

Once all proposal sections (e.g., narrative, budget, and application forms) are complete, several decisions must be made before reproducing the required number of copies specified by the funding agency. The final layout of grant proposals must follow RFP/RFA guidelines.

Proposal directors should check and re-check grant proposals against RFP/RFA requirements for compliance. If funding agencies require an abstract of 500 words or less, applicants should not provide 650 words. If funding agencies require double-spaced text, applicants should not format in single-spaced text. If funding agencies require 12-point text, applicants should not use 10-point text. If funding agencies require no more than 40 pages of text, applicants should not submit 44 pages of text (and do not reduce the font size or margins to accommodate additional pages). Provide exactly what is required in the RFP/RFA.

Exhibit 7-1

Producing, Reproducing, Packaging, and Delivering Proposals

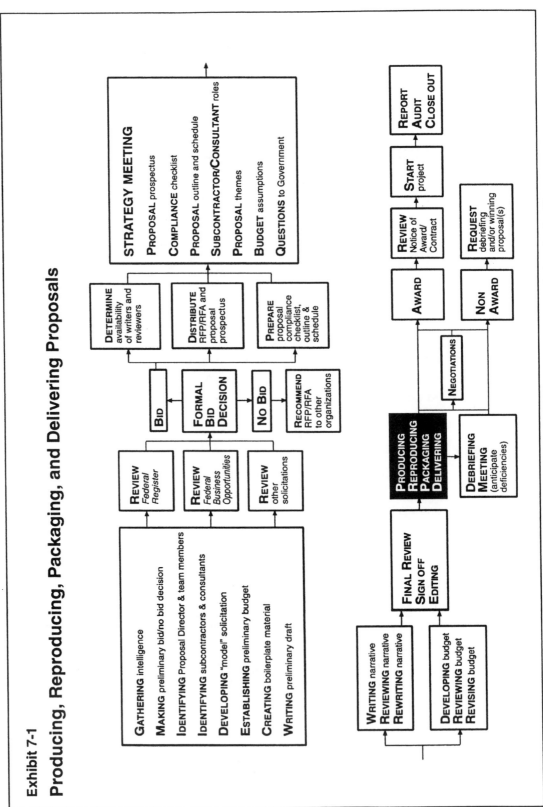

Grant applications must be produced, reproduced, packaged, and delivered to the government agency before the deadline.

Assemble the proposal cover sheet, table of contents, narrative, budget, application forms, and appendix material in the exact manner specified in the RFP/RFA guidelines. Complete a quality control check of the table of contents (TOC) to ensure that major heads and page numbers used in the narrative are included in the TOC. Major heads should generally match the RFP/RFA evaluation criteria. Include a list of tables, figures, or exhibits for the funding agency readers' reference. If the proposal is large, consider using tabs so readers can easily locate specific proposal sections.

Résumés, letters of support, and other supplemental material should be organized in a logical manner in proposal appendices. A table of contents should precede appendix documents. If there are numerous support materials, applicants might consider using tabs so reviewers can easily locate specific appendix items. Always check the RFP/RFA before using tabs.

A *quality control check* of grant applications from cover-to-cover should be completed before proposal reproduction. If grant applications have numerous sections with a large appendix, proposal directors should use a checklist to track all proposal components before and after proposal reproduction. **See Exhibit 7-2**.

Reproducing Proposals

After assembly, proposals should be reproduced to provide the necessary copies required by the funding agency as well as sufficient copies for internal use by proposal team members. Proposal directors must determine the: (1) total number of proposal copies required by the funding agency, (2) type of duplication (e.g., single-sided or double-sided copying), (3) tabs needed, if any, and (4) binding type. Custom or generic tabs should be ordered prior to proposal reproduction. Proposal binding should consider RFP/RFA specifications and cost. Grant application binding should allow proposals to be easily reassembled and to lie flat when being read. After reproduction, another quality control check of each proposal copy should be made prior to submission to the funding agency. Often, a "fresh pair of eyes" can spot overlooked mistakes. Don't allow reproduction errors to hurt your chances of delivering a winning proposal that you worked so hard to prepare. **See Exhibit 7-3**.

Packaging and Delivering Proposals

After proposal reproduction, grant applications are packaged and delivered to funding agencies. If an original proposal is required, it should be clearly marked "original" on the cover of the grant application. Proposals must be carefully packaged to prevent damage. Follow exact packaging and delivering specifications provided in the RFP/RFA guidelines and include any special markings (e.g., solicitation number) on containers. Finally, applicants should carefully recheck the delivery address for accuracy. **See Exhibit 7-4**.

Exhibit 7-2

Proposal Tracking Checklist

Proposal Name: Innovative Programs to Increase Information Technology

CFDA/RFP/RFA#: 42702

Contact/Phone: David Johnson / 219-838-3599

Address: 1001 Main Street, Hoosierville, IN 65432

Due Date/Time: March 15, 20xx / 4:00 p.m. CST

(It is very important to note whether the due date is a delivery date or a postmark date)

Proposal Component	Receive	Produce/ Assemble	Quality Control	Reproduce	Quality Control	Pack	Final Check/ Deliver
Cover Sheet	✓	✓	✓				
Abstract	✓	✓	✓				
Application Forms	✓	✓	✓				
TOC	✓	✓	✓				
Introduction	✓	✓	✓				
Problem/Need	✓	✓	✓				
Goals/Objectives	✓	✓	✓				
Methods/Activities	✓	✓	✓				
Evaluation Plans	✓	✓	✓				
Budget	✓	✓	✓				
Appendices TOC	✓	✓	✓				
Résumés	✓	✓	✓				
Support Letters	✓	✓	✓				
Mission Statement	✓	✓	✓				

Checklists are used to track all proposal components before and after proposal reproduction.

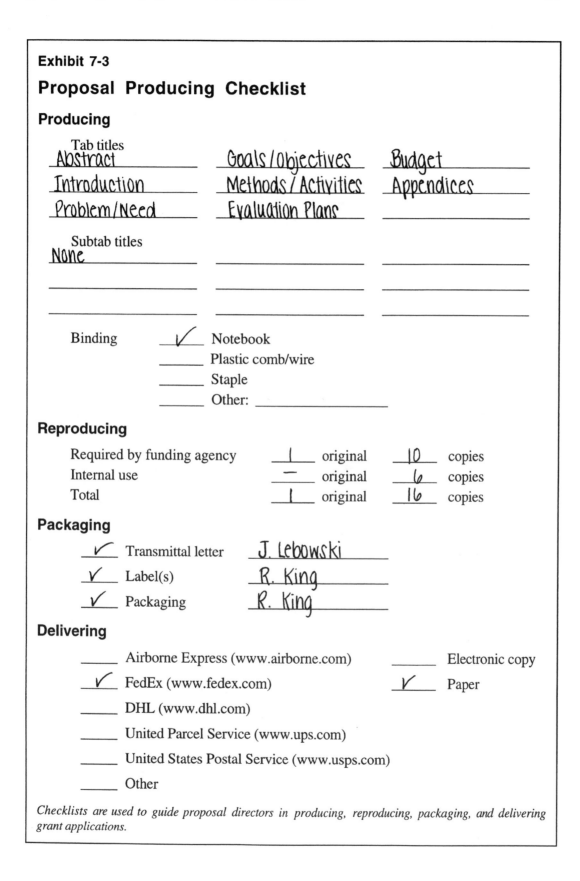

Exhibit 7-3

Proposal Producing Checklist

Producing

Tab titles

Abstract	Goals/Objectives	Budget
Introduction	Methods/Activities	Appendices
Problem/Need	Evaluation Plans	

Subtab titles

None

Binding   _✓_ Notebook

            _____ Plastic comb/wire

            _____ Staple

            _____ Other: _____

Reproducing

Required by funding agency	_1_ original	_10_ copies	
Internal use	_—_ original	_6_ copies	
Total	_1_ original	_16_ copies	

Packaging

_✓_ Transmittal letter   J. Lebowski

_✓_ Label(s)   R. King

_✓_ Packaging   R. King

Delivering

_____ Airborne Express (www.airborne.com)   _____ Electronic copy

_✓_ FedEx (www.fedex.com)   _✓_ Paper

_____ DHL (www.dhl.com)

_____ United Parcel Service (www.ups.com)

_____ United States Postal Service (www.usps.com)

_____ Other

Checklists are used to guide proposal directors in producing, reproducing, packaging, and delivering grant applications.

Exhibit 7-4

Final Checklist Before Delivering Grant Applications

✓ **Due Date and Time.** Check and recheck RFP/RFA guidelines concerning the date and time when grant applications are due and allow adequate time for delivering applications to funding agencies.

✓ **Number of Copies.** Check RFP/RFA guidelines to determine the number of proposal copies required by funding agencies. The required number of proposal copies will vary from agency to agency. Some funding agencies require one original and multiple copies while other agencies will only require a single copy. Provide exactly what is requested in the RFP/RFA guidelines.

✓ **Funding Agency Address.** Check and recheck the address where proposals are to be submitted. Be sure to check spelling and zip code.

✓ **Authorized Signatures.** Check all grant application pages that require signatures. Most applications require upper administration signatures on cover sheets and assurance and certification forms. Some applications require signatures on budget forms. All forms should be signed in blue ink to make originals stand out from copies. Signatures are a requirement because proposals will become part of a legally binding contract if you win.

✓ **Packaging and Markings.** Proposal size and number of copies required by funding agencies will dictate if submissions will require an envelope, box, or multiple boxes. Use sturdy packaging that will protect your grant submission. Properly mark each envelope or box with the specific RFP/RFA number, project name, and quantity of proposals inside the package. If multiple boxes are submitted, indicate the number of boxes sent (e.g., 1 of 3 boxes, 2 of 3 boxes, and 3 of 3 boxes). Include a transmittal letter with grant applications.

Funding seekers should make a final check of the grant application before submission.

Transmittal Letters

Transmittal or cover letters with an authorized signature (e.g., President of the organization) should normally accompany grant application submissions to funding agencies. Prepare letters on organizational letterhead and address them to the POC identified in the RFP/RFA. Transmittal letters should include the RFP/RFA or CFDA number and identify the number of proposals included in the package as well as the contents of each proposal. In addition, letters should identify a knowledgeable grant application contact person who can be reached for questions. **See Exhibits 7-5 and 7-6.**

Exhibit 7-5

Sample Transmittal Letter 1

March 15, 20XX

Carol Dean, Grant Coordinator
42nd Street and Elm
New York, NY 10014   ⟵ **RFP Number**

Re: Grant Application in Response to RFP# 0005321

                                                               ⟵ **Copies Required**
Dear Ms. Dean:

Anytown State College (ASC) is pleased to submit three copies of our application to the Anderson Health Trust to support the Nursing Education Wellness Service (NEWS) project. This project will enhance the knowledge and clinical expertise of faculty in the area of community-based health and will also provide our students with a clinical experience that will improve their ability to function in community health care settings.

The NEWS project planning has energized the nursing faculty to look at new ways to present the theoretical and clinical competencies necessary to prepare students for community-based care. By developing a clinical setting on campus, students will be afforded hands-on nursing experiences that have not been previously available. Additionally, nursing students will have the opportunity to serve ASC faculty, students, and staff in a very meaningful way.

ASC is totally committed to assist in making NEWS a reality by contributing in-kind funds in the amount of $63,800 for administrative personnel, purchased services, construction, and renovation. Facility plans have been altered to accommodate the space necessary for the NEWS project.

ASC has administered more than 100 grants in a wide variety of educational and service areas. If awarded, ASC will commit high-level administrators to the successful completion of the NEWS project. If you have project oversight questions, please contact Dr. Patrick W. Smith, Vice President of Academic Affairs at (555) 312-3333 or e-mail: psmith@anytown.cc.us. If you have specific questions regarding implementation of the NEWS project, please contact Ms. Gwen Olson, Chairperson of Nursing at (555) 312-3344 or e-mail: golson@anytown.cc.us. We look forward to hearing from you.

Sincerely,   ⟵ **Authorized Signature**

Abdul J. Kaakaji

Dr. Abdul J. Kaakaji, President

c: Dr. Patrick W. Smith
      Ms. Gwen Olson

Transmittal letters should accompany grant application submissions.

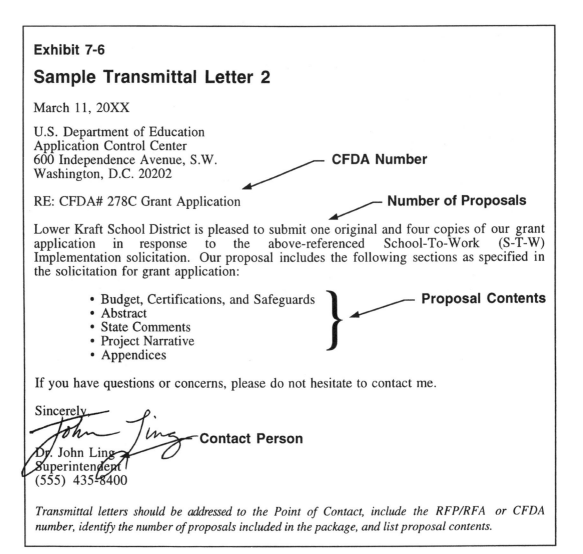

Exhibit 7-6

Sample Transmittal Letter 2

March 11, 20XX

U.S. Department of Education
Application Control Center
600 Independence Avenue, S.W.   ⟵ **CFDA Number**
Washington, D.C. 20202

RE: CFDA# 278C Grant Application   ⟵ **Number of Proposals**

Lower Kraft School District is pleased to submit one original and four copies of our grant application in response to the above-referenced School-To-Work (S-T-W) Implementation solicitation. Our proposal includes the following sections as specified in the solicitation for grant application:

- Budget, Certifications, and Safeguards
- Abstract   } ⟵ **Proposal Contents**
- State Comments
- Project Narrative
- Appendices

If you have questions or concerns, please do not hesitate to contact me.

Sincerely,

John Ling ⟵ **Contact Person**

Dr. John Ling
Superintendent
(555) 435-8400

Transmittal letters should be addressed to the Point of Contact, include the RFP/RFA or CFDA number, identify the number of proposals included in the package, and list proposal contents.

Proposal Delivery Options

Always deliver grant applications in a timely fashion. Many institutions spend a considerable amount of time and money developing grant applications, but skimp on delivery costs. Institutions should spend the necessary dollars to ensure that grant applications are delivered to funding agencies before the due date and time. For grant applications that are critical to your institution, personal delivery should be a viable consideration. When delivering in person, be sure to obtain a receipt from funding agency representatives to verify that applications were received on time.

If proposals do not warrant personal delivery, overnight express services provide a reasonably safe and cost effective way to deliver proposals. There are several reliable express shipping companies that will deliver proposals overnight to most U.S. cities for a relatively inexpensive rate. Most express shipping companies provide delivery rates and shipping charges by delivery zone. Check the express courier's Web site to learn about delivery costs to the final destination. Example shipping couriers include:

- Airborne Express (www.airborne.com)
- FedEx (www.fedex.com)
- United Parcel Service (www.ups.com)
- DHL (www.dhl.com)

Before using an express courier, funding seekers should know the package dimensions (height, width, and length) and weight as well as the specific address where the package will be sent (including zip code). Obtain a tracking number from express courier representatives for each package that is shipped. Use the Internet to track the package delivery to the final destination. Always obtain a delivery confirmation. If you are running late or if unexpected circumstances (e.g., inclement weather) could delay the delivery of grant application packages, consider sending two complete application packages using two different carriers. Even though these express couriers guarantee "on time delivery or your money back," the financial courier's reimbursement will hardly compensate your institution for grant funds lost due to late delivery.

Many funding agencies are allowing electronic grant application submissions. When submitting grant applications through electronic means, always follow the specific agency guidelines. Grant applications that appear perfect on your computer screen may not necessarily be the same formatted document received by funding agencies. If submitting electronically, get an e-mail or fax receipt that states the grant application was received in readable form by the funding agency. Experienced funding seekers send a backup paper copy of the grant application (in addition to the electronic submission) to ensure the application was delivered to the funding agency before the announced deadline date and time.

Do not assume that grant applications submitted by fax or e-mail will be accepted by funding agencies. Always check with the funding agency's POC before using these electronic delivery methods for submitting applications.

Chapter 7 Review

(Chapter 7 Review answers are found on page 212)

Directions: For statements 1 through 10, circle T for True or F for False.

T F   1. Grant applications delivered after the due date and time specified in the RFP/RFA will generally be considered for funding.

T F   2. Final proposal layout must follow RFP/RFA guidelines.

T F   3. A table of contents should always be part of proposals submitted to funding agencies.

T F   4. If grant proposals have numerous sections and a large appendix, it is advisable to use a checklist to track all proposal components.

T F   5. Letters of support, résumés, and other supplemental material should be placed in the proposal narrative.

T F   6. Proposal binding should consider RFP/RFA specifications and cost.

T F   7. Grant proposals should go through a quality control check before and after reproduction.

T F   8. Applicants should always submit two additional grant proposals to funding agencies.

T F   9. Grant application transmittal letters should identify a contact person who can be reached for questions about proposal submissions.

T F   10. Considering today's technology, it is highly advisable to submit grant applications by fax or e-mail to ensure delivery on time.

Exercise 7-1

Transmittal Letter and Proposal Delivery

(Exercise 7-1 answers are found on page 240)

Directions: Write a grant application transmittal letter based on the situation below.

Situation: You are a senior faculty member at Sears Tower College, 233 South Wacker Drive, Chicago, Illinois 60606. You and a team of faculty in your department have been working on grant application CFDA# 255G for the last month and it must be delivered tomorrow to the U.S. Department of Education in Washington, DC. The proposal is requesting $100,000 to enhance your current instructional programs, which may be eliminated due to insufficient college funds.

It is February and the temperature is below freezing. It is currently 5:10 p.m. CST and weather forecasters are predicting a snowstorm starting at 12:00 midnight with the accumulation of several inches. Grant applications are due tomorrow at 2:00 p.m. EST in Washington DC.

The funding agency requires 1 original and 11 copies of the proposal. After reproduction, the approximate weight of 12 proposals (225 pages each) is 27 pounds. The packing material and shipping box (approximate dimensions: 12" x 12" x 12") weigh an additional 3 pounds.

Proposals must be delivered to the following address:

> U.S. Department of Education
> CFDA #255G
> Application Control Center
> 1990 K Street NW
> Washington, DC 20202-4725
> Attn: Ms. Jean E. Miller, POC

You must deliver the grant application package before the due date and time specified above. The U.S. Department of Education is open from 9:00 a.m. to 4:30 p.m. EST Monday through Friday except for federal holidays. The agency will not accept electronic or fax submissions.

Exercise 7-1 continues on the next page

Exercise 7-1 (Continued)

Transmittal Letter and Proposal Delivery

(Exercise 7-1 answers are found on page 241)

Directions: Based on the situation presented on page 135, determine the delivery method you will use to ensure the grant application package is delivered in a timely fashion.   Indicate the cost associated with the delivery method and identify the pros/cons associated with this delivery method considering the weather, deadline date, and time to deliver the package to Washington, DC.

Delivery Method (Attach all delivery documentation forms)

Cost

Pros/Cons

Chapter 8
Postsubmission Activities

After the grant application has been delivered to the funding agency, all writers and reviewers should meet to debrief and discuss the proposal submission. Grant proposals received by funding agencies undergo a thorough review that may take six months or more before a funding outcome is determined. After the review process, funding agencies make award decisions based on recommendations from funding agency readers. Funding agencies may: (1) fund all or part of a proposed project, (2) request clarification about the proposal narrative or budget, or (3) not fund the proposed project. **See Exhibit 8-1**.

Holding Debriefing Meetings

Once grant applications have been delivered, there is a natural tendency to relax and go back to normal activities, but this is a mistake. Immediately after grant applications have been delivered to funding agencies, proposal directors should hold *debriefing meetings* and organize and file all documents in anticipation of questions from funding agencies. Debriefing meetings should be held in an effort to identify proposal strengths and weaknesses. Prior to debriefing meetings, writers and reviewers should review applications and identify potential deficiencies. Writers and reviewers should focus on answers to the following questions:

- Is the proposal compliant?
- Are project claims substantiated?
- Are project benefits emphasized?
- Are costs appropriate?

Debriefing meetings are scheduled to identify and respond to proposal problems and deficiencies while they are fresh in the minds of proposal team members; thus the rationale for having the meeting immediately after proposal submission. Strategies for improving proposal narrative and budgets are noted at debriefing meetings and used later to clarify any concerns by funding agencies.

Original RFPs/RFAs and all other funding agency documents and correspondence should be stored for safekeeping. Computer files of the proposal narrative and budget should be backed up and kept in a separate location for security purposes.

Exhibit 8-1

Postsubmission Activities

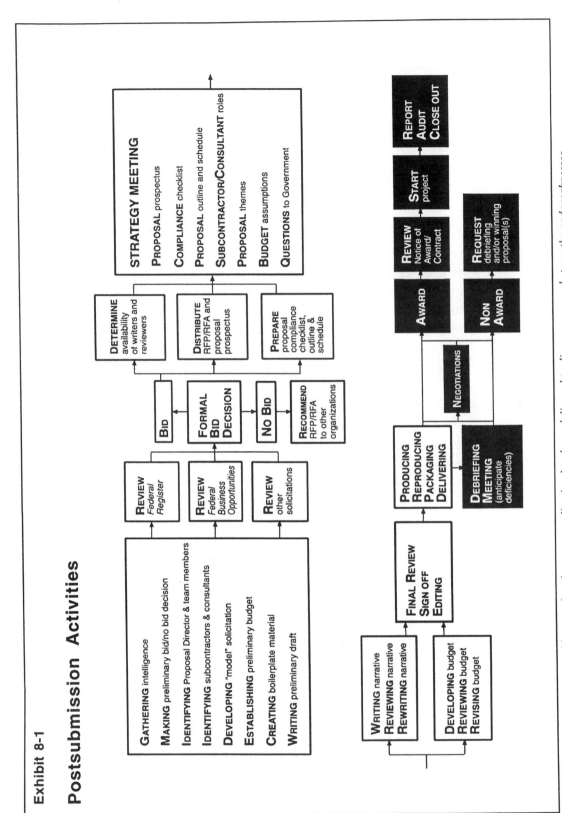

All writers and reviewers should meet after the grant application has been delivered to discuss proposal strengths and weaknesses.

Tracking Proposal Submissions

Organizations applying for multiple grants should use spreadsheets or databases to track submissions and create end-of-the-year reports. These spreadsheets or databases should identify the grant title; CFDA or RFP/RFA number; institutional (internal) proposal tracking number; project director; funding agency and POC; performance period; amount of funding requested; and whether proposals were awarded, denied, or pending. Financial amounts awarded by funding agencies should also be recorded. **See Exhibit 8-2.**

Proposal Review by Funding Agencies

Grant proposals received by funding agencies are evaluated and scored by a panel of funding agency (field) readers who are selected because of their education, experience, and geographic representation. Most funding agencies welcome letters and résumés from potential readers interested in reviewing grant applications.

Panel readers travel to common locations to read and evaluate proposals or they may read proposals at home and send results back to funding agencies. Several agencies conduct proposal evaluations using the Internet and panel member discussions by conference calls or Internet chat rooms to avoid travel expenses. Grant application field readers often receive training from funding agencies about reader activities and responsibilities prior to evaluating and scoring proposals. **See Exhibit 8-3.** Readers must sign an assurance form to ensure that they do not have a conflict of interest with respect to proposals included in the competition. **See Exhibit 8-4.**

Most panel reader teams consist of three readers with various skill levels and experiences. Readers use their experience, training, and professional judgment to rate each grant application using an assessment form based on the same weighted criteria published in the RFP/RFA. Grant application readers must provide written comments addressing the strengths and weaknesses of the applicant's proposed project. Readers' comments must not include personal biases that hinder the integrity of the review process. **See Exhibit 8-5.** Grant applications are evaluated on the basis of how well applicants responded to criteria in the RFP/RFA and the quality of proposed project ideas. Basic review questions might include:

- Is the project consistent with the agency's funding priorities?
- Were proposal guidelines followed?
- Is there a compelling problem/need for this project and is it well documented?
- Is the project's purpose (goals and objectives) clearly identified?
- Do the methods describe specific tasks to meet the project's goals/objectives?
- Will the proposed evaluation plans determine project effectiveness?
- Is the budget within the average funding range, well justified, and accurate?
- Is the proposal well-written, logical, reasonable, and free from errors?

Exhibit 8-2

Sample Proposal Tracking Spreadsheet

Title of Grant CFDA/RFP/RFA#	Internal Proposal Number	Department Contact/Phone	Agency/POC Performance Period	Amount Requested	Awarded Denied Pending	Amount Awarded
Early School Program RFP 203136	201	Social Science Brooks/5920	STATE / J. Marshal April 1, XX–June 30, XX	$16,201	Awarded	$16,201
Career Opportunities in Biology NSF 02-36	202	Science Ash/6489	NSF / M. James July 1, XX–June 30, XX	$208,500	Pending	0
Hispanic Serving Institutions RFP 14621	203	Social Science Richards/7090	HUD / K. Watkins July 1, XX–June 30, XX	$154,320	Denied	0
Excellence in Electronics NSF 03-27	204	Technology Howard/4452	NSF / M. Ellis July 1, XX–June 30, XX	$4,330,232	Pending	0
Work Study Program RFP 555102	205	Technology Wheeler/4487	HUD / D. Studdert July 1, XX–June 30, XX	$263,920	Awarded	$263,920
School-to-Work CFDA 84-2788	206	Technology Michaels/2732	EDUC / K. Addel July 1, XX–June 30, XX	$487,215	Awarded	$487,215
YouthNet Project RFP 454521	207	Social Science Collins/8816	DHS / L. Green July 1, XX–June 30, XX	$160,000	Awarded	$160,000
Community Development RFP 133421	208	Social Science Collins/8816	EDUC / T. Foreman July 1, XX–June 30, XX	$48,711	Awarded	$48,711

Funding seekers use spreadsheets or databases to track multiple grant submissions.

Most funding agencies include solicitation guidelines and expect funding seekers to follow them diligently when submitting grant applications. Funding seekers who win consistently pay special attention to content and format criteria before submitting proposals. Content criteria identify the composition of components and sub-components expected in proposals. Normally, content criteria include the same weighted point system that funding agency readers use to rate proposals. Format criteria identify the layout of content that is expected in grant submissions. Some RFPs/RFAs specify the number of pages allowed for each content area (e.g., 500 words or less for the abstract, problem/need statement not to exceed 5 pages). In other instances, RFPs/RFAs provide a specific outline of content and format guidelines for proposals. Grant applications must carefully follow these guidelines if you expect to score high and be recommended for funding.

Exhibit 8-3

Sample Funding Agency Readers' Responsibilities

• Read criteria published in the RFP/RFA.

• Evaluate each grant application based on rating criteria published in the RFP/RFA.

• Assign a numerical rating to each application section (based on criteria).

• Write detailed comments relating to the application's strengths and weaknesses.
  • Comments must be evaluative, not descriptive.
  • Comments must be directly tied to rating criteria.
  • Comments must be thorough and objective since they are used in funding decisions and debriefing of unsuccessful grant applicants.

• Meet with other funding agency readers to discuss each application. The purpose of this meeting is to allow readers the opportunity to discuss scores and provide justification of those scores. This is the only opportunity to revise scores if readers see differences based on ambiguous language within a proposal.

• Keep all review proceedings confidential. Readers are not permitted to discuss applicants, contents or scoring of grant applications, identity of other readers, or any other part of the review process with anyone – either during or after the review.

Funding agency readers must agree to specific responsibilities prior to evaluating grant applications.

Exhibit 8-4

Sample Funding Agency Readers' Agreement

Freedom of Information Act

I understand that under the Freedom of Information Act the government may release my reviews verbatim to the public. The government may also release individual readers' names in conformance with the government's disclosure policy, but generally will not identify an individual reader with a particular review. However, to avoid complicating the release of reviews, I agree *not* to make comments that could be seen as offensive or constitute an invasion of privacy.

Confidentiality of Documents and Restriction on Contact

I understand that grant applications are made available to grant readers solely for the purpose of reviewing against the selection criteria.

I agree *not* to discuss the information, concepts, and procedures contained in grant applications after the review process, and to discuss only with the panel readers and in the context of and under the procedures for application review. I agree to follow all written instructions provided by the government for the completion of review forms. I also agree to return all grant applications to the government. I agree *not* to contact the originator of the grant application being reviewed concerning any aspects of its contents.

Conflict of Interest

I hereby certify that to the best of my knowledge I do not have a conflict of interest and that my particular circumstances are not likely to raise the appearance of a conflict of interest (or have received a waiver) with respect to any grant application in this competition. For purposes of this agreement I recognize that I will have a conflict of interest, if any of the following has a financial interest in an application:

- I, my spouse, minor child, or partner,
- a profit or nonprofit organization in which I serve as an officer, director, trustee, partner, or employee; or
- any person or organization with whom I am negotiating or have an arrangement concerning prospective employment.

I acknowledge that this agreement is in effect at all times until I have completed all work to be performed.

If I discover that I might have a conflict of interest or the appearance of a conflict of interest with any grant application in the competition, I will inform the appropriate program official immediately.

Agreement on Scope of Work

Before reviewing and scoring grant applications, I will read all instructions, regulations, criteria, and review forms, all of which will be made available to me by the appropriate program official.

- I will read and score all grant applications;
- I will score each grant application solely on its content and the degree to which the application meets the appropriate priorities and criteria; and
- I will sign and date a review form for each grant application and return it to the appropriate program official.

Funding agency readers must sign assurance forms to ensure that they do not have a conflict of interest with respect to grant applications included in the competition.

Exhibit 8-5

Sample Grant Application Evaluation Form

Applicant: Hoosier State College

Reader Team #: 3

Points Awarded

Criteria (Possible Points)

Problem/Need (30)

• Problem/need description	12	12
• Problem/need rationale	5	5
• Population affected by project	5	5
• Vision for solving the problem	8	8

Goals/Objectives (10)

• Goals/objectives are realistic and measurable	5	5
• Goals/objectives are related to the plan	5	5

Methods/Activities (45)

• Project strategy	10	10
• Project rationale	10	10
• Project timetable	5	5
• Key personnel	10	9
• Project management procedures	10	9

Evaluation Plans (10)

• Data elements/data collection	5	5
• Data analysis	5	5

Budget (5)

• Necessary and reasonable project costs	5	5

Total | 100 | 98

Funding agency readers evaluate grant applications using a review form with the same weighted criteria that was published in the RFP/RFA.

After evaluating proposals on an independent basis, funding agency readers meet and discuss grant application ratings. The purpose of the panel discussion is to: (1) share professional judgments and ratings, (2) assist readers in the re-evaluation of his/her ratings, if necessary, (3) clarify information in grant applications that may have been overlooked, and (4) eliminate, where possible, wide differences between the highest overall rating and the lowest rating where those differences result from lack of information, misinformation, or misunderstanding. While funding agency readers use this meeting time to discuss proposal deficiencies and variations in ratings, a consensus is not required. Readers may revise their ratings and comments if the panel discussion provides new insight and a different conclusion. If necessary, an arbitrator intervenes to resolve disagreements about grant application sections. Readers should provide a courteous, straightforward, and specific analysis that justifies their score for a particular evaluation criterion. In addition, readers must be sure that points awarded correspond with narrative comments. Since the Freedom of Information Act (FOIA) allows all applicants the opportunity to request copies of readers' scores and comments about grant applications, funding agency readers must write substantive and analytical comments that directly relate to criteria published in RFPs/RFAs. **See Exhibit 8-6**.

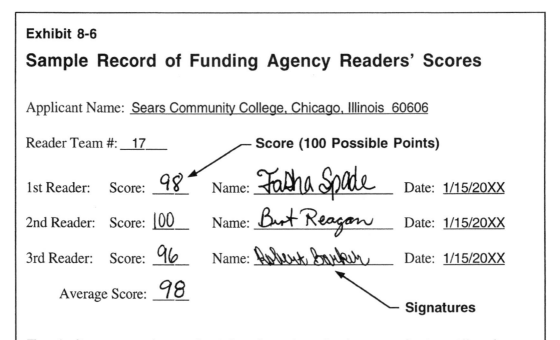

Exhibit 8-6

Sample Record of Funding Agency Readers' Scores

Applicant Name: <u>Sears Community College, Chicago, Illinois 60606</u>

Reader Team #: <u>17</u>   ⎡ **Score (100 Possible Points)**

1st Reader: Score: <u>98</u> Name: <u>Fatha Spade</u> Date: <u>1/15/20XX</u>

2nd Reader: Score: <u>100</u> Name: <u>Burt Reagan</u> Date: <u>1/15/20XX</u>

3rd Reader: Score: <u>96</u> Name: <u>Robert Barber</u> Date: <u>1/15/20XX</u>

Average Score: <u>98</u>

⎣ **Signatures**

Three funding agency readers complete independent reviews of each grant application. All readers meet and discuss the strengths and weaknesses of the application and final scores are recorded. The highest-scoring applications are recommended for funding.

Winning Proposals

After grant applications have been reviewed, funding agencies send notifications to funding seekers regarding proposal outcomes. If your proposed project was selected for funding, you will receive a *notice of award* letter or a detailed contract that specifies the funding amount to complete the proposed work identified in the grant application. **See Exhibit 8-7**. Notice of award letters may also include attachments that delineate the terms and conditions of the award and provide further guidance about administrative procedures.

Exhibit 8-7

Sample Notice of Award Letter

Title: Forging Connections between Business, Education, and Government for Strengthening Technological Skills Among Urban Students

⌐ Award Amount

Dear Dr. Brown:

The National Science Association (NSA) hereby awards a grant of $84,427 to Jackson University to support the project referenced above, under the direction of Dr. Nancy Brown. This award is effective July 1, 20XX and expires June 30, 20XX.

— Grant Period

This grant is awarded pursuant to the authority of the National Science Association Act of 1950 and is subject to the following terms and conditions:

- Administration of NSA conference and group travel award grant special conditions.

  ⌐ Cost Sharing
- The grantee agrees to provide cost sharing as specified in the referenced proposal in the amount of $56,162. No NSA funds may be used to meet the grantee's cost sharing obligation for this project.

The cognizant NSA program official for this grant is Ms. Janet Hall (703) 306-1100. Please contact Ms. Hall if you have questions or concerns about this award.

∟ Agency Contact

Sincerely,

Lynette Winterbaum
Lynette Winterbaum
Grant Officer

c: Janet Hall

Notice of award letters specify the funding amount and outline the terms and conditions of the award.

Grant award terms and conditions are binding and must be followed by the grantee. Some awards have relatively few restrictions, while others are laden with significant limitations and extensive reporting requirements. Most grant awards require periodic progress and financial reports that provide detail about the completion of proposed activities in relation to project objectives. Most award documents contain narrative regarding the: (1) amount of funds awarded, (2) period of performance, (3) work to be done, (4) *financial and performance reports* and due dates, and (5) contractual conditions. Other terms and conditions may also be included by reference. Detailed contracts may contain clauses that should be reviewed by legal counsel prior to signing.

In some cases, funding agencies may determine through cost analysis that certain proposal activities are unnecessary and recommend deleting them and their associated costs from the award. In other cases, funding agencies might determine that amounts requested for particular items are excessive and will want to negotiate a lower funding amount with your organization. Always prepare before a contract negotiation session. Decide beforehand who will attend the negotiation meeting, what documents are necessary to take to the meeting (proposal narrative and support documents, direct, indirect, and cost sharing contributions as well as calculations to support budget items), and be prepared to both give and take.

If you receive an award amount that was less than what you proposed and there is no room for negotiating, it is strongly suggested that you reread the proposal narrative and make appropriate corrections to the proposed activities. A letter should then be sent to the POC explaining exactly what activities have been changed to meet the financial limitations of the award. **See Exhibit 8-8**.

Always notify internal staff and administrators as well as partners, subcontractors, and consultants about awards. After the official award notification has been *fully executed* (signed by the funding agency and your organization), proposal directors should adjust the project schedule, if necessary, and begin hiring staff and purchasing equipment and supplies necessary to start the project.

Proposal Negotiation and Clarification

In some cases, additional information about grant proposals is needed prior to funding decisions. Funding agencies may ask questions that require funding seekers to clarify points in proposals, correct errors, or respond to suggestions made by proposal readers. Questions may require written and/or oral responses. Potential award recipients must be responsive to funding agency questions. Funding seekers should not over interpret questions. If funding agencies ask questions about submissions, it is a very positive sign and should be treated favorably, not defensively. The length of discussion or *negotiation* sessions will depend on the number of fiscal or regulatory issues pertaining to grant applications and the proposal's complexity. Funding seekers should strive to prepare responses that: (1) eliminate deficiencies, (2) provide clarification, and (3) improve proposals. Keep in mind that during negotiation sessions, proposal funding is still pending. An award is not official until an award notification is fully executed.

Exhibit 8-8

Sample Letter to POC After Receiving a Low Budget Award

June 20, 20XX

⟵ **Agency/POC**

State Community College Board
Attention: Dr. Jean E. Thomas, CFO
401 East Highway Road
Capital City, IN 58765-1234

⟵ **RFP Number/Title**

Re: RFP# 42702
    Innovative Programs to Increase Information Technology Graduates

Dear Dr. Thomas:

Thank you for your comments concerning our Information Technology (IT) Special Initiative Grant (SIG). Hoosier State College was very pleased to receive the Notice of Award letter indicating that we received $40,000 to implement the IT project.

We have altered several proposal tasks to account for the $10,000 difference between our $50,000 original budget submission and the $40,000 award from your agency. Specifically, instead of sending IT faculty for out-of-state training, we were able to negotiate an understanding with 3-Com to have them come to Hoosier State College and train both college and high school instructors at a savings of $7,000.

Other funding will be used to provide outreach materials to local high schools, which will result in a $3,000 savings. Enclosed is a revised proposal and budget to reflect the $40,000 award. Specifically note the changes to proposal activity items 1.1a and 2.1d under measurable outcomes of the project overview and timeline.

If you have questions or concerns about these project changes, please do not hesitate to contact me. Thank you.

Sincerely,

Janet J. Passmore

Dr. Janet J. Passmore,
President
219-834-5555

⟵ **Contact Person/Phone Number**

c: Dr. Patrick Smith
       Mr. David Johnson

enclosures

When awarded a budget amount less than expected, you should make appropriate corrections to the original proposal and write a letter to the POC explaining what activities have been changed to meet the financial limitations of the award. When making these changes, take care not to alter the core purpose of the grant. The funding agency Program Officer must approve all changes.

Tracking Grant Costs

If you have been awarded grant funding, your work has just begun. Now, you must complete the proposed project activities for the costs previously identified in the proposal budget. It is very important that accurate financial records be maintained. Spreadsheets or databases can be used to track costs for most small grant awards. More sophisticated software packages can be used for complicated multi-year awards. Spreadsheets or databases should be set up to track budget items on a quarterly basis for budget reports and final grant *closeout* activities. **See Exhibit 8-9**.

Exhibit 8-9

Sample Grant Expenditures Spreadsheet

Quarterly Expenditures				
Budget Line Items	**7/1 – 9/30**	**10/1 – 12/31**	**1/1 – 3/30**	**4/1 – 6/30**	**Total**
Personnel	3,525	3,525	3,525	3,525	14,100
Fringe Benefits	860	860	860	860	3,440
Travel	3,225	2,225	1,250	1,250	7,950
Equipment	5,856	5,777	6,435	6,555	24,623
Supplies	2,559	2,010	4,445	1,245	10,259
Contractual	3,660	3,660	3,660	3,660	14,640
Other	500	1,239	1,250	0	2,989
Total	$ 20,185	$ 19,296	$ 21,425	$ 17,095	$ 78,001

Spreadsheets or databases are used to track grant expenditures on a quarterly basis.

Losing Proposals

Grant applications may not receive funding even though a tremendous amount of work and effort went into developing the proposal. *"You never really lose until you quit trying" (Mike Ditka).* If you lose, it is extremely important that you find out why you were denied funding. **See Exhibit 8-10.** If your federal or state grant application was not funded, you should request: (1) a debriefing meeting with the Point of Contact (POC), (2) reviewers' comments, and (3) copies of several winning proposals. **See Exhibit 8-11.**

Requesting a Debriefing Meeting With the Point of Contact (POC)

If your organization was not selected to receive an award, a *debriefing meeting* should be set up with the POC immediately after grant award winners have been selected. Ask the POC to explain the basis for selecting grant recipients and discuss the shortcomings of your proposal submission. In the same conversation, ask the POC about specific suggestions to improve and strengthen your grant proposal narrative and budget. Take careful meeting notes and discuss this feedback information with proposal writers and reviewers.

Exhibit 8-10

What to Do When Proposals Are Not Funded

If your grant application was not funded, you should find out the reasons behind the denial and then try again. By law, most public agencies are required to provide adequate reasons for turning down a grant application (policies do not apply to private grants).

Reapplication

Agencies generally look favorably upon reapplications. Some funding agencies specifically state that reapplications are welcome and declare no bias against them. Many reapplications succeed because applicants had requested a "why not" letter and improved their proposals on the basis of reviewers' comments. In some cases you may need to file a FOIA request to receive a written response.

Not every request for feedback produces improvement in proposals. Nor does every reapplicant, however persistent, eventually win. Most funding officials will tell you, unless the reapplication involves excessive labor, there is no harm in trying.

"Why Not" Requests

Some federal agencies such as The Department of Health and Human Services inform all applicants automatically of reasons why grant applications are not funded. Other agencies, such as the National Endowment for the Humanities, respond to letters from educators or schools that request "why not" as a matter of courtesy and a matter of course. The letter need not be complex–a short written request is sufficient. A "why not" request, however, must be in writing due to the private nature of the content.

Adapted from: If You Don't Get a Grant, Get Reasons, and Try, Try Again. (1997). Capitol Publications, 8204 Fenton St., Silver Spring, MD 20910

If grant funds are not awarded, it is important to find out why, make appropriate corrections, and reapply for the next round of competition.

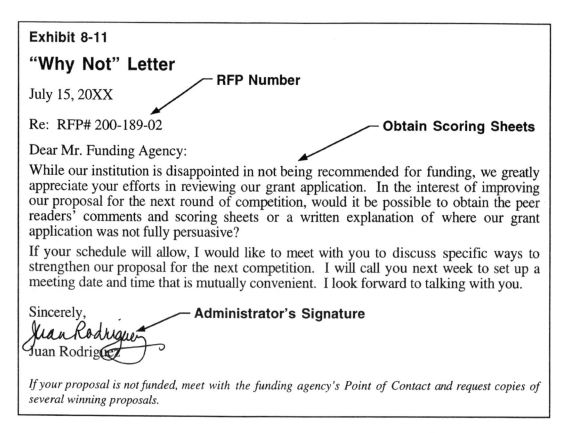

Exhibit 8-11

"Why Not" Letter

RFP Number

July 15, 20XX

Re: RFP# 200-189-02

Obtain Scoring Sheets

Dear Mr. Funding Agency:

While our institution is disappointed in not being recommended for funding, we greatly appreciate your efforts in reviewing our grant application. In the interest of improving our proposal for the next round of competition, would it be possible to obtain the peer readers' comments and scoring sheets or a written explanation of where our grant application was not fully persuasive?

If your schedule will allow, I would like to meet with you to discuss specific ways to strengthen our proposal for the next competition. I will call you next week to set up a meeting date and time that is mutually convenient. I look forward to talking with you.

Sincerely, *Administrator's Signature*

Juan Rodriguez

If your proposal is not funded, meet with the funding agency's Point of Contact and request copies of several winning proposals.

Requesting Reviewers' Comments

Always request readers' comments if they were not previously provided by the funding agency. **See Exhibit 8-12**. Based on an analysis of 700 proposals that were *not* funded from the U.S. Public Health Services, the following errors were the basis for rejection.

- Inadequate planning led to carelessly prepared applications (39%). Simple mistakes such as too many pages or failure to specifically address funding priorities were apparent.

- Competency of applicants were not shown (38%). Note the problem was not applicant qualifications, but that qualifications were not clearly identified and tied to proposed projects.

- Unclear presentation of project ideas (18%). Most agencies receive more proposals with good ideas than they can fund; the difference between an accepted and rejected proposal is attention to detail and presentation of proposed project ideas (*Federal Assistance Monitor*, June, 1998).

Requesting Winning Proposal(s)

It is usually worthwhile to request a list of winning grant applicants and one or more winning grant applications from funding agencies. With some agencies, a simple telephone call is all that is needed to obtain copies of winning proposals. Other agencies require a formal letter that references the FOIA before they will send information.

Exhibit 8-12

Sample Proposal Debriefing Letter

July 15, 20XX

U.S. Department of Education
Application Control Center   ┌─ **CFDA Number**
600 Independence Avenue, S.W.
Washington, DC 20202   ┌─ **Cite FOIA**
RE: CFDA# 278C Grant Application

Based on the Freedom of Information Act, Anytown School District requests a written debriefing of its School-To-Work (S-T-W) Implementation Project grant application submitted earlier this year. We would appreciate the scoring sheets and specific reader comments in order to strengthen our proposal for the next round of S-T-W applications. Please send the specified information to:

> Dr. John Ling
> Anytown School District
> 1311 Northwest Main Street
> Anytown, USA 98765

Please contact me at (555) 435-8400 if you have questions. Thank you.

Sincerely,   ── **Contact Person**

John Ling
Dr. John Ling
Superintendent

Always request a copy of the readers' comments if your proposal was not funded.

Winning proposals and other information received from funding agencies as a result of FOIA letters may provide new insights and ideas that can be incorporate into grant applications. Agencies are supposed to respond to FOIA letters within 10 working days of receipt. While some may delay, no agency can completely ignore a legitimate FOIA request. The best strategy to use with funding agency staff members is to ask politely but immediately for everything related to funding competitions that will be helpful to you in resubmitting other proposal applications. However, note that funding agencies can legally limit the number of pages sent to funding seekers without charging for clerical and/or duplication costs. In addition, information about other applicants and internal agency memoranda or review materials are not covered by FOIA.

When reviewing grant proposal feedback, determine which comments are valid and make appropriate corrections. Armed with a revised grant application, past winning proposals, and knowledge about the competition, consider resubmitting a grant proposal for future funding competitions.

Winning Strategies for Funding Seekers: Final Thoughts

Funding seekers must remember that patience, persistence, and a positive attitude are needed to win grant funding. Keep in mind these final thoughts:

- Use the Internet and get on free mailing lists to obtain early alerts about state and federal grant opportunities so you have time to prepare winning applications.

- Be extremely choosy about grants you go after. State funds are often the easiest to obtain; federal funds are more difficult.

- Research potential funding agencies thoroughly. Contact the agency's POC before and during the proposal development process.

- Attend preproposal conferences and technical workshops offered by agencies.

- Develop boilerplate materials that can be used and reused in grant applications. Collect appendix material and sign partner agreements before funding agency solicitations are released.

- Preview successful grant applications that are similar to your project. You will obtain some good ideas and an understanding of the competition.

- Always follow application directions that are provided by funding agencies.

- Don't just tell funding agencies about the existence of a problem you intend to solve–demonstrate it with recent and relevant statistics, case studies, and other measurable data. Use the Internet to collect data to support your problem/need.

- Demonstrate that you have appropriate management skills and experience that can deliver successful projects.

- Use proposal schedules to meet funding agency deadlines. If you don't have time to do it right, don't compete for grant funds.

- Use rules of writing that make the proposal narrative shine.
    - Use current funding agency language.
    - Use reviewers and editors to check and recheck written work.

- Make budgets realistic and credible.
    - Check all calculations.
    - Keep a record of how specific costs were determined.
    - Don't ask for more than you need.
    - Keep budget narrative clear, factual, supportable, and professional.

- Don't underestimate the importance of a strong cover letter. Letters should provide an overview of major proposal components and identify a contact person who is knowledgeable about the proposed project.

- Complete all necessary assurance and certification forms. Sign them in blue ink.

- Grant proposals may be turned down by one agency and funded by another. Always know the needs and wants of the funding agency.

- Grant competitions are becoming more rigorous; funding seekers should revise and resubmit grant proposals that were not funded.

- Be realistic in what you propose to do. Remember that someone must actually execute what is proposed in the project narrative.

Chapter 8 Review

(Chapter 8 Review answers are found on page 212)

Directions: For statements 1 through 15, circle T for True or F for False.

T F   1. Immediately after submission, proposal writers and reviewers should meet and discuss the grant proposal's strengths and weaknesses.

T F   2. Most funding agencies welcome letters of interest and résumés from potential grant application readers.

T F   3. The grant proposal review process is subjective.

T F   4. All funding agency readers have equal educational background and experience.

T F   5. Organizations applying for multiple grants should used spreadsheets or databases to track submissions.

T F   6. Funding agency readers must provide written comments about the strengths and weaknesses of grant applications.

T F   7. Funding agency readers must reach a consensus when scoring grant proposals.

T F   8. The Freedom of Information Act (FOIA) allows funding seekers the opportunity to obtain copies of funding agency readers' scores and written comments.

T F   9. Funding agencies provide financial assistance to support grant projects through a notice of award letter or a signed contract.

T F   10. Grant award terms and conditions are binding and must be followed by grant recipients.

T F   11. If you receive a grant award for an amount that was less than what was proposed in the budget and there is no room for negotiating, it is strongly suggested that you make appropriate corrections to the proposed grant activities to meet the financial limitations of the award.

T F   12. Grant awards are not official until an award notification has been *fully executed.*

T F   13. If your proposal did not receive funding, you should always request copies of winning proposals.

T F   14. Funding agencies are supposed to respond to FOIA letters within five working days of receipt.

T F   15. Funding seekers should revise and resubmit grant proposals that were not funded.

Exercise 8-1

Evaluating Proposal Components in Response to Criteria

(Exercise 8-1 answers are found on pages 242 - 244)

Directions: Read the situation below and evaluate the 10 responses to proposal criteria on pages 155 through 164.

Situation: You are serving as a funding agency reader to evaluate proposals submitted in response to a solicitation to provide supervisory skills training to small business owners. The potential grant recipients have been narrowed to two organizations: Lincoln Department of Development and Jefferson Chamber of Commerce.

The following pages contain grant criteria with corresponding responses from the two organizations. Identify the strengths and weaknesses of each response and determine the lessons learned from each of the 10 proposal criteria.

_____

Adapted from: *Writing Winning Grant Proposals: Simulation Learning Workshop for Non-Profit Organizations* (1995). Westinghouse Electric Corporation, Carlsbad, New Mexico

Exercise 8-1 continues on the next page

Criteria #1
The proposal clearly describes the need for supervisory training for small business owners.

Lincoln Department of Development

Lincoln Department of Development conducted a survey of small business needs in April. Nearly 90 percent of small business owners indicated that they needed more supervisory skills to improve their business operations. Nearly 78 percent indicated that they would attend supervisory training if it were offered in the Lincoln community.

Strengths/Weaknesses:

Jefferson Chamber of Commerce

The primary reason for the proposed activities is that Jefferson Chamber of Commerce believes that education is a key element to continually improve economic development. Jefferson Chamber of Commerce is committed to use supervisory training to help all businesses in the Jefferson area.

Strengths/Weaknesses:

Lessons Learned:

Exercise 8-1 continues on the next page

Criteria #2
The proposal clearly describes a schedule for analyzing, designing, developing, implementing, and evaluating the training.

Lincoln Department of Development

Lincoln Department of Development will adhere to the following training schedule.

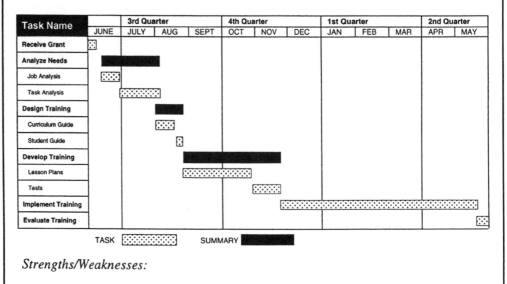

Strengths/Weaknesses:

Jefferson Chamber of Commerce

Upon receipt of the grant funds, Jefferson Chamber of Commerce will develop a schedule for the project. We plan to hire a consultant to assist us in developing the schedule and training. Be assured that Jefferson Chamber of Commerce recognizes the importance of having a detailed project schedule.

Strengths/Weaknesses:

Lessons Learned:

Exercise 8-1 continues on the next page

Criteria #3
The proposal clearly describes time commitments of key personnel who will be responsible for completing proposed activities.

Lincoln Department of Development

The following table shows time commitments of key personnel who will be responsible for carrying out the proposed activities.

Table 1: Time Commitments of Key Personnel

Key Personnel	Position	Hours Per Week
John Smith	Executive Director	5
Sharon Jones	Administrative Assistant	10
Greg Miller	Executive Board Representative	2
Becky Wilson	Small Business Owner	1
David Shields	University Liaison	1
Bruce Wills	Training Consultant	20

Strengths/Weaknesses:

Jefferson Chamber of Commerce

Key personnel who will be responsible for carrying out the proposed activities have committed a considerable amount of time for the project duration: the Executive Director will commit five hours per week, the Administrative Assistant will commit ten hours per week, the Executive Board Representative will commit two hours per week, the Small Business Owner Representative will commit one hour per week, the University Liaison member will commit one hour per week, and the Training Consultant will commit 20 hours per week.

Strengths/Weaknesses:

Lessons Learned:

Exercise 8-1 continues on the next page

Criteria #4

The proposal clearly describes the involvement that stakeholder groups (administration, staff, board members, small business owners, and the educational community) will have in training.

Lincoln Department of Development

All stakeholder groups will participate in the supervisory skills training project. The Executive Director will coordinate the project, ensuring it stays on schedule and produces desired deliverables and outcomes. The administrative assistant will provide desktop publishing support for material development. The board, small business owners, and educational representatives will meet weekly as a steering group to guide the project through the five phases: (1) analysis, (2) design, (3) development, (4) implementation, and (5) evaluation.

Strengths/Weaknesses:

Jefferson Chamber of Commerce

All stakeholder groups will participate in the training project. Coordination of the project to ensure that it stays on schedule and produces desired deliverables and outcomes will be the responsibility of the Executive Director. Desktop publishing will be the responsibility of the administrative assistant. Guidance of the project through the five phases–analysis, design, development, implementation, and evaluation–will be ensured by a steering group. Weekly steering group meetings will be attended by the board, small business owner, and educational representatives.

Strengths/Weaknesses:

Lessons Learned:

Exercise 8-1 continues on the next page

Criteria #5
The proposal clearly describes the proposal director's experience and training in strategic planning.

Lincoln Department of Development

The Lincoln Department of Development Executive Director has had no formal education in strategic planning. However, the Executive Director has over 20 years of on-the-job experience in developing long-range (5-10 year) plans, helping over 100 small businesses. His planning contributions helped him earn a quality contributor award from the state association of Chambers of Commerce last year.

Strengths/Weaknesses:

Jefferson Chamber of Commerce

The Executive Director has a vast amount of experience in strategic planning, from designing the department's calendar to scheduling daily activities for staff members. The Executive Director was involved in the project, which, of course, was a huge success. The Executive Director has also been involved in other plans, and is recognized as one of the best planners in the field of economic development.

Strengths/Weaknesses:

Lessons Learned:

Exercise 8-1 continues on the next page

Criteria #6
The proposal provides evidence of dedication to the project that indicates the training program will be successful.

Lincoln Department of Development

The amount of time and money donated by the Department of Development, small businesses, and community representatives provides evidence of dedication to the project that indicates that it will be successful. We have raised over $45,000 in contributions from the community to be used for the project. Community volunteers have agreed to donate over 2,000 hours to this project.

Strengths/Weaknesses:

Jefferson Chamber of Commerce

Jefferson Chamber of Commerce personnel have read and heard quite a bit about the benefits of supervisory skill training and find the concept to be interesting. The grant will allow Jefferson Chamber of Commerce to offer training that could be valuable in the future.

Strengths/Weaknesses:

Lessons Learned:

Exercise 8-1 continues on the next page

Criteria #7
In a single sentence, the proposal clearly describes the project mission.

Lincoln Department of Development

The supervisory skills training program will help small businesses in Lincoln grow and improve by providing small business owners with knowledge, skills, and abilities to effectively manage their employees.

Strengths/Weaknesses:

Jefferson Chamber of Commerce

Jefferson Chamber of Commerce will develop a world-class training program. The program will be viewed as one of the best plans ever developed. Jefferson Chamber of Commerce will receive awards for the training and national recognition.

Strengths/Weaknesses:

Lessons Learned:

Exercise 8-1 continues on the next page

Criteria #8

In 30 pages or less, the proposal clearly addresses the following required factors: Required Forms, Need, Proposed Activities, Evaluation Plans, Allocations of Key Personnel, Commitment to Broad-Based Participation, and Budget.

Lincoln Department of Development

Proposal Table of Contents

	Page
1. Required Forms	1
2. Need	5
3. Proposed Activities	9
4. Evaluation Plans	20
5. Allocations of Key Personnel	21
6. Commitment to Broad-Based Participation	23
7. Budget	26

Strengths/Weaknesses:

Jefferson Chamber of Commerce

Proposal Table of Contents

	Page
1. Needs Analysis	1
2. Finance	7
3. Activities	11
4. Assessment Plan	25
5. Commitment	27
6. People	31
7. Forms	35

Strengths/Weaknesses:

Lessons Learned:

Exercise 8-1 continues on the next page

Criteria #9
The proposal clearly describes what materials will be produced during the development phase of the project.

Lincoln Department of Development
During the development phase, the Lincoln team will produce the following materials:

- 20 lesson plans (one per training session)
- 60 case studies (three per training session)
- 20 student handouts (one per training session)
- 40 examinations (two per training session)
- Course evaluation form

Strengths/Weaknesses:

Jefferson Chamber of Commerce
The Jefferson team will coordinate activities to ensure that all required training materials are produced on schedule. The consultant will focus on lesson and examination development. The educational representative and small business representative will work on case studies. The administrative assistant will work on student handouts.

Strengths/Weaknesses:

Lessons Learned:

Exercise 8-1 continues on the next page

Criteria #10
The proposal clearly describes what performance indicators will be used to monitor the effectiveness of the program.

Lincoln Department of Development
The Lincoln team has identified the following performance indicators to monitor program effectiveness:

- Sales volume/income
- Employee turnover rate
- Employee absenteeism rate
- Customer satisfaction rate

Strengths/Weaknesses:

Jefferson Chamber of Commerce
With the benefit of a practiced statistician, the Jefferson Chamber of Commerce will determine absenteeism, turnover, sales, and customer satisfaction parameters. We really think it's important to do this. State-of-the-art analytical engines will be utilized to originate key data. This should give us some neat numbers to crunch.

Strengths/Weaknesses:

Lessons Learned:

Exercise 8-1 continues on the next page

Exercise 8-2

Evaluating Two Proposals

(Exercise 8-2 answers are found on pages 245 - 246)

Directions: You work for EagleEye Analysts. Your company specializes in aerial/ satellite photograph analysis. You employ many technicians to analyze photographs for a variety of purposes and you need a training program in aerial/satellite photograph analysis for entry- and mid-level employees.

EagleEye Analysts has received two proposals in response to a Request for Proposal (RFP). One proposal is from Instructors, Inc. (pages 167 - 176) and the other is from Technical Trainers, Inc. (pages 178 - 191). You know little about either firm, but have been assigned to an evaluation panel to read and score the two proposals. Your specific assignment is to evaluate the part of each proposal that addresses the firms' training philosophy and approach.

You will not have access to other parts of the proposals or to cost information. At this point you will not be able to ask questions of either training firm. Your evaluation must be made strictly on the basis of information in the proposals.

Proposal Preparation Instructions

The RFP provided the following proposal preparation information to all firms:

1. Describe your training philosophy and the principles your firm considers important in the development of training programs.

2. Describe your firm's approach to training program development and instruction.

3. Provide a detailed project plan for the development of a training program that includes: (1) methods and time schedules for delivering the training, and (2) a comprehensive description of the experience and role of key members of the project team.

Evaluation Criteria

1. Does the firm's training philosophy seem appropriate to EagleEye Analysts' needs? Does it seem sound to you?

2. Does the firm present a sound training program based on a clear understanding of recent evidence from the literature?

3. Are proposed deliverables clearly described, and do they appear to be adequate?

4. Has the firm proposed an appropriately organized project team?

5. Are you persuaded that this firm has a sound approach overall?

Adapted from The Winning Proposal Student Workbook, ESI. Used with permission.

Exercise 8-2 continues on the next page

Exercise 8-2

Evaluating Two Proposals

Use this form to evaluate Instructors Inc.'s proposal on pages 167 to 176.

Proposal Scoring Sheet for Instructors, Inc.

Ratings	
Superior	I am convinced that this is a capable training firm. They may not be perfect, but they have a sound philosophy and approach.
Good	I think this training firm might be able to do the job, but I would not select them without asking more questions.
Marginal	I am not persuaded that this training firm could do the job. Their plan is unclear and lacking in important details.
Poor	I am convinced that this training firm cannot do the job.

Evaluation Criteria

Directions: Evaluate the proposal on the following criteria.

1. Does the firm's training philosophy seem appropriate to EagleEye Analysts' needs? Does it seem sound to you?

   Rating:_____

2. Does the firm present a sound training program based on a clear understanding of recent evidence from the literature?

   Rating:_____

3. Are proposed deliverables clearly described, and do they appear to be adequate?

   Rating:_____

4. Has the firm proposed an appropriately organized project team?

   Rating:_____

5. Are you persuaded that this firm has a sound approach overall?

   Rating:_____

Recommendation: Yes   No

Evaluator's name: _____

Exercise 8-2 continues on the next page

Exercise 8-2: Evaluating Two Proposals

Instructors, Inc.'s Proposal

Training Philosophy

> Aerial photography analysis is a skill that must be learned by doing. Instructors, Inc. devotes at least half of class time to practical exercises. As a result, EagleEye Analysts' employees will return from our courses able to perform tasks, not just describe them.

Training experts agree: The best way to teach someone how to do a job is to show them how, let them try, and give them feedback.[1] A lecture may provide an informative and engaging account of how to analyze a satellite image, but will employees remember the lecture's instructions back at the workbench? Will employees be able to actually identify terrain and manmade features based on that memory? Experience has taught us that the answer is no.

Aerial/satellite photography analysis traditionally has been taught by lecture, with an occasional case study, demonstration, or practical exercise thrown in for variety. Instructors, Inc. has learned from a sampling of courses on aerial/satellite photography analysis that other training companies devote an average of 75 percent of class time to lecture.[2] Figure 1 contrasts our use of class time with that of our competitors.

Most trainers we observed emphasized concepts and theory. They described procedures but provided participants with few opportunities to practice them. We suspect that, back at their workbenches, employees from those classes stared at their notes, tried to remember the lecturer's instructions, and found applying what they "learned" harder than anticipated.

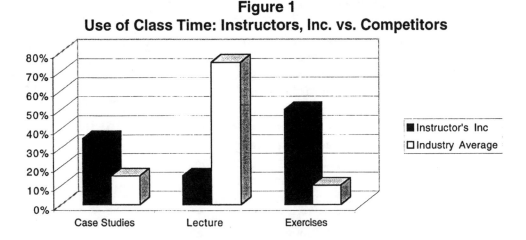

Figure 1
Use of Class Time: Instructors, Inc. vs. Competitors

Instructors, Inc., unlike most of its competitors, devotes at least 50% of class time to practical exercises, rather than lecture. Instructors, Inc. usually allocates at least 30% of class time to demonstrations and case studies.

Exercise 8-2 continues on the next page

Instructors, Inc. training is task-oriented. Our philosophy is that aerial/satellite photography analysis training should teach participants how to perform workday tasks. Some lecture about concepts and theories is necessary, but even the most entertaining lecturer can become tiresome after a while. Research has shown that after an hour or so the average participant's attention span deteriorates.[3] Exercises, case studies, and demonstrations are keys to cost-effective training and on-the-job performance. Instructors, Inc. guarantees that EagleEye Analysts' training dollars will pay for experience, not just information.

Instructors, Inc. devotes no less than 50% of class time to realistic practical exercises in on-the-job tasks. The remaining time is allocated to demonstration, case studies, and lecture in that order of priority. Our market research indicates that no other trainer we studied devoted as much time to practice of work tasks.

Instructors, Inc.'s approach means that when EagleEye Analysts' employees attend our classes they will spend most of their time *doing*, instead of just listening and trying to memorize. In the five-day, seven-hour-a-day aerial photography analysis courses we developed for Orbitronics, participants spent no less than 18 hours doing procedures they had come to learn. Orbitronics' training dollars bought experience under the eye of skilled instructor-practitioners.

Exercise 8-2 continues on the next page

Supervised practice is the key to effective on-the-job performance and it is the philosophy underlying the approach we offer to EagleEye Analysts.

Instructors, Inc.'s Approach: Systematic, Phased, and Thorough

Instructors, Inc. will confirm EagleEye Analysts' needs, specify what employees will be able to do after training, and develop a means of testing the training program *before* we design courses.

Thus, Instructors, Inc. will design a training program to well-defined objectives. And we will have clear standards and methods for evaluating the program effectiveness.

Instructors, Inc. uses a proven instructional systems development approach to training design and presentation based on a systems engineering approach to project management.[4] The key to our success has been the concentration of effort in up-front analysis, specification of objectives, and test development before beginning detailed program design. This approach helps us avoid costly mistakes and extra work during training.

Figure 2 shows our work breakdown structure for the EagleEye Analysts Training Program Development Project. The remainder of this section details each element in the figure.

Figure 2
EagleEye Analysts' Training Program Development Project
Work Breakdown Structure

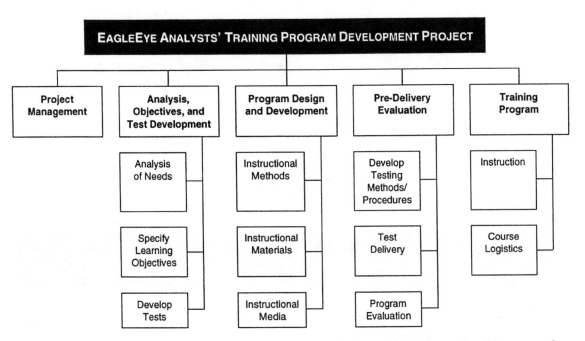

Instructors, Inc. training program provides a breakdown of the major project tasks. The proposal narrative addresses each task in detail, describing levels of effort and products.

We have broken the project down into five major elements, or tasks: (1) project management; (2) analysis, objectives, and test development; (3) program design and development; (4) pre-delivery evaluation; and (5) training. These tasks are divided into subtasks as shown in Figure 2. This work breakdown structure is the foundation for our project planning, scheduling, and controlling, and is the basis for our project organization.

Approximately 30 percent of our effort will consist of up-front analysis and specification of objectives. We will dedicate XXX hours of aerial/satellite photography analysis expert and program design specialist labor [5] to this phase of the training.

Exercise 8-2 continues on the next page

Upfront analysis is important, because it reduces the risk of unnecessary and costly rework during the design and development and program evaluation phases.

Figure 3 shows our schedule for completing each phase of the project.

Note that the design and development work of Phase II will not commence until the analytical and specification work of Phase I has been approved. Training will not commence until we have established the validity of our program design through test and evaluation.

Figure 3
Program Schedule

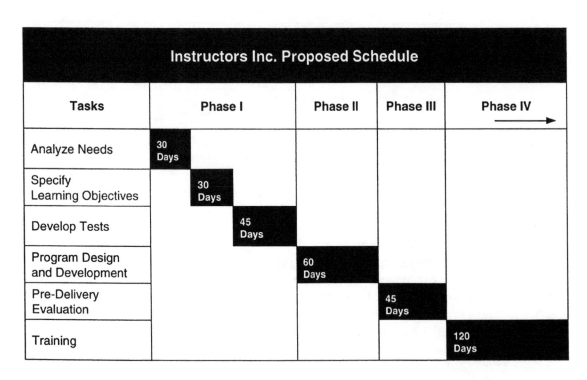

Instructors Inc. Proposed Schedule					
Tasks	**Phase I**		**Phase II**	**Phase III**	**Phase IV** →
Analyze Needs	30 Days				
Specify Learning Objectives		30 Days			
Develop Tests			45 Days		
Program Design and Development				60 Days	
Pre-Delivery Evaluation					45 Days
Training					120 Days

Instructors, Inc. will proceed with the work in four phases. We will proceed with each phase only after EagleEye Analysts' representatives have approved the work of the preceding phase. EagleEye Analysts will be assured that training is proceeding toward the achievement of clearly defined objectives.

Exercise 8-2 continues on the next page

Phase I: Analysis, Objectives, and Test Development

Phase 1 has three stages. First, we assess EagleEye's training needs. Our aerial/satellite photography analysis experts will spend at least XX hours interviewing managers, supervisors, and employees and observing them at work in order to understand their tasks and problems.

We will be especially concerned with distinguishing the differing needs of entry- and mid-level analysts. We will discuss with Eagle Eye management the knowledge and skills that should be taught. In this way, we will confirm the learning objectives for the training program.

Second, we specify the learning objectives. Our aerial/satellite photography analysis experts and program design specialists will spend at least XXX hours writing a clear and detailed *Specification of Learning Objectives*–a description of what EagleEye's employees will be able to do after they have attended the training.[6] This document will be available for review and approval by (date). EagleEye's approval will ensure that our design efforts will address employees' needs.

Third, we will develop testing methods. Our test development specialists, working from the *Specification of Learning Objectives*, will spend no less than XXX hours designing written and performance tests to measure the level of participants' analytical skills after training. These tests will be described in a *Student Achievement*

and Program Evaluation Test Specification. This document will be available for review and approval by (date).

Approved *Specification of Learning Objectives* and *Student Achievement and Program Evaluation Test Specification* will be used as the baseline during Phase II: Program Design and Development.

Phase II: Program Design and Development

Only after approval of the learning objectives and testing methods will we design and develop training methods and media. Products of this phase will be an *Instructor's Statement of Work and Methods* and workbooks and media that will be used in the classroom.

Instructors, Inc. will allocate at least 50% of class time to skills practice. Demonstrations and discussions of sample analyses will consume at least another 30%. We will use lecture to present only those concepts, theories, and facts essential to achieve the learning objectives. As a result, employees sent to classes will return with actual analytical experiences.

Our program design specialists and instructors will work with the documentation developed during Phase I: Analysis, Objectives, and Test Development. They will spend at least **XXX hours** developing practical exercises in aerial/satellite photography analysis that give employees feedback on their learning and performance progress.

Exercise 8-2 continues on the next page

They will also develop a participant workbook and sample analyses that will provide useful reference material back on the job. Finally, they will develop instructional media: transparencies, prepared charts, power point presentations, slides, and demonstration materials.

Instructors, Inc. will complete phase II by (date). The *Instructor's Statement of Work and Methods* and the course media will be made available for review at that time.

We will develop instructional methods and media based on clearly specified learning objectives that EagleEye Analysts has reviewed and approved. Our design effort will focus on EagleEye's training needs. The development of testing methods and procedures will give EagleEye a way to evaluate the effectiveness of our program design. Our task-oriented design will ensure that EagleEye employees will learn not only what to do, but how to perform the necessary tasks to be effective workers.

Phase III: Pre-Delivery Evaluation

With clearly defined learning objectives, course methods and media, and evaluation methods and procedures in hand, we will test the program. Instructors, Inc. will conduct a demonstration training session for a group of employees selected by EagleEye Analysts. At the conclusion of the course, we will test these participants to determine the effectiveness of our instructional methods and media in achieving the specified learning objectives. The

demonstration session will be conducted no later than (date).

Two weeks later, after employees have had an opportunity to apply their skills on the job, our aerial/satellite photography analysis experts and program development specialists will interview them. They will determine whether the results of the earlier tests are confirmed by actual work experiences. We will complete these post-training debriefings no later than (date).

Instructors, Inc. will use the testing results and post-training debriefings to evaluate program effectiveness. We will provide you with results of our analysis and findings by (date). If necessary, we will modify the course design. If modifications are necessary, we will provide EagleEye Analysts with modification plans by (date). We will complete any necessary redesign, and submit the final design for EagleEye's approval no later than (date). This work will require an estimated XXX hours of labor.

We will deliver the following on (date), after EagleEye Analysts' approval of the training design:

• Specification of Learning Objectives

• Student Achievement and Program Evaluation Test Specification

• Instructor's Statement of Work and Methods

• Course workbook and instructional media

Exercise 8-2 continues on the next page

Our systematic approach assures you of program effectiveness before we deliver any training. EagleEye will know that precious training dollars are being used to purchase results.

Phase IV: Training Program

After the proposed instructional program has been approved, we will conduct training in accordance with EagleEye Analysts' schedule, at the specified site(s). Our staff will handle the logistics of facility arrangements and shipment of materials to the site. A complete listing of all training seminars we have managed in the past (which provide detailed information about our training and logistical experiences) are presented in the appendix.

All our instructors have had hands-on experience in aerial/satellite photography analysis, meet all requirements in the RFP, and are skilled trainers. Comprehensive résumés of all key staff proposed for this project are located in the appendix.

> Phase IV will continuously evaluate the effectiveness of the training program and seek recommended improvements.
>
> EagleEye Analysts' management staff will always know what employees are supposed to be able to do after training and whether objectives are being met.

Instructors, Inc.'s Key Project Staff are Skilled, Experienced, and Responsive

Colby Haverstock will manage this project on a full-time basis. He will have complete authority over all project controls–quality, schedule, and cost. He will also be our principal liaison with EagleEye Analysts. Mr. Haverstock is a training development specialist and instructor with more than 25 years of industrial training experience.

Pamela Keaton will work full-time on this project and will manage the needs analysis, specification of objectives, and program design and development under Mr. Haverstock's direction. Ms. Keaton has designed 12 programs for Instructors, Inc., and has 10 years of training development experience.

Regina Clark, an U.S. Navy-trained expert with 20 years of experience in aerial/satellite photography analysis, will assist Ms. Keaton in needs analysis and program development.

Mary Gutierrez, Director of Program Evaluation for Instructors, Inc., will manage program test development and pre-delivery evaluation. Although her staff will support Mr. Haverstock, Ms. Gutierrez will report independently to corporate management and EagleEye Analysts. Ms. Gutierrez has been evaluating industrial training programs for 16 years and is the author of several articles on the subject.

Exercise 8-2 continues on the next page

Richard McMahon will be chief instructor for the program. Mr. McMahon will teach the initial courses and he will train and supervise all other course instructors. Mr. McMahon has been lead instructor for several technical training programs and was a cartographer and photographic analyst for the Defense Mapping Service for 25 years before joining Instructors, Inc.

Albert Cabriales, Instructors, Inc.'s Chief of Administration, will be in charge of course logistics. He will report to Mr. Haverstock. Mr. Cabriales has managed the administrative aspects of Instructors, Inc. programs throughout the United States and in foreign countries for seven years. See Figure 4.

Figure 4
Project Organization for EagleEye Training Program Development

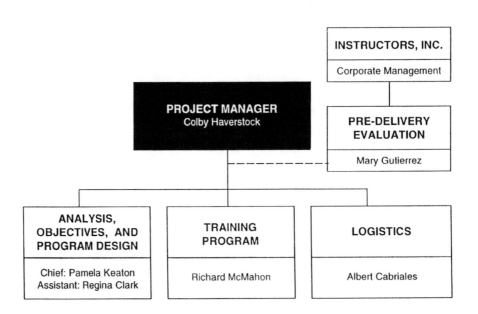

Instructors, Inc.'s project organization is led by a team with a combined total of more than 83 years of experience in technical training, program development and delivery. The project manager has full authority over project control and contractual relations and will deal directly with EagleEye's representatives. Résumés of key personnel are located in the appendix.

Exercise 8-2 continues on the next page

Conclusion

Instructors, Inc. will provide Eagle Eye Analysts' employees with on-the-job skills necessary for effective analysis of aerial/satellite photographs. We will achieve result through a systematic phased approach that specifies program learning objectives and evaluation criteria before program design begins. Throughout the design process EagleEye Analysts will have opportunities to check and evaluate the progress toward clearly defined goals. We will conduct no scheduled training until EagleEye Analysts has had a chance to verify our ability to achieve the results desired.

Figure 5 shows the program deliverables. Our record of past performance with other aerial/ satellite photography clients is located in the appendix.

Figure 5
Deliverables for EagleEye Analysts Training Program

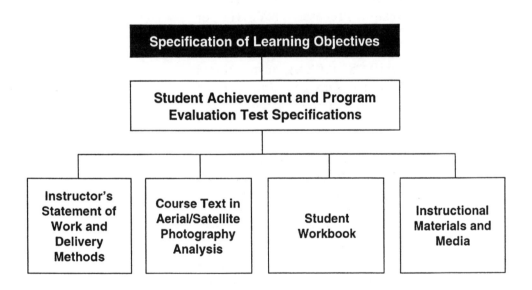

After program objectives and evaluation criteria have been clearly described and approved by representatives from EagleEye Analysts we will design course methods and media. Scheduled training will not begin until deliverables have been inspected and accepted. EagleEye can be assured that the design is objective-driven and effective.

Exercise 8-2 continues on the next page

Footnotes

1. Gagne, R.M. (20XX). *Designing Instructional Programs*. Hillsdale, NJ: Capital Publishing.

    Earl, C.M. (20XX). *Intstruction in Action*. Hillsdale, NJ: Capital Publishing.

2. Miller, D.D. (20XX). *Training Designed for Aerial/ Satellite Photography Analysis*. (In the appendix of this proposal).

3. Wilson, B.G. (20XX). Techniques for Teaching Technical Subjects. *Journal of Training and Development, (18)1, 2-5.*

4. Kemp, J. (20XX). Instructional Design Process. NY: Harper Publishing.

    Schiff, S. (20XX). Instructional Systems Design. *Journal of Instructional Development. (19)2, 14-21.*

5. Position titles and comprehensive responsibilities of all project staff are provided in the appendix.

6. Specific examples of program documents to be used in this project as well as materials developed for other satellite photography analysis clients are provided in the appendix.

Exercise 8-2 continues on the next page

Exercise 8-2

Evaluating Two Proposals

Use this form to evaluate Technical Trainers, Inc.'s proposal on pages 178 to 191.

Proposal Scoring Sheet for Technical Trainers, Inc.

Ratings

Superior   I am convinced that this is a capable training firm. They may not be perfect, but they have a sound philosophy and approach.

Good   I think this training firm might be able to do the job, but I would not select them without asking more questions.

Marginal   I am not persuaded that this training firm could do the job. Their plan is unclear and lacking in important details.

Poor   I am convinced that this training firm cannot do the job.

Evaluation Criteria

Directions: Evaluate the proposal on the following criteria.

1. Does the firm's training philosophy seem appropriate to EagleEye Analysts' needs? Does it seem sound to you?

   Rating:_____

2. Does the firm present a sound training program based on a clear understanding of recent evidence from the literature?

   Rating:_____

3. Are proposed deliverables clearly described, and do they appear to be adequate?

   Rating:_____

4. Has the firm proposed an appropriately organized project team?

   Rating:_____

5. Are you persuaded that this firm has a sound approach overall?

   Rating:_____

Recommendation: Yes   No

Evaluator's name: _____

Exercise 8-2 continues on the next page.

Exercise 8-2: Evaluating Two Proposals

Technical Trainers, Inc.'s Proposal

The central focus of Technical Trainers, Inc.'s business since 1991 has been developing and conducting training courses in aerial/satellite photography analysis addressing the needs of both industry and government for audiences reflecting a wide range of professional orientation and experience. This section of our proposal describes the teaching philosophy, capabilities, techniques, and modes of instruction employed by Technical Trainers, Inc. in presenting training courses.

Instructional Methodology

Technical Trainers, Inc.'s Approach

Aerial/satellite photography has traditionally been taught in lecture format, with the occasional use of samples, films, or case studies to retain student interest and illustrate practical applications. Technical Trainers, Inc., on the other hand, has designed training courses that emphasize experiential learning and effectively use a variety of instructional techniques and media. To ensure effective implementation, we have identified and retained individuals who are comfortable in leading dynamic learner-oriented, rather than passive instructor-oriented, training sessions.

Technical Trainers, Inc. favors the use of case studies, simulations, and other practical exercises. Such exercises can be used effectively to "break up" or "wrap up" instructor presentations and class discussions: first, students are presented with concepts, policies, and procedures; then, an exercise is used to illustrate application. However, it is a mistake to employ practical exercises solely in this manner. We have found that participants need opportunities to learn by doing–that is, opportunities to identify, through experience, the issues and problems that arise in the course of a certain task and then reflect on the experience and arrive at key learning points. When used in this way, practical exercises challenge and strengthen the ability of students to exercise judgment in coping with situations they face on the job. Exercises provide practice in identifying and using resources, developing and weighing alternatives, and reaching and implementing decisions.

All courses presented by Technical Trainers, Inc:

- Present aerial/satellite photography analysis as a process with successive, interrelated steps.

- Devote an appropriate portion of class time to learning experiences in which participants encounter situations that typically arise on the job and in which they learn by doing.

- Use instructional methodologies appropriate to the knowledge or skills being taught.

- Convey basic principles or needed guidance through introductory or summary lectures, coupled with visual aids to increase retention.

- Demonstrate procedures, such as completion of forms and other "paper skills," using step-by-step visual aids.

Exercise 8-2 continues on the next page

- Simulate actual tasks to develop skills.

- Hone issue identification and decision-making abilities through videotaped simulations and other activities based on actual cases.

- Improve research skills by providing, in the classroom, a comprehensive library of resource documents–all the references normally available in an aerial/satellite photography analysis office–which students will use in completing case studies and other activities.

- Develop communication skills through the use of role-playing.

- Use exercises as both skill-building and diagnostic tools.

- Use quizzes as checkpoints so students can assess their own comprehension.

- Stress learning competencies that students need to attain for successful workplace performance.

- Use, to best advantage, the space and equipment provided by the instructional facility.

Variation in Approach from Course to Course

We believe that the interplay of four primary factors–(1) course length, (2) subject matter, (3) training objectives, and (4) class composition–shape the approach to be taken in designing and presenting a given course.

A one-day session aimed at orienting aerial/satellite photography analysts to their role and responsibility, for example, would necessarily rely on lecture/discussion, with ample opportunity for question-and-answer periods, and a limited number of exercises illustrating practical applications. A two-week course on basic aerial/satellite photography analysis principles and practices, however, would need to be highly experiential, taking participants through their responsibilities from A to Z, with a large amount of hands-on practice and substantial variety in instructional methods. An intensive case study and discussion approach, on the other hand, would be suitable for a one-week course in the subject for legal and management personnel.

The level of coverage that is intended–basic and advanced–is a critical aspect of the training objectives. The challenge of a basic-level course is "beginning at the beginning"–ensuring that those who truly need a thorough, ground-level introduction to the subject matter get one–while at the same time maintaining a pace that challenges those with some knowledge and experience. Well-structured and skillfully led lecture/discussion/question-and-answer sessions are critical. So are exercises and quick quizzes that give participants frequent feedback and reinforcement. Group exercises tend to work better than individual exercises, in that less-experienced students can work along with those who have more experience.

Even when all participants have been carefully screened or required to complete a basic course or courses as a prerequisite, the challenge of addressing varying levels of knowledge, experience, and interest inevitably arise in presenting an advanced course. Instructors must take care in establishing a common baseline of information from which to launch into more sophisticated or complex treatments.

Exercise 8-2 continues on the next page

Instructors must also be clear in adhering to the course objectives, and at the same time be flexible in working with individuals who need help in mastering the basics. Lectures/discussions can generally be faster-paced in basic courses. A greater proportion of class work can be done on an individual basis and more responsibility given for homework assignments. Whatever the methods used, students' knowledge, experience, and expertise must be acknowledged and respected.

Handling of Practical Exercises

Technical Trainers, Inc. sees the use of practical exercises as essential. To enhance interest and retention, such exercises should be used in all courses, even those of only one or two days' duration. Small exercise groups (two to six persons) are usually best, as participants can learn much from their interaction with one another.

To be effective, exercises must be introduced properly. Participants must understand the purpose of the exercise and how it fits in with the overall learning objectives. Students must also understand precisely what is expected from them, and the timeframe in which they must work. Written instructions should be provided, but instructions should also be communicated by the instructor, with opportunities to ask questions before starting and while doing exercises. Instructors should be active observers while exercises are being done so as to become better acquainted with stumbling blocks and intervene to keep participants from going off in a totally nonproductive direction.

"Processing" of participants' solutions to problems posed by exercises is also critical. All Technical Trainers, Inc. instructors are skilled in encouraging participants to present outcomes of their work. They know how to question why each step presented was taken, reinforce creative thinking and good judgment, and allot adequate, but not excessive time for the discussion of each exercise.

Instructor's Skill and Style

We have found that no factor is as critical to the success of a training course as a skilled instructor. Further, we have discovered that the best instructors are those individuals who know their subject, know their audience, and have the ability to convey that they both know and care about each.

Technical Trainers, Inc. use instructors who possess both technical expertise and highly developed instructional skills. Personal style is critical and each person's style is different. We have found, however, that the best instructors have certain characteristics and competencies in common:

- Ability to convey that, for the duration of the course, they are fully committed to helping participants master the subject at hand, however that can best be accomplished.

- Ability to help participants see specifically "what's in it for them"–how it will make them better at what they do, make their job easier for them, improve their work product and the like.

- Ability to perceive, as the class progresses, where participants' on-the-job problems actually lie and where reinforcement of information and skills is most critically needed–as well as flexibility in adapting the agenda and approach to meet those needs.

Exercise 8-2 continues on the next page

- Ability to capture interest and increase understanding by providing pertinent, realistic examples and illustrations.

- Ability to engender a classroom atmosphere of camaraderie and collaboration–despite the inevitably wide range of skill and interest levels that participants bring to the learning experience.

- Ability to make the learning process an active one, even when participants are in a listening mode (by raising thought-provoking questions and pausing to allow for student responses).

It is these kinds of abilities, along with instructional format variations that keep a class of adult learners interested, whether for one day or three weeks.

Skillful fielding of questions is another facet of an instructor's capability that both sustains class interest and enhances learning. Our instructors believe that asking questions is a vital element of the learning process–that a class that raises questions, even hard ones, is much to be preferred over one that sits back passively.

All Technical Trainers, Inc. instructors are adept in the basics of fielding questions:

- Creating an atmosphere where participants feel comfortable raising questions.

- Repeating/paraphrasing the question to make sure that all other participants hear it and, as necessary, to make sure that the instructor himself or herself understands its nature and purpose.

- Saying "I don't know, but I'll get the answer and get back to you" when necessary, and then taking steps to get the information as promptly as possible (with assistance as needed from staff at the Technical Trainers, Inc. office).

- Achieving the appropriate balance between responsiveness to a given individual's often limited or tangential concerns and adherence to the overall class objectives and agenda.

Other Training Elements

Class Discussion

Class discussion plays a central role in Technical Trainers, Inc.'s approach to training. As we see it, all lectures should actually be lectures/discussions. As they present their material, our instructors are open to, and take steps to elicit comments and questions from participants. Also, they are mindful of the fact that participants can often learn as much from one another as they can from the instructor. In processing the results of practical exercises, they encourage an interplay of ideas and approaches among the participants, intervening only as warranted to keep the discussion constructive and on track.

Exercise 8-2 continues on the next page

Visual Aids

Our experience has shown that visual aids should be of two kinds: pre-prepared and generated-in-process. Pre-prepared visual aids can include overheads, slides, videos, films, and demonstration equipment (such as computers). Through experience, we have developed the following guidelines concerning the use of visual aids:

- Visual aids must closely track the instructor's lesson plan and the course materials.

- Their most effective use is generally in providing a coherent overview of coverage and highlighting key points.

- Overuse of visuals is just as much to be avoided as underuse.

- Participants may be given handouts mirroring visual aids for note-taking purposes, but only in instances where complex information (math needed in price analysis or cost analysis, for example) is being conveyed.

- Any videotape or film used must be relevant and current if it is to be worthwhile.

- All visual aids must be interesting and easily readable by every participant.

Technical Trainers, Inc.'s design staff use the most recent software to produce attractive, legible, and professional-quality instructional materials. We generally prefer to develop overhead transparencies because the classroom need not be darkened and the instructor can use markers to point out critical material.

All Technical Trainers, Inc. instructors are adept not only at using pre-prepared visual aids but also at generating visual aids spontaneously during the instructional process. They frequently make flip charts for noting key points raised by class members and outlining examples; these aids are very useful in focusing attention and enhancing comprehension during class discussion. Technical Trainers, Inc. instructors are skilled in using video recording equipment to tape and play back class participant role-plays–an invaluable way of reinforcing interactive communication skills, especially negotiation techniques.

Pretests, Quizzes, and Examinations

Technical Trainers, Inc. endorses the use of pretests. Preliminary testing can provide the instructor with a valuable indicator of participants' initial knowledge levels. Pretests also can serve to alert participants to the course content and to inadequacies in their own mastery of it, thereby heightening their interest and participation. On the other hand, they can threaten, discourage, and "turn off" participants. To be effective, pretests must: (1) represent course content, (2) be aimed at "middle level" difficulty, and (3) be presented in a non-threatening manner.

Instructors must explain the purpose of pretests from both the participants' and instructors' point of view. Pretest scores should be between the instructor and learner, not put on record, and should be provided to participants the first day of class. To make this possible, participants may be allowed to grade their own tests as the instructor reviews the answers; then, tests should be collected for verification of scores and reviewed by the instructor.

Exercise 8-2 continues on the next page

We also favor the use of periodic quizzes, both written and oral, to reinforce key learning points and give participants needed feedback on their progress.

Technical Trainers, Inc. is experienced in constructing course examinations that are fair and valid indicators of both how well an individual has comprehended and retained the information conveyed in a course, and how well prepared he or she is to apply that information on the job. A well-designed examination is an outgrowth of a well-designed course: accurate analysis of the on-the-job competencies (knowledge, skills, and abilities) needed in a given subject area lays the groundwork for realistic learning objectives. Those learning objectives are, in turn, the basis for both sound lesson plans and valid tests of what has been learned. Technical Trainers, Inc. favors the use of multiple-choice test questions over true-false test questions, as they provide learners with greater direction, less chance of guessing correctly, and when devised with care, a more thought-provoking task. We employ the services of an expert in test construction who carefully screens question terminology and format.

Tailoring Teaching Methods to Learning Objectives

Instructional design experts, whether in public or private sectors, agree that there are three cardinal rules for successful course development and instruction and, consequently, good training.

1. *Establish learning objectives.* It must be clear, from the outset, what students are expected to know at the conclusion of the course.

2. *Teach to reach the learning objectives.* The plans the teacher develops or uses during the course must be sufficiently flexible that the style of teaching can be tailored to suit students who constitute a particular class and learning experience.

3. *Test for achievement of the learning objectives.* Test results must demonstrate that students have acquired the skills and knowledge they need to operate competently within the course area.

Technical Trainers, Inc. instructors use various techniques to ensure student and teacher success in any class situation. These techniques are not, of course, used wholesale in every teaching situation. Rather, a skillful teacher will use a combination of those techniques to ensure a learning environment that accomplishes the course learning objectives.

Motivation

Students must enter the course emotionally prepared to learn, or the teacher must stimulate the desire to learn. Students can be warmed up for a lesson by doing an activity that starts them thinking in the way that they will be asked to think during the course. The Technical Trainers, Inc. instructor will use this method to determine the students' backgrounds, positions and organizational affiliations, individual strengths and weaknesses, and the like. The instructor will then adjust lesson plans to meet the needs of students.

Exercise 8-2 continues on the next page

Application and Participation

The more meaningful and relevant a task or set of information is to the students' world, the easier it is to learn. Based on information obtained about students at the beginning of the first day of class, the instructor will make explicit references to students' work experiences as a way of connecting content with students' experience, or in some other way embed the content in the students' framework of meaning. It is critical that students operate, respond, move about, and talk during the course of the learning experiences embodied in the principle of active participation.

Goal Setting

The Technical Trainers, Inc. instructor may involve students in goal setting; the instructor could ask them what they expect to get from the course and what they plan to do with what they learn. When students become involved in goal setting for their learning, they learn more and both their motivation to accomplish and their ability to self-evaluate increase.

Role-Playing

Students should practice new skills in the setting and manner in which they will be used in real life. The instructor may divide the class into small groups to enable them to participate in simulations of specific tasks that arise on the job. The use of videotaping is encouraged during these sessions. It is important that instructors provide detailed guidance in learning new tasks and withdraw such guidance gradually with demonstrated student proficiency.

Feedback and Self-Critiquing

Feedback to students on their work should be given as rapidly as possible after completion. Playing the videotape of a practice session immediately after the experience and involving students in critiquing it is an example of immediate feedback. The instructor will ask questions throughout the session to see whether students understand the process, to correct errors in the process, and so on. At the conclusion of small-group problem-solving sessions, a useful approach is to have a representative from one or more of the groups present the group's response to the problem. The instructor will ask questions and review key points of the lesson.

Positive Reinforcement

It is important during any question-and-answer session that the instructor never says, "That's wrong." Students get powerful messages from our responses to their answers, and it is these messages that influence the way they participate. As influential as an instructor's questions may be in getting students interested, in stretching their thinking, and in guiding discussions, the questions alone do not account for the quality of the discourse. The instructor must respond in a way that keeps students open and thinking rather than shut down and afraid.

Whatever the mix of instructional techniques, they must always be directed toward achieving the established learning objectives.

Exercise 8-2 continues on the next page

Project Plan and Project Controls

Phase I: Training Materials Development

Our approach to completing Phase I–Training Materials Development—involves the following steps:

- Confirmation of objectives
- Development
- Review and finalization
- Production

Confirmation of Objectives

During a post-award meeting, we will meet with EagleEye personnel to:

- Establish and confirm detailed requirements and schedule Phase I tasks.
- Identify and obtain all published policy and procedural guidance applicable to the course material to be developed.
- Identify EagleEye personnel to be interviewed in developing course materials.
- Establish criteria for editorial style and format.
- Establish procedures for communications between Technical Trainers, Inc. and EagleEye analysts.

Development

A draft of each course manual will be developed by one or more assigned researchers/writers working closely with the Technical Trainers, Inc. Project Manager.

The Project Manager will meet with EagleEye personnel to define the outline, scope, and coverage of the course material and the length of the course.

The Project Manager will be cognizant of the current status and extent of completion of each objective and will report promptly to the Technical Trainers, Inc. Officer-in-Charge concerning any problems encountered or anticipated, with their proposed resolution, obtaining guidance from EagleEye as needed.

Review and Finalization

Complete drafts of each course manual will be submitted to EagleEye for review. Course manuals will be revised as necessary to incorporate any changes or additions requested by EagleEye and resubmitted in final form.

Production

Upon receipt from EagleEye that a draft is final, and that no other changes need to be made, Technical Trainers, Inc. will produce the course material in final form, and deliver printed copies and computer disks as called for by the contract.

Exercise 8-2 continues on the next page

<u>Time-Based Planning Chart</u>

Attached, as Exhibit 1, is a time-based planning chart representing actions to complete the training materials.

<u>Progress Reporting</u>

All project staff members will be required to report the status of their assigned projects to the Project Manager on a weekly basis. In addition, any unforeseen developments that might impact the completion of a task will be reported to the Project Manager immediately.

Phase II: Conducting the Training Program

Our approach to performance of Phase II–Conducting the Training Program–is based on these proven principles:

- An in-place, dedicated organization of professional and support resources is the key to effective management of a training program.

- Effective administration and review are critical to program success.

- Continuity in instructors is vital to maintaining consistency and quality of classroom presentations.

- Production processes must be available to support the preparation, production, and distribution of course materials.

<u>Orientation of Instructors</u>

The Project Manager together with a team of researchers/writers, who prepared the course materials in Phase I, will conduct an orientation briefing for all instructors. The briefing will cover an overview of:

- EagleEye's mission, organization, and operating environment.

- Training curriculum and specific materials for each course.

- Issues of critical concern to EagleEye management.

<u>The Highest Level of Teaching Skills</u>

Technical Trainers, Inc. employs only instructors of proven quality and dynamism. Students evaluate the class and instructor at the conclusion of each course. The Project Manager "sits in" on courses and reviews all instructor evaluation forms and student test results; based on this first-hand observation and student feedback, instructors are given specific directions and advice as what might be needed to improve their performance. Any instructor receiving an average evaluation score of less than 8 (on a scale of 1 to 10) receives counseling to improve performance. Any instructor receiving less than an average rating of 7 on two occasions, or 5 on one occasion is immediately replaced.

Technical Trainers, Inc.'s instructors, over a period of years, have consistently achieved course evaluation ratings averaging 9 and above. Student comments have consistently demonstrated enthusiasm for courses presented by Technical Trainers, Inc.'s instructors.

Exercise 8-2 continues on the next page

Timely Production of Course Materials

Technical Trainers, Inc. publishes its own course materials and produces video courses for a number of customers.

Technical Trainers, Inc. will provide all services and materials, including tabbed binders with a complete set of course materials for each student scheduled to attend a particular course. Specifically, Technical Trainers, Inc. will take responsibility for:

- Assembling all materials for reproduction. Technical Trainers, Inc. will assure that all course materials are current and that all approved changes and updates have been incorporated into the package.

- Reproducing and assembling course materials (including printing, collating, and binding).

- Assuring quality. The Project Manager will perform a quality review of course material to ensure the highest standards of workmanship. Course material will also be inspected after production and before shipment.

- Packing and appropriate labeling of boxes before shipment.

- Storing all course materials at Technical Trainers, Inc. until the appropriate time for shipment.

- Shipment of course materials to the training site.

Technical Trainers, Inc. has a full-scale in-house production facility that can easily accommodate these requirements. Each month, Technical Trainers, Inc. runs 500,000 or more copies and produces hundreds of course packages.

Project Staffing

Phase I: Training Materials Development

For Phase I–Training Materials Development–we have proposed a core staff of researchers/writers selected on the basis of their previous successful experience on similar projects for Technical Trainers, Inc. Core staff will be available for the duration of the assignment. Additional fully-qualified personnel may supplement core staff, if needed to complete several tasks concurrently.

Janice Roberts, Corporate Officer-in-Charge of Phase I, and Tim Reed, the Project Manager, have proven credentials and extensive experience on similar projects, as have the researchers/writers assigned. All these personnel have worked together on previous projects and have proven their ability to work together as a team.

Exercise 8-2 continues on the next page

Phase II: Conducting the Training Program

For Phase II–Conducting the Training Program–we have assembled an experienced management and teaching team. Technical Trainers, Inc.'s president, Janice Roberts, will serve as Corporate Officer-in-Charge, and will be fully accessible to the Project Manager, Tim Reed. Reflecting the importance of this project to both Technical Trainers, Inc. and EagleEye, Ms. Roberts will also serve as a course instructor. Ms. Roberts' experience as Officer-in-Charge of the course materials development effort will greatly enhance her management of the teaching effort, and will enable her to provide substantive guidance.

We have selected a core group of instructors who are subject-matter experts as well as seasoned teachers; they have consistently received outstanding ratings from their students and will bring a wealth of experience to the program. They will be available for the duration of the training program, and will be supplemented by equally-qualified teachers if needed to meet the requirements of multiple, simultaneous, or overlapping course presentations.

Course Administration

Technical Trainers, Inc.'s administrative staff is thoroughly experienced in all tasks associated with effective course administration, such as processing student enrollment forms, preparing class rosters, making travel arrangements for instructors, tabulating test and evaluation results, preparing and mailing course completion certificates, and getting the proper course materials to the place of instruction on time.

Staffing Plan

Exhibits 2 and 3 are our staffing charts for Phase I: Training Materials Development and Phase II: Conducting the Training Program. Résumés for project personnel and references for previous similar projects are located in the appendix.

Exercise 8-2 continues on the next page

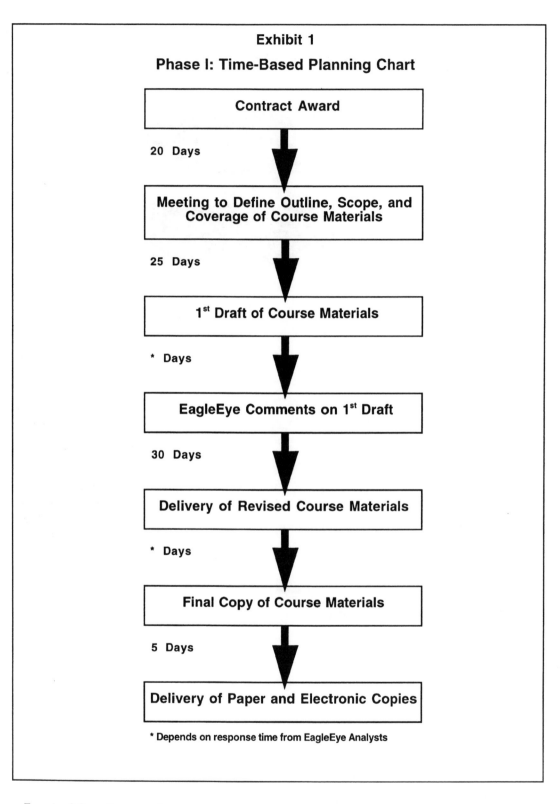

Exhibit 1

Phase I: Time-Based Planning Chart

Contract Award

20 Days

Meeting to Define Outline, Scope, and Coverage of Course Materials

25 Days

1st Draft of Course Materials

* Days

EagleEye Comments on 1st Draft

30 Days

Delivery of Revised Course Materials

* Days

Final Copy of Course Materials

5 Days

Delivery of Paper and Electronic Copies

* Depends on response time from EagleEye Analysts

Exercise 8-2 continues on the next page

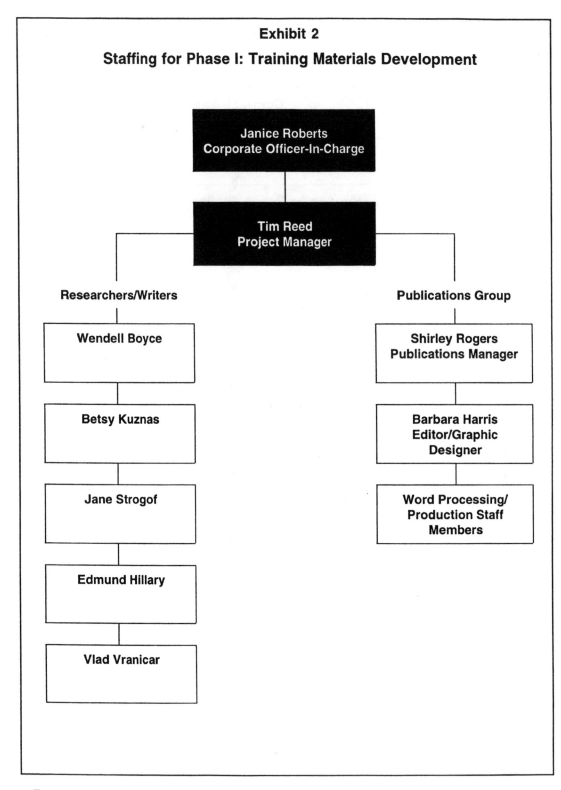

Exercise 8-2 continues on the next page

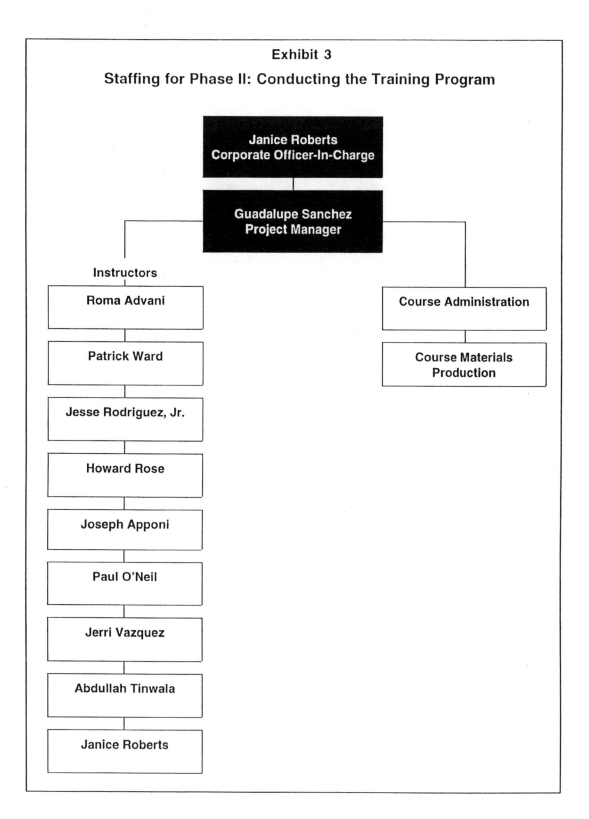

Exhibit 3

Staffing for Phase II: Conducting the Training Program

Bibliography

Baker, B. & Thomas, J.J. (20XX). *Evaluation and Assessment of Technical Training*. Chicago, IL: G. Disc Worldwide.

Coates, D.D. (20XX). *Training Designed for Aerial/Satellite Photography Analysis*. New York: Technical Press.

Lebec, L. (20XX). *Training for Entry-level Employees in Technical Subjects*. Alexandria, VA: Capitol Publications.

Perez, M. (20XX). *Contemporary Aerial/Satellite Photography for Professionals*. Atlanta, GA: Get Smart Book Company.

Wilson, B.G. (20XX). *Industrial and Business Training*. New York: Springer Publishing.

Yu, P. (20XX). *Aerial/Satellite Photography for Professionals*. San Francisco: Browning Press.

Glossary

Abstract — Cogent summary of a proposed grant project. Most abstracts are brief statements of 500 words or less that highlight the features and benefits of major grant proposal components (e.g., problem/need, goals/objectives, methods/activities, evaluation plans, and costs).

Acquisition — Procurement function to fulfill a funding agency's needs.

Amendment — Modification or change to a solicitation.

Appendix — Back section of a proposal that contains supplemental information too detailed to include in the main body of the application. Appendices are used especially when funding agencies impose proposal page limits.

Application Notice — Grant notice published in the Federal Register that includes: (1) program rules and regulations, (2) guidelines for proposal development, (3) application forms, and (4) mailing instructions.

Assurances and Certifications — Government agency conditions agreed to by an organization when submitting a prospective proposal. These may include anti-discrimination requirements; drug-free workplace requirements; lobbying restrictions; environmental protection assurances; public employee standards; health, safety, and welfare of human subjects; and other miscellaneous assurances and certifications that must be met by the organization responding to solicitations.

Bid/No-Bid Decision — Decision to proceed toward submitting a proposal or to terminate all activity in response to a solicitation. Bid decisions should be based on the funding seeker's: (1) estimated value of the proposed work, (2) estimated proposal effort in terms of hours and cost, (3) probable competition, (4) major institutional strengths and weaknesses, (5) arguments for and against bidding, and (6) estimated probability of winning.

Bid/No-Bid Decision Form — Form used to guide funding seekers in making a decision to submit or not submit a proposal in response to a solicitation.

Bid/No Bid Decision (Preliminary) — Initial bid/no bid decision made prior to release of the RFP/RFA.

Boilerplate — Narrative and budget material used and reused in preparation of proposal drafts.

Budget — Line-item expenditures that will be used to complete a grant project.

Budget Detail — Brief narrative description of budget line items.

Budget Narrative — Thorough written explanation of cost expenditures for a proposed project.

Budget (Preliminary) — Proposal budget that is based on the model solicitation and other intelligence gathering activities and is prepared prior to the release of the RFP/RFA.

Callout — Label used to describe parts of a figure, exhibit, chart, or table.

Caption — Brief one or two sentence description of a figure, exhibit, chart, or table.

Catalog of Federal Domestic Assistance (CFDA) — Publication provided by the General Services Administration that lists the domestic assistance programs of all federal agencies. The CFDA provides information about the program's authorization, fiscal details, regulations, eligibility requirements, and award process.

CFDA Number — Federal assistance identification number consisting of a two-digit prefix that indicates the federal agency and a three-digit code for the authorized program.

Closeout — Administrative and financial wrap-up tasks associated with completing a discretionary grant or cooperative agreement.

Compliance Checklist — List of requirements obtained from a solicitation that is used by proposal writers and reviewers as a guide in developing a grant application.

Consultant — Outside expert hired to assist fund-seeking institutions in completing specific project tasks.

Contract — Legal document indicating the amount as well as terms and conditions of an award for a grant or cooperative agreement.

Contract (Fully Executed) — Official award notification that has been signed by the funding agency and the grantee.

Cooperative Agreement — Federal assistance awarded to a recipient to accomplish a proposed project where substantial involvement is expected between the federal agency and recipient during the performance period.

Cost-Plus-Fixed-Fee Contract — Contract where funding seekers have minimal responsibility for performance costs and the negotiated fee (profit) is fixed.

Cost-Reimbursement Contract — Contract that provides payment of allowable incurred costs to the extent prescribed in the contract.

Cost Sharing — Grant seeking institution's financial commitment to project costs. Cost sharing is the difference between the actual cost and amount requested.

Deadline (Due Date and Time) — Specified date and time the funding agency must receive the grant application for it to be considered for funding.

Debriefing Meeting (With Funding Agency) — Conference between funding agency personnel and losing institution representatives after grant recipients have been selected. During this meeting, funding agency personnel explain the basis for grant selection and discuss the shortcomings of the proposal submitted by the losing institution. The losing institution uses the information gained from this meeting to improve the grant application for subsequent competitions.

Debriefing Meeting (With Proposal Writers and Reviewers) — Meeting held immediately after the grant application has been delivered to the funding agency in an effort to identify the proposal's strengths and weaknesses. Prior to the meeting, writers and reviewers should review the entire grant application and identify potential deficiencies.

Deficiency — Proposal component that fails to satisfy a solicitation's minimum requirement.

Direct Costs — Costs that are specifically identified with a proposed project (e.g., personnel, supplies, and equipment).

Evaluation Plans — Procedures used to measure the success of a proposed grant project in direct relation to project goals/objectives.

FedBizOpps (FBO) — Single point of electronic public access to government wide procurement contract opportunities.

Federal Acquisition Regulations (FAR) — Primary document used by federal agencies that contains uniform policies and procedures for governing acquisition activity.

Federal Register (FR) — Daily publication by the National Archives and Records Administration that lists all federal agency regulations and legal notices, including details about grant competitions. The FR is available in most major libraries.

Field Readers — Professional subject area experts (also referred to as peer reviewers) used to review discretionary grant applications. Readers are selected based on education, experience, and geographic representation. Most funding agencies welcome letters of interest and résumés from potential readers. Prior to selection, readers must sign an assurance form to confirm that they do not have a conflict of interest with respect to grant applications in the competition.

Final Proposal Review Team — Team of experienced personnel who review the final proposal draft. The team's mission is to check the final proposal against the solicitation requirements before submitting it to the funding agency.

Financial Report — Report by the funding recipient that indicates the amount and type of expenditures made during a budget period.

Firm-Fixed-Price Contract — Contract where funding seekers have full responsibility for performance costs and resulting profit or loss.

Fixed-Price Contract — Contract that provides a firm (fixed) price for work specified in the proposal.

Formative Evaluation — Ongoing process of providing feedback about the quality and effectiveness of the grant project.

Freedom of Information Act (FOIA) — Administrative Procedures Act that allows the public to have access to agency records maintained by the government (www.foia.state.gov).

Fringe Benefits — Personnel costs that include medical and dental coverage, life insurance, workman's compensation and unemployment, Medicare, and retirement pension.

Full-Time Equivalent (FTE) — Cost to replace faculty or staff members. One full-time equivalent is one person working eight hours per day, five days per week for the entire year.

Funding Agency's Needs — Basic requirements sought by funding agencies that are normally included in RFPs/RFAs.

Funding Agency's Wants — Subtle requirements that funding agencies would ideally like to see mentioned in a winning proposal, but may or may not be included in RFPs/RFAs.

Goals/Objectives — Measurable project outcomes that relate to the funding agency's wants and needs. Goals/objectives indicate what will be done, under what conditions, and how the target population will be affected as a result of the proposed activities.

Grant — Financial assistance to an eligible recipient to accomplish a proposed project where there is no substantial involvement between the federal agency and recipient during the performance period. Applicants are allowed to indicate both what they want to do and how in response to the solicitation. Notices inviting applications and review criteria are published in the Federal Register. Multiple awards are usually made.

Grant (Continuation) — Additional funding awarded to recipients for budget years after the initial budget year of a multi-year grant or cooperative agreement.

Grant (Discretionary) — Competitive grants where funding agencies have the discretion to determine the award amount and recipients. Awards are made to those institutions whose applications ranked the highest based on review criteria published in the Federal Register. Funding agencies base award decisions on a peer review process.

Grant (Entitlement, Mandatory, or Formula) — General revenue or federal pass-through funds allocated by state agencies to institutions based on a pre-determined formula. Agencies make awards so long as statutory and regulatory conditions are met. Once these conditions are met, the state agency must make the award.

Grant Officer — Person with authority to award discretionary grants on behalf of the funding agency.

Indirect Cost Rate Agreement — Indirect cost rate approved by a federal agency that is used by grant seeking organizations that regularly apply for grants.

Indirect Costs — Costs often called overhead or facilities and administrative (F&A) expenses incurred for common project objectives that are not identified with a particular project (e.g., heating, lighting, and air conditioning of a facility).

Job Description — Comprehensive presentation of duties and responsibilities for key personnel to be hired for a proposed grant project.

Methods/Activities —Specific tasks and procedures to be completed to meet proposed project goals and objectives. Methods/activities are project means to meet the goals/objectives (project ends).

Model Solicitation — Solicitation developed by funding seekers that is based on information obtained from intelligence gathering activities and an analysis of similar RFPs/RFAs. The "model" solicitation is used as a proposal guide until the funding agency's RFP/RFA is released.

Negotiation — Discussion about the proposal prior to a funding decision. Negotiation may involve answering questions to clarify points in a proposal, correct errors, or respond to changes suggested by the funding agency. Negotiation with funding agency representatives may require written and/or oral responses.

Notice of Award — Legal document indicating the amount as well as terms and conditions of an award for a grant or cooperative agreement.

Office of Management and Budget (OMB) Circulars — Policy documents that provide instructions about the administration of federal grants and cooperative agreements.

Partners — Personnel from other institutions, business and industry, and/or local community organizations that have made financial and in-kind commitments to assist with the proposed grant project.

Per Diem — Cost per day that an organization allows an individual to spend on lodging, meals, and incidental expenses during travel. Per diem rates are established annually by the United States General Service Administration (www.govexec. com/travel/) for most U.S. cities.

Performance Period — Amount of time authorized to complete a project approved by a funding agency.

Performance Report — Report of activities performed during a specified budget period for a discretionary grant or cooperative agreement. These reports may be used to judge if the grant will continue.

Person Hours — Total number of hours an individual will dedicate to a funded project.

Point of Contact (POC) — Funding agency staff member to be contacted for questions related to a specific solicitation.

Postsubmission Activities — Proposal activities that occur after grant applications are submitted to funding agencies.

Pre-proposal Conference — Conference held by funding agency personnel to answer questions and provide explanations regarding a solicitation. Information provided at the conference is usually published and disseminated to all RFP/RFA recipients. This conference may also be referred to as a bidder's conference or technical workshop.

Problem/Need Statement — Persuasive essay that convinces the reader that a problem exists that needs to be resolved. Problem/need statements must establish the importance of the problem and identify the population to be served by the proposed project.

Procurement Contract — Legal instrument for acquiring products or services governed by the Federal Acquisition Regulations (FAR) for the direct benefit of or use by the federal government.

Project Director — Key staff member who will manage the grant project; also referred to as the Principal Investigator.

Proposal — Written offer submitted in response to a solicitation.

Proposal Director (PD) — Person chosen to lead the development of a proposal in response to a solicitation.

Proposal Draft (Preliminary) — Proposal narrative that is based on a model solicitation and other intelligence gathering activities and is prepared prior to release of the RFP/RFA.

Proposal Introduction — Description of the local or regional area to be served and how the institution's professional and organizational qualifications relate to the proposed grant project.

Proposal Outline — Outline of proposal narrative to be completed by writers. Proposal outlines should correspond with RFP/RFA requirements and identify proposal authors for each narrative section to be written.

Proposal Prospectus — Planning tool used to communicate basic project ideas developed before proposal writing.

Proposal Review Process — Funding agency readers evaluate proposals and make recommendations to the funding agency about which grant applications should be funded.

Proposal Reviewers — Grant seeking staff members who read each proposal draft in an effort to ensure that writers have addressed the evaluation criteria in the RFP/RFA and presented a comprehensive, coherent, and persuasively-written document. Reviewers must make sure that the proposal is compliant and that all information requested by the funding agency is included in the grant narrative and budget.

Proposal Schedule — Schedule used in proposal development to determine when proposal writing, reviewing, and rewriting as well as budgeting, reviewing, and rebudgeting will take place. Schedules must also take into account proposal production, reproduction, packaging, and delivery.

Purchased Services — Direct costs that include consultant fees, rentals, tuition, service contracts, equipment repairs, and other contractual services.

Quality Control Checks — Checks before and after grant proposals have been reproduced to ensure complete and error-free submissions.

RFA (Request for Application) — Solicitation used to obtain applications from prospective organizations.

RFP (Request for Proposal) — Solicitation used to obtain proposals from prospective organizations.

Solicitation — Request for Proposal (RFP) or Request for Application (RFA) that invites organizations to submit proposals in response to the funding agency's requirements, terms, and conditions.

Strategy (Kickoff) Meeting — Initial meeting of proposal writers and reviewers that serves as a strategy session for responding to a solicitation. Discussion should focus on writing assignments and other responsibilities, adhering to the proposal schedule, questions to the funding agency, and the formulation of budget assumptions.

Style Sheets — Format and style guidelines that writers and editors follow in preparing proposals. Style sheets usually include guidelines for text, levels of heads, lists, references, figures and tables, and terminology specific to the solicitation.

Subcontractors — Outside organizations or personnel that agree to work with funding seekers to complete proposed project tasks, if the grant is awarded.

Summative Evaluation — Process of assessing the degree to which the grant project has accomplished the predetermined goals and objectives.

Synopsis — Brief description of a proposed procurement contract prepared according to the FAR and published in the FedBizOpps (FBO). The purpose of a synopsis is to notify prospective sources about government contracting activity.

Teaming Agreement — Written document that identifies the terms and conditions between two or more organizations that plan to respond to a solicitation.

Transmittal (Cover) Letter — Letter signed by the CEO of an organization that is included with grant applications sent to funding agencies. Transmittal letters should include the RFP/RFA or CFDA number and identify the number of proposals included in the package as well as the contents of each proposal. In addition, the transmittal letter should identify a knowledgeable contact person who can be reached for possible questions.

Uniform Contract Format — Prescribes the organizational format (parts and sections) for procurement contract solicitations and contracts.

Work Breakdown Structure (WBS) — Hierarchical analysis of RFP/RFA requirements into basic components. Work breakdown structures provide an understanding of the underlying nature of the funding agency's needs as well as the relationship among RFP/RFA parts.

Resources

Books

Barber, D. M. (2002). *Finding Funding: The Comprehensive Guide to Grant Writing*. Long Beach, CA: Bond Street.

Bauer, D.G. (1999). *Successful Grants Program Management*. San Francisco: Jossey-Bass.

Bauer, D.G. (1999). *The Grantwriter's Start-up Kit: A Beginner's Guide to Grant Proposals*. San Francisco: Jossey-Bass.

Bauer, D.G. (1998). *The Teacher's Guide to Winning Grants*. San Francisco: Jossey-Bass.

Blum, L. (1996). *The Complete Guide to Getting a Grant: How to Turn Ideas into Dollars*. New York: John Wiley.

Brown, L.G., Brown, M.J. & Nichols, J.E. (2001). *Demystifying Grant Seeking: What you Really Need to Do to Get Grants*. New York: John Wiley.

Browning, B. (2001). *Grant Writing for Dummies*. Foster, CA: IDG Books Worldwide.

Browning, B. (2001). *How to Become a Grant Writing Consultant*. Hot Springs, AR: Bev Browning and Associates.

Carson, M. (1995). *Winning Grants Step by Step: Support Centers of America's Complete Workbook for Planning, Developing, and Writing Successful Proposals*. San Francisco: Jossey-Bass.

DeAngelis, J. (Ed) (1996). *The Grantseeker's Handbook of Essential Internet Sites*. Alexandria, VA: Capitol.

Gitlin, L.N. & Lyons, K.J. (1996). *Successful Grant Writing: Strategies for Health and Human Service Professions*. New York: Springer.

Golden, S.L. (1997). *Secrets of Successful Grantsmanship: A Guerrilla Guide to Raising Money*. San Francisco: Jossey-Bass.

Government Information Services (1994). *A Insider's Guide to Writing Proposals for Federal Dollars*. Arlington, VA: Government Information Services.

Hale, P.D. (1999). *Writing Grant Proposals that Win*. Alexandria, VA: Capitol Publications.

Holcomb, J. H. (1995). *Proposing Projects and Finding Funds: Guide to Grants.* Lancaster, PA: Technomic.

Holtz, H. & Schmidt, T. (1993). *The Winning Proposal: How to Write It.* New York: McGraw-Hill.

Jasmine, J. (1996). *Writing Grants: A Complete Guide to Educators.* Huntington Beach, CA: Teacher Created Materials.

Lauffer, A. (1997). *Grants, etc.* Thousand Oaks, CA: Sage.

Locke, L.F. (2000). *Proposals That Work: A Guide for Planning Dissertations and Grant Proposals.* Thousand Oaks, CA: London: Sage.

Miner, L. E. & Griffith, J. (1993). *Proposal Planning and Writing.* Phoenix, AZ: Oryx Press.

New, C.C. & Quick, J.A. (1998). *Grantseeker's Toolkit: A Comprehensive Guide to Finding Funding.* New York: John Wiley.

Orlich, D.C. (1996). *Designing Successful Grant Proposals.* Alexandria, VA: Association for Supervision and Curriculum Development.

Pequegnat, W. & Stover, E. (1995). *How to Write a Successful Research Grant Application: A Guide for Social and Behavioral Scientists.* New York: Plenum.

Porter-Roth, B. (1998). *Proposal Development: How to Respond and Win the Bid.* Grants Pass, OR: Oasis.

Porter-Roth, B. (2001). *Request for Proposals: A Guide to Effective RFP Development.* Boston, MA: Addison Wesley.

Quick, J.A. & New, C.C. (2000). *Grant Winner's Toolkit: Project Management and Evaluation.* New York: John Wiley.

Reif-Lehrer, L. (1995). *Grant Application Writer's Handbook.* Boston, MA: Jones and Bartlett.

Ries, J.B. & Leukefeld, C.G. (1995). *Applying for Research Funding: Getting Started and Getting Funded.* Thousand Oaks, CA: Sage.

Ries, J.B. & Leukefeld, C.G. (1998). *The Research Funding Guidebook: Getting it, Managing it, and Renewing it.* Thousand Oaks, CA: Sage.

Ruskin, K. & Achilles, C.M. (1995). *Grantwriting, Fundraising, and Partnerships: Strategies that Work!* Thousand Oaks, CA: Corwin.

Salit, V.L. & Manatt, K. (1997). *How to Write Winning Grant Proposals.* Upper Saddle River, NJ: Center for Professional Development and Resources.

U.S. Department of Education (1998). *What Should I Know About ED Grants?* Washington DC: U.S. Department of Education.

Publications

Aid for Education Report
CD Publications
8204 Fenton Street
Silver Spring, MD 20910-9935
Phone: 301-588-6380 or 800-666-6380
Fax: 301-588-6385
www.cdpublications.com

Chronicle of Higher Education
1255 23rd Street, NW, Suite 700
Washington, DC 20037
Phone: 800-466-1000
Fax: 202-452-1033
www.chronicle.com

Federal Assistance Monitor
CD Publications
8204 Fenton Street
Silver Spring, MD 20910-9935
Phone: 301-588-6380 or 800-666-6380
Fax: 301-588-6385
www.cdpublications.com

Federal Grants and Contracts Weekly
Aspen Publishers, Inc
7201 McKinney Circle
Frederick, MD 21704
Phone: 800-234-1660
Fax: 800-901-9075
www.aspenpublishers.com

Federal Register
U.S. Government Printing Office
Superintendent of Documents
P.O. Box 371954
Pittsburgh, PA 15250-7954
Phone: 202-512-1800 or 866-512-1800
Fax: 202-512-2250
www.access.gpo.gov/su_docs/aces/aces140.html

Nyquist Report on Funding for Community, Junior, and Technical Colleges
140 Huguenot Street
New Paltz, NY 12561-1018
Phone: 845-255-3003
Fax: 845-256-9609
www.nyquistassoc.com

The Grantsmanship Center Magazine
1125 W. Sixth Street, Fifth Floor
P.O. Box 17220
Los Angeles, CA 90017
Phone: 213-482-9860
Fax: 213-482-9863
www.tgci.com

Web Sites

General Resources

A Grant Seeker's Guide to the Internet
www.nonprofit.net/info/guide.html
Grant information guide for nonprofit organizations.

American Association of State Colleges and Universities Grants Resource Center
www.aascu.org/ofpopen/ofpopen.htm
Information and services to help state colleges and universities secure grant funds.

Community of Science, Inc.
www.cos.com
Information about funding opportunities for research professionals.

Catalog of Federal Domestic Assistance (CFDA)
www.cfda.gov
Government-wide compendium of federal programs, projects, services, and activities, which provide assistance to the public.

Federal Information Exchange (FEDIX)
www.sciencewise.com/fedix
Free grant information for education and research organizations.

GrantsNet (U.S. Department of Health and Human Services)
www.hhs.gov/grantsnet
Grant resources and other information for funding seekers.

HTML Links for Fundamentals of Grant Writing
www.tecweb.org/funding/grant.html
Resources, organizations, agencies, and references to assist funding seekers.

Internet Resources for Nonprofits
www.ai.mit.edu/people/ellens/Non/online.html
Academic, governmental, and scientific resources for individuals at nonprofits in housing, health, and human service areas.

Official U.S. Executive Branch Web Sites
www.lcweb.loc.gov/global/executive/fed.html
Library of Congress resources.

National Institution of Standards and Technology (NIST)
www.atp.nist.gov
NIST advance technology program website.

School Grants
www.schoolgrants.org
Comprehensive listing of K-12 grant opportunities.

ScienceWise.com
www.sciencewise.com
Funding sources for science research and engineering professionals.

U.S. Nonprofit Gateway
www.nonprofit.gov
Network of links to federal government information and services.

Society of Research Administrators International
www.srainternational.org
Resources and other information for funding seekers.

Federal Agencies

Food and Drug Administration (FDA)
www.fda.gov
Funding available for projects that advance the health of Americans.

National Aeronautics and Space Administration (NASA)
www.nasa.gov
Funding available for projects that provide space-related education and research.

National Endowment for the Arts (NEA)
www.arts.gov
Funding available for outcome-based projects in arts and literature.

National Endowment for the Humanities (NEH)
www.neh.gov
Funding available for projects in humanities including funds for libraries, museums, and media.

National Institutes of Health (NIH)
www.nih.gov
Funding available for projects on a wide variety of health-related topics as well as training grants (including fellowships) to support research at the graduate and postdoctoral levels.

National Science Foundation (NSF)
www.nsf.gov
Funding available for projects in science, engineering, and education.

U.S. Department of Agriculture (USDA)
www.usda.gov
Funding available for projects in rural areas.

U.S. Department of Commerce (DOC)
www.doc.gov
Funding available for projects that promote job creation and economic growth.

U.S. Department of Education (DOED)
www.ed.gov
Funding available for projects that support improvement in teaching and learning.

U.S. Department of Energy (DOE)
www.energy.gov
Funding available for projects to support energy savings.

U.S. Department of Health and Human Services (HHS)
www.dhhs.gov
Funding available for projects that provide human services and health care.

U.S. Department of Housing and Urban Development (HUD)
www.hud.gov
Funding available for housing projects.

U.S. Department of Justice (DIJ)
www.usdoj.gov
Funding available for law-enforcement projects.

U.S. Department of Labor (DOL)
www.dol.gov
Funding available for projects that assist welfare recipients.

U.S. Department of Transportation (DOT)
www.dot.gov
Funding available for transportation improvement projects.

U.S. Environmental Protection Agency (EPA)
www.epa.gov
Funding available for environmental projects.

Others

Federal Acquisition Regulations (FAR)
www.arnet.gov/far

Office of Management and Budget (OMB) Circulars
www.whitehouse.gov/omb/circulars/index.html

U.S. Government Printing Office (GPO)
www.access.gpo.gov

Comprehensive Review

(Comprehensive Review answers are found on pages 247 - 254)

Directions: For items 1 through 40, write responses in the spaces provided.

1. In addition to grants, identify two other forms of funding provided by the U.S. government.

2. Name the primary document that funding seekers use to locate information about grant opportunities.

3. In addition to the *Federal Register*, name three resource publications used to locate solicitations.

4. Name two categories of grants.

5. Name the Web site where government agencies post all public notices about federal procurement contract solicitations over $25,000.

6. Name two broad categorical groupings of procurement contracts.

7. Identify the major differences between grants and procurement contracts.

Comprehensive Review continues on the next page

8. Name six distinct proposal development phases that funding seekers should go through to prepare winning proposals.

9. Name the common components found in most grant applications.

10. Describe the difference between funding agency's needs and wants.

11. List eight activities that experienced funding seekers will complete six months to one year prior to release of RFPs/RFAs.

12. Identify three individuals who should be questioned by funding seekers before bid/no bid decisions are made.

13. Identify three questions you would ask a Point of Contact (POC) before release of RFPs/RFAs.

14. Identify the main members of a proposal development team.

15. Identify the pros and cons of using external grant writers to develop grant proposals.

16. Identify three "boilerplate" documents that would be helpful in preparing grant proposals.

17. Name two major activities that should be completed the first day after release of RFPs/RFAs.

Comprehensive Review continues on the next page

18. Name four organizational tools developed prior to holding a proposal strategy (kickoff) meeting.

19. Describe the major topics discussed at a proposal strategy (kickoff) meeting.

20. Identify four skills that winning proposal writers possess.

21. Identify four "Cs" of proposal writing.

22. Identify the major narrative sections contained in most grant proposals.

23. Identify the guidelines for writing good problem/need statements.

24. Identify the guidelines for developing good goals/objectives.

25. Describe the components found in a good methods/activities section of a grant application.

26. Name two forms of evaluation used in most grant applications.

27. Identify five documents that might be found in proposal appendices.

28. Describe two types of proposal editing.

Comprehensive Review continues on the next page

29. Name three government agency assurances or certifications that are often submitted with grant applications.

30. Describe two reasons for using graphics in grant proposals.

31. List three *direct* cost items used in proposal budgets.

32. List three *indirect* cost items used in proposal budgets.

33. Describe what is meant by an "indirect cost rate agreement."

34. Identify and provide examples of two types of cost sharing used in grant proposals.

35. Describe what is meant by budget detail and budget narrative.

36. List three common proposal budget problems.

37. Identify five items that should be checked before grant applications are delivered to funding agencies.

38. List three components found in a good proposal transmittal letter.

39. List two reasons to hold a debriefing meeting with writers and reviewers after proposal submission.

40. Identify three activities that should be completed if proposals are not funded.

Appendices

Chapter Review Answers

Chapter 1 Review (page 11)

1. True	(page 1)	6. False	(page 6)	11. True	(page 7)
2. True	(page 1)	7. False	(page 6)	12. False	(page 7)
3. False	(page 3)	8. True	(page 6)	13. True	(page 7)
4. True	(page 4)	9. True	(page 6)	14. True	(page 9)
5. False	(page 6)	10. True	(page 6)	15. False	(page 10)

Chapter 2 Review (page 33)

1. False	(page 25)	4. False	(page 28)	7. True	(page 31)
2. True	(page 25)	5. True	(page 28)	8. False	(page 31)
3. True	(page 28)	6. True	(page 30)	9. True	(page 31)
				10. True	(page 32)

Chapter 3 Review (page 47)

1. True	(page 35)	4. True	(page 37)	7. False	(page 42)
2. True	(page 35)	5. True	(page 37)	8. False	(page 44)
3. False	(page 35)	6. True	(page 40)	9. True	(page 46)
				10. True	(page 46)

Chapter 4 Review (page 60)

1. True	(page 49)	4. True	(page 51)	7. True	(page 56)
2. False	(page 49)	5. True	(page 53)	8. True	(page 56)
3. False	(page 49)	6. True	(page 56)	9. True	(page 58)
				10. True	(page 59)

Chapter 5 Review (page 100)

1. True	(page 73)	6. True	(page 79)	11. True	(page 90)
2. True	(page 73)	7. True	(page 81)	12. False	(page 92)
3. False	(page 75)	8. True	(page 87)	13. True	(page 93)
4. True	(page 76)	9. True	(page 88)	14. False	(page 94)
5. False	(page 76)	10. False	(page 89)	15. True	(page 95)

Chapter Review answers continue on the next page

Appendices

Chapter Review Answers (Continued)

Chapter 6 Review (page 118)

1. True	(page 103)	4. False	(page 106)	7. True	(page 110)
2. False	(page 105)	5. True	(page 106)	8. False	(page 113)
3. False	(page 106)	6. True	(page 107)	9. True	(page 117)
				10. True	(page 117)

Chapter 7 Review (page 134)

1. False	(page 125)	4. True	(page 127)	7. True	(page 127)
2. True	(page 125)	5. False	(page 127)	8. False	(page 130)
3. True	(page 127)	6. True	(page 127)	9. True	(page 130)
				10. False	(page 133)

Chapter 8 Review (page 153)

1. True	(page 137)	6. True	(page 139)	11. True	(page 146)
2. True	(page 139)	7. False	(page 144)	12. True	(page 146)
3. False	(page 139)	8. True	(page 144)	13. True	(page 149)
4. False	(page 139)	9. True	(page 145)	14. False	(page 151)
5. True	(page 139)	10. True	(page 145)	15. True	(page 151)

Appendices

Chapter Exercise Answers

Author's Note

The majority of answers to exercises are based on feedback from numerous grants writing workshop participants. Although the answers provide a good sample of possible answers, there are always other possible responses that may be appropriate.

Exercise 1-1: Locating and Reviewing Solicitations
(Chapter 1, page 12)

Sample Federal Register Solicitation

1. CFDA#/Title: CFDA# 84.339A/Learning Anytime Anywhere Partnerships

2. Sponsoring agency: Fund for the Improvement of Postsecondary Education (FIPSE) U.S. Department of Education

3. Publication date: January 16, 2001 (Volume 66, Number 10)

4. Eligible applicants: Partnerships of two or more agencies or organizations, including institutions of higher education.

5. Funding allocations: $15,500,000* ($333,333 per year)/30 to 40 awards

6. Selection criteria: Selection criteria include the following: need, significance, quality of design, quality of evaluation plan, quality of management plan, quality of personnel, and adequacy of resources for the proposed project.

7. Solicitation summary:
To enhance the delivery, quality, and accountability of postsecondary education and career-oriented lifelong learning through asynchronous distance education.

* Federal funds may not pay for more than 50 percent of the project costs.

Sample FedBizOpps (FBO) Solicitation

1. Title: Transitional Drug Abuse Treatment Services

2. Solicitation number: RFP# 200-0677-NE

3. Sponsoring agency: Department of Justice, Bureau of Prisons, Federal Bureau of Prisons, Procurement and Property

4. POC/Phone #/e-mail: Jacqueline Ponders/202-307-3069/jponders@bop.gov

5. Publication date: April 18, 2001

6. Solicitation summary:
Provide outpatient assessment and counseling sessions for transitional drug abuse treatment services for male/female federal offenders in or near Bangor, Maine held under the authority of various United States statutes.

Exercise 1-2: Analyzing Grant Solicitations
(Chapter 1, pages 14-22)

Answers and Location Within Grant Solicitation

1. **Identify the contact person and telephone number to obtain further information about this solicitation.**

    Christine Camillo   Telecommunication device for deaf
    202-401-6222   1-800-877-8339

    (Page 18202; 1ˢᵗ column under "For Further Information Contact:")

2. **Where should the application be hand delivered?**

    U.S. Department of Education
    Application Control Center
    Room 3633
    Regional Office Building 3
    7ᵗʰ and D Streets, SW
    Washington, DC

    (Page 18204; 2ⁿᵈ column under "Applications Delivered by Hand")

3. **Where will the bidders' conferences be held? Please provide dates, times, and locations.**

    May 9, 1997   May 12, 1997
    1:00 to 4:00 p.m.   1:00 to 4:00 p.m.
    Dallas, Texas   Chicago, Illinois

    (Page 18205; 2ⁿᵈ column under "Section G. Bidders' Conferences")

4. **How many days do states have to review applications?**

    30 days or the local partnership may submit the application without State comments, with proof the State received the application at least 30 days prior to the due date.

    (Page 18203; 2ⁿᵈ column under "State Comments")

5. **How long is the period of performance? How many years may the grant be extended?**

    Period of performance is 60 months. Grants may be extended up to four additional years.

    (Page 18203; 3ʳᵈ column under "Period of Performance" and "Option to Extend")

Exercise 1-2 answers continue on the next page

Exercise 1-2: Analyzing Grant Solicitations (continued)
(Chapter 1, pages 14-22)

6. **What is the total amount of money available for this competition?**

   Approximately $14 million dollars is available for this competition.
   (Page 18203; 3rd column under "Available Funds")

7. **Approximately how many awards will be made?**

   Departments expect to make 30 to 40 awards.
   (Page 18203; 3rd column under "Estimated Number of Awards")

8. **What is the range of first-year awards? The amount of an award depends on what criteria?**

   Departments expect that first-year award amounts will range from a minimum award of $200,000 to a maximum award of $500,000. The amount of an award under this competition will depend upon the scope, quality, and comprehensiveness of the proposed initiative and the relative size of the community to be served by the local partnership. Individual grants will effectively serve high poverty areas of no more than a total of 50,000 in population.

   (Page 18203; 3rd column under "Estimated Range of Awards")

9. **What are the six distinct parts of the application?**

   Part I: Eligibility Requirements
   Part II: Budget and Certifications
   Part III: Abstract
   Part IV: State Comments
   Part V: Program Narrative
   Part VI: Appendices
   (Page 18204; 2nd column under "Section D. Organization and Content of Applications")

10. **What items should be included in "Part II: Budget and Certification" of the application?**

    Standard Form SF 424 "Application for Federal Assistance"
    Standard Form SF 524 "Budget"
    Detailed cost breakout of each line item on SF 524
    All assurances and certifications
    (Page 18204; 2nd column under "II. Budget and Certifications")

Exercise 1-2 answers continue on the next page

Exercise 1-2: Analyzing Grant Solicitations (continued)
(Chapter 1, pages 14-22)

11. What are the five selection criteria and point value for Part V "Program Narrative" of the application?

Criterion 1: Comprehensive Local S-T-W Opportunities System (40 points)

Criterion 2: Quality and Effectiveness of the Local Partnership (20 points)

Criterion 3: Participation of All Students (15 points)

Criterion 4: Collaboration with State (15 points)

Criterion 5: Management Plan (10 points)

(Page 18206; 1ˢᵗ column under "Selection Criteria")

12. Explain what "administrative costs" may include.

Administrative costs may be either personnel or non-personnel costs, and may be either direct or indirect. Costs of administration include those costs that are related to this grant in such categories as:

A. Costs of salaries, wages, and related costs of the grantee's staff engaged in:

- Overall system management, system coordination, and general administrative functions, except evaluation activities;

- Preparing program plans, budgets, and schedules, as well as applicable amendments;

- Monitoring of local initiatives, pilot projects, subrecipients, and related systems and processes;

- Procurement activities, including the award of specific subgrants, contracts, and purchase orders;

- Developing systems and procedures, including management information systems, for ensuring compliance with the requirements under the Act;

- Preparing reports and other documents related to the Act;

- Coordinating the resolution of audit findings;

B. Costs for goods and services required for administration of S-T-W opportunities system;

C. Costs of system-wide management functions; and

D. Travel costs incurred for official business in carrying out grants management or administrative activities.

(Page 18205; 3ʳᵈ column under "Definition of Administrative Costs")

Exercise 2-1: Determining Winning Grant Proposal Characteristics
(Chapter 2, page 34)

Sample Winning Grant Proposal Characteristics

Compliant With RFP/RFA Requirements
The first and most important characteristic of any winning grant proposal is that it must follow the RFP/RFA directions and guidelines and meet specific criteria identified in the solicitation. Organizations must provide exactly what government agencies require. If the proposal fails to include specific requirements or is not organized in the manner specified in the solicitation, the agency may consider the proposal non-compliant and refuse to consider it for funding. At the very least, grant readers may subtract points for missing proposal components or lack of proper organization.

Clear Problem/Need Statement
The problem/need section will often start with a brief profile of your institution followed by a statement that clearly describes a need and how the proposed project will correct or reduce the problem. This section should use test results, local statistics, feedback from questionnaires, and various data-based reports and records to justify the problem and support the project need.

Measurable Goals and Objectives
The primary purpose of the goals and objectives section is to provide readers with a better understanding of the proposed project's intended outcomes. Goals and objectives must be clear and quantifiable statements that are realistic and responsive to the funding agency's wants and needs.

Clear Project Activities/Procedures
Proposals should describe the activities that will be accomplished to achieve the proposed goals and objectives. The methods/procedures section should indicate the who, what, where, when, and how of the project. Good project activities include a timetable and indicate what will be done and by whom. Project activities must be realistic and reasonable; remember someone must complete what is being proposed. This section should also address collaborations with other institutions, consultants, subcontractors, and partners from business and industry.

Strength and Expertise of Personnel
The proposed project should included information about the role and responsibilities of key personnel. Résumés should be included in the appendix and indicate the education, content expertise, and previous grant management experience of proposed personnel. This section should also identify the project management structure and reporting lines within the grant seeking organization.

Strong Evaluation Plans
Evaluation plans should include formative and summative measures that detail how the project goals and objectives will be assessed. Plans should indicate procedures to collect and analyze data in an effort to demonstrate what has been achieved. In addition, plans should indicate how the project would continue after grant funding ends.

Exercise 2-1 answers continue on the next page

Exercise 2-1: Determining Winning Grant Proposal Characteristics (continued)
(Chapter 2, page 34)

Appropriate Cost

Budgets are fundamental components of all grant applications and should indicate financial responsibility. Budgets must include accurate and reasonable costs to complete proposed project activities. Proposal reviewers assess budgets in relationship to project objectives, proposed activities, and RFP/RFA requirements. Incomplete budgets signal poor preparation, inflated budgets indicate waste, and low budgets cast doubt on the planning ability of applicants. All project expenditures must be justified. Do not assume project costs will be obvious to funding agency readers. Always use agency budget worksheets and include budget narrative to provide detail and explanation. Provide direct and indirect costs as well as cost sharing funds, if applicable. In addition, be prepared to prioritize budget needs if the funding agency provides only partial financial support for the grant project.

Comprehensive Abstract, Strong Letter, and Complete Application Forms

Abstracts are usually the last proposal section written, but the first document seen by grant readers. Abstracts must represent a cogent summary of the proposed project, emphasizing key proposal components, and complying with length restrictions.

Cover letters should always include the RFP/RFA or CFDA number, indicate the proposal contents, and identify the name, telephone number, and e-mail address of the institution's contact person.

Grant proposals must follow all instructions when completing application materials. Check all forms for completeness and accuracy. Have all forms and application materials signed in blue ink by institutional administrators/managers.

Strong Appendices

Appendices should include documentation to support the proposal narrative. Typical appendix components include: (1) institution's mission statement; (2) résumés of key staff; (3) letters of support/commitment from partners, subcontractors, and consultants; (4) reports and papers; and (5) other documents too bulky for inclusion in the main body of the proposal narrative.

Professional Appearance

Proposal applications should have a professional appearance. Fancy covers and excessive materials should be avoided. Proposals should use heads and subheads to provide a neat and organized delivery of material requested in the solicitation. A table of contents should precede the proposal narrative. Grammar, spelling, and punctuation should be checked and rechecked before final submission.

Exercise 3-1: Planning Activities Before the Solicitation's Release
(Chapter 3, page 48)

Sample Planning Activities

Planning activities are essential prerequisites if funding seekers are going to successfully win grants on a regular basis. Funding seekers must (1) gather intelligence, and (2) make smart decisions about the match between the government's wants and institution's needs.

Gather Intelligence

Funding seekers must gather intelligence before the release of RFPs/RFAs. Grant seekers should review newsletters, journals, reports, and other publications that disclose information about upcoming grant solicitations. Experienced grant seekers also review comprehensive solicitation lists that are available on the Internet. When reviewing potential grant solicitations, care should be taken to understand the funding program's purpose, applicant eligibility, deadline date, specific regulations, application selection criteria, and budget range of awards.

Funding seekers should always contact state and federal agency representatives that oversee potential grant solicitations. It is estimated that chances for success go up 300% when funding seekers contact an agency representative before proposals are developed. In addition, funding seekers should attempt to contact past award winners and proposal readers in an effort to gather information that may not be available elsewhere. Questions should be prepared prior to contacting these individuals.

Make Smart Bid/No Bid Decisions

After gathering intelligence from various sources, funding seekers must make a decision to submit a proposal or look at other sources of funding that provide a better match between what the funding agency requires and the problem the funding seeker is attempting to resolve. Ultimately, the decision to go forward with developing or not developing a proposal is based on knowledge about the funding agency's wants and needs and the funding seeker's ability to prepare a winning proposal. A decision not to proceed may be the correct decision if the funding seeker: (1) is not prepared to write a winning proposal, (2) does not have adequate support from upper administration, or (3) cannot carry out the proposed grant activities in a timely manner.

If the decision is to go forward and develop a proposal, the funding seeker should:

- use the information gained from the intelligence gathering effort to develop a model solicitation that will serve as a guide for developing the proposal.

- identify a proposal director who will serve as the leader for the proposal development effort and proposal writers and financial staff who will develop the narrative and budget sections of the grant application. Upper administration must determine if there are internal staff members who have the knowledge and time to develop a proposal or if they need to hire outside grant writers to do the activities associated with developing a grant application.

Exercise 3-1 answers continue on the next page

Exercise 3-1: Planning Activities Before the Solicitation's Release (continued)
(Chapter 3, page 48)

- identify partners, subcontractors, and consultants. Upper administration/ management must understand their organization's capabilities and deficiencies when responding to funding agency solicitations. If your organization has specific deficiencies, you should immediately identify partners, subcontractors, and/or consultants who can fill those voids. Partners, subcontractors, and consultants should be included only when it enhances your project. Formal written teaming agreements should be established with partners, subcontractors, and consultants before grant applications are submitted to funding agencies.

- create boilerplate materials that can be used and reused in proposals. Boilerplate materials should not be thought of as final proposal documents. Rather, these materials must be customized to meet the funding agency's needs and wants (specified in the RFP/RFA) in order to be effective.

- write a preliminary proposal draft based on information from intelligence gathering activities. Preliminary proposal drafts should follow model solicitation guidelines, address proposal evaluation criteria, and provide information that is easy for the reader to locate. Simple language that communicates clearly to the intended audience is the best.

- prepare a preliminary proposal budget. Preliminary budgets should provide an estimate of costs associated with proposed activities to be completed during the performance period.

Exercise 4-1: Preparing Compliance Checklists
(Chapter 4, pages 61-66)

Requirements and RFP Location

Requirements	RFP Location
Include background statement about the offeror's experience and qualifications to perform the contract.	L-12-D
Include résumés of all principal staff and consultants involved in tasks under the RFP as well as the primary contact for inquiries relating to contract compliance issues. Résumés shall include technical qualifications, such as duties, education, and experience.	L-12-D
List recent private and government clients (contract names and numbers, client name, address, phone number, and contact person).	L-12-E
Describe the quality control procedures that will be followed for data entry, data prep, data editing, site training, editing, and graphics.	L-12-F
Present a detailed management and staffing plan, including hours or percentage of time for each individual or position.	L-12-G
List all equipment used in accomplishing the work set forth in the RFP.	L-12-H
Present a plan to accomplish project objectives.	L-12-I-1
Demonstrate a detailed understanding of pertinent problems and methods for overcoming them.	L-12-I-2
Address each of the specific tasks in Section C, specifying methodology/approach for accomplishing each task. Indicate the number of person hours estimated for each task.	L-12-I-2
Provide approach to tasks including procedures, format, and designs to indicate how they will meet requirements.	L-12-I-2
Show expertise in SPSS or SPSSPC and ability to modify data entry programs and log programs.	L-13-A-2
Describe procedures to ensure quality and demonstrate experience in maintaining data integrity during data entry, multi-source data merging, and data reporting.	L-13-A-3
Identify other problems which may occur in completing tasks specified in this RFP and recommend procedures to prevent or resolve them.	L-13-A-3
Show an understanding and mastery of the complex practical issues involved in organizing, tracking, processing, and reporting results from a national multi-site data collection program.	L-13-A-3-a
Demonstrate successful implementation of quality control measures and availability of personnel to respond to diverse quality control issues.	L-13-A-3-b

Exercise 4-1 answers continue on the next page

Exercise 4-1: Preparing Compliance Checklists (continued)
(Chapter 4, pages 61-66)

Requirements and RFP Location

Requirements	RFP Location
Propose procedures for attaining the following goals and cite recent experience in successfully accomplishing similar goals on projects involving collection of data from multiple independent sites:	L-13-A-3-b
(1) ensure that the total number of interviews per gender/age group received from a site are processed.	L-13-A-3-b-(1)
(2) ensure that all interview data are reported.	L-13-A-3-b-(2)
(3) ensure that the total number of specimen results received from the laboratory are processed.	L-13-A-3-b-(3)
(4) ensure that the total number of specimen results received from the laboratory are reported.	L-13-A-3-b-(4)
(5) ensure that data are reported separately for each site and quarter.	L-13-A-3-b-(5)
(6) ensure that data are reported separately for gender and age groups.	L-13-A-3-b-(6)
(7) ensure that data are entered accurately.	L-13-A-3-b-(7)
(8) ensure contract compliance with schedules outlined in the RFP.	L-13-A-3-b-(8)
(9) ensure confidentiality of site results.	L-13-A-3-b-(9)
(10) ensure confidentiality of Drug Use Forecasting (DUF) data (DUF data cannot be released without written approval).	L-13-A-3-b-(10)
(11) ensure accuracy in matching interview data and urine data when merging files.	L-13-A-3-b-(11)
(12) ensure that data sets are free from errors for all files (e.g., data files, systems files, and merged files).	L-13-A-3-b-(12)
Enforce quality control issues concerning editing of DUF publications.	L-13-B-1
Suggest problems, which may occur in the publication tasks specified in the RFP, and propose solutions or procedures to prevent them.	L-13-B-1
Propose new graphic formats.	L-13-B-2-a
Propose procedures to ensure high-quality presentation of data.	L-13-B-2-b
Demonstrate experience in accurately representing quantitative data and provide points of contact for substantiation.	L-13-B-2-b
Demonstrate experience in and an understanding of issues involved in publishing results from a national program under tight time schedules.	L-13-B-3-a

Exercise 4-1 answers continue on the next page

Exercise 4-1: Preparing Compliance Checklists (continued)
(Chapter 4, pages 61-66)

Requirements and RFP Location

Requirements	RFP Location
Demonstrate experience in design, editing, and report development.	L-13-B-3-b
Demonstrate that sufficient quality control measures are in place and that personnel are available to respond to diverse quality control issues.	L-13-B-3-b
Propose procedures for attaining the following goals and cite recent experience in successfully accomplishing similar goals on projects involving quantitative information for publication:	L-13-B-3-b
(1) ensure that data received from the National Institute of Justice (NIJ) are accurately transposed into graphic layouts.	L-13-B-3-b-(1)
(2) ensure that all materials are presented according to NIJ specifications.	L-13-B-3-b-(2)
(3) ensure that data presented in tables, graphs, or charts are consistent with corresponding text.	L-13-B-3-b-(3)
(4) ensure that a final review of the entire publication is conducted with emphasis on accuracy.	L-13-B-3-b-(4)
(5) ensure contract compliance with respect to time lines in the RFP.	L-13-B-3-b-(5)
(6) ensure confidentiality of data until the publication is released.	L-13-B-3-b-(6)
Include samples of weekly, monthly, and quarterly financial reports.	L-13-C-2
Meet with the Contracting Officer Technical Representative (COTR) in Washington, DC on a regular basis and sometimes at short notice. Enter into an agreement with a pool of consultants to provide a number of diverse tasks.	L-13-C-3
Describe managerial staff.	L-14-A
Demonstrate the degree of importance attached to projects of this nature.	L-14-A
Include "organizational structure" as part of the Management Plan.	L-14-B
Include résumés of key personnel.	L-14-C

Exercise 4-2: Preparing Proposal Outlines and Schedules
(Chapter 4, pages 67-72)

Sample Proposal Outline

1. Application and Project Abstract *(P. Smith)*

2. Problem/Need *(P. Smith)*
    2.1   Critical shortage of qualified information technology (IT) workers
    2.2   Lack of Hoosier State College students preparing for IT jobs
    2.3   High school students not prepared for IT curriculum

3. Project Leadership and Partners *(D. Johnson)*
    3.1   College leadership
    3.2   High school partners
    3.3   Educational support organizations
    3.4   Business and industry partners

4. Goals/Objectives, Project Activities, and Timeline *(P. Smith and D. Johnson)*
    4.1   Increase awareness among high school students of IT career opportunities
    4.2   Develop dual credit program that begins in the junior year of high school
    4.3   Develop partnerships with business, industry, and professional groups

5. Budget *(P. Smith and D. Johnson)*
    5.1   Direct costs
            5.1.1 Salaries and benefits
            5.1.2 Contractual services
            5.1.3 Supplies and materials
            5.1.4 Training workshops and meetings
            5.1.5 Capital outlay
    5.2   Cost sharing (cash matching funds)

6. Appendices *(S. Gorbitz)*
    6.1   Résumés
    6.2   Organizational chart
    6.3   Letters of support
    6.4   Proposed training curriculum
    6.5   Agreement with 3Com

(Indicates author[s])

Exercise 4-2 answers continue on the next page

Exercise 4-2: Preparing Proposal Outlines and Schedules (continued)
(Chapter 4, pages 67-72)

Sample Proposal Schedule

Distribution: February 15, 20XX
Agency: State Community College Board (SCCB)
Issue Date: February 15, 20XX
Due Date: March 15, 20XX

Tentative Schedule

Activity	Date	Time	Place/Person
Strategy (kickoff) meeting	2/18	10:00 a.m.	Conference Rm. 210
1st draft to reviewers	2/24	5:00 p.m.	Turner
Reviewers' meeting	2/26	11:00 a.m.	Conference Rm. 210
2nd draft to reviewers	3/5	5:00 p.m.	Turner
Reviewers' meeting	3/8	1:00 p.m.	Conference Rm. 210
Final draft to edit/production	3/11	flow basis	Turner
Final draft to reproduction	3/13	1:00 p.m.	Turner and Rice
To SCCB	3/13	5:00 p.m.	Smith and Johnson
Proposal due	3/15	4:00 p.m.	

Writers

Gorbitz, Johnson, Smith [1,2]

Reviewers

Baker, Johnson, Passmore,[2] Smith[2]

Support Staff

Turner, Rice

---

[1] Proposal Director
[2] Final Review Team Member

Exercise 5-1: Preparing Grant Applications
(Chapter 5, page 101)

Sample Transmittal (Cover) Letter

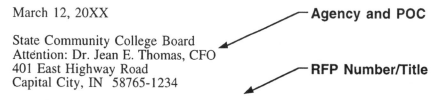

March 12, 20XX ────────────────────────── **Agency and POC**

State Community College Board
Attention: Dr. Jean E. Thomas, CFO
401 East Highway Road ──────────────── **RFP Number/Title**
Capital City, IN 58765-1234

Re: RFP# 42702 / Innovative Programs to Increase Information Technology Graduates

Dear Dr. Thomas:

Hoosier State College (HSC) is pleased to submit six copies of our grant application (*Information Technology: Program Linkages Between Hoosier State College and District High Schools*) in response to the above referenced solicitation. Our proposal addresses the focus categories of recruitment, high school/college program linkages, and employer linkages. The grant proposal includes the following sections:

- Application and Project Abstract
- Problem/Need
- Project Leadership and Partners   **Proposal Contents**
- Goals/Objectives, Project Activities, and Timeline
- Budget
- Appendices

Hoosier State College is totally committed to assist in making the IT proposed project a reality by contributing $17,700 for salaries, contractual services, supplies and materials, training workshops, and capital outlay.

Hoosier State College has administered more than 100 grants in a wide variety of education and service areas. If awarded, HSC will commit high-level administrators to the successful completion of the IT project. If you have oversite questions, please contact Dr. Patrick Smith, Associate Vice President of Academic Affairs. Dr. Smith has an extensive background in managing the successful completion of numerous large-scale grants and will serve as the administrative supervisor of the IT project. He can be reached at (219) 838-3536 or e-mail: psmith@hoosier.edu. If you have specific questions regarding the implementation of the IT project, please contact Mr. David Johnson, IT Project Coordinator at (219) 838-3599 or e-mail: djohnson@hoosier.edu. We look forward to hearing from you.

Sincerely,   **Contact Person**

Janet J. Passmore
Dr. Janet J. Passmore
President

c: Dr. Patrick Smith
    Mr. David Johnson

Exercise 5-1 answers continue on the next page

Exercise 5-1: Preparing Grant Applications (continued)
(Chapter 5, page 101)

Sample Application and Project Abstract

Name of College: Hoosier State College

Contact Person: Dr. Patrick W. Smith

Office Address: 1001 Main Street, Hoosierville, IN 65432-8226

Telephone: 219-838-3536

Fax: 219-838-3774

e-mail: psmith@hoosier.edu

Descriptive Title of Application:

Information Technology: Program Linkages Between Hoosier State College and District High Schools

Abstract (no more than 200 words):

Hoosier State College's project will: (1) increase awareness among high school students about career opportunities in Information Technology, (2) enhance our existing hands-on Tech Prep program that provides employability for our students, and (3) add local IT business partners to our internship pool. Hoosier State College, four local high schools (Hoosierville North, Hoosierville South, Eastland, and Richton Fields), the Career Preparation Network, 3Com corporation, and local businesses will provide students with IT experiences to meet the current and future IT workforce needs. We will complete a marketing plan to disseminate information about IT courses available for high school and college students, which will include hosting informational meetings and visitation programs for high school students in the area. From this plan, we anticipate 150 students will be enrolled in the IT program in fall, 20XX. In order to increase high school and college linkages, we will develop four dual credit courses, send nine instructors to Westnet training, and develop advanced IT courses. We will also provide 60 high school students with IT workplace experiences. During this same time we will establish an Information Technology club on campus that will involve college students and community business leaders.

Exercise 5-1 answers continue on the next page

Exercise 5-1: Preparing Grant Applications (continued)
(Chapter 5, page 101)

Sample Proposal Narrative

Proposal Title

Information Technology: Program Linkages Between Hoosier State College and District High Schools

Special Initiative Grant
March 15, 20XX

Due Date

Funding Agency

Submitted to

State Community College Board
401 East Highway Road
Capital City, IN 58765-1234

Funding Seeker

Submitted by

Hoosier State College
1001 Main Street
Hoosierville, IN 65432-8226

Exercise 5-1 answers continue on the next page

Exercise 5-1: Preparing Grant Applications (continued)
(Chapter 5, page 101)

Introduction

Hoosier State College (HSC) is a publicly supported, comprehensive community college located in Northwest Indiana approximately 25 miles southeast of Chicago. The College's student population is culturally diverse with over 52% of the population either African American or Hispanic. The economic strata of the College is equally diverse

> **HOOSIER STATE COLLEGE**
> **Fall 20XX**
>
> - 6,934 Total Students
> - Mean Age 26; Median Age 24
> - 60% Female; 40% Male
> - 34% African American
> - 48% Caucasian; 18% Hispanic

with the district spanning from the impoverished community of Eastland (one of the poorest communities in the United States to fairly affluent communities of Hoosierville and Richton Fields. The College's primary purpose is to provide excellent educational opportunities for all students in occupational areas.

Problem/Need

The virtual explosion of information technology (IT) job opportunities, coupled with the dearth of students who are preparing for these jobs, provides a unique challenge for HSC. Many of the students who enroll at HSC are most likely to have graduated from under funded, under equipped, "property tax poor" high schools. Because of this situation, HSC has the difficult task of shaping these minimally prepared students into skilled workers for tomorrow.

According to the Information Technology Association of America (ITAA), more than a million new IT jobs have been created in the last decade with more than 840,000 IT jobs unfilled this year. Toby Richards, Educational Customer Programs Director at Microsoft Education Solutions Group, stated that IT represents some of the best paying jobs available – "the average high tech job pays 78% more than the average non-high tech job." He continues, "this will present a tremendous challenge and opportunity for schools to develop new curriculum and to prepare teachers to teach new subjects." According to a study conducted by ITAA and William M. Mercer (a leading human resources consulting firm), it takes 37% longer to fill IT jobs than non-IT jobs. All employers from large corporations to small retail stores require competent IT workers to maintain a smooth running business.

Exercise 5-1 answers continue on the next page

Exercise 5-1: Preparing Grant Applications (continued)
(Chapter 5, page 101)

Richard Greenberg, in his article, "Filling the Gap" in the October 20XX issue of *Techniques*, claims that successful IT training programs are driven by industry needs. Hoosier State College's Computer Information Systems Program and their advisory board members have been discussing the rapid technological changes in the workplace with implications for curriculum for several years. In response to the changing technology and in an effort to prepare students for IT careers, Hoosier State College, in collaboration with four district high schools, has teamed up with 3Com Corporation (one of the world's pre-eminent suppliers of data, voice, and video communications technology) to train a generation of network workers. See the appendix for our NetPrep Regional Training Center Agreement. The Computer Information Systems – NetPrep Network Technology Program will lead to an industry-recognized certification, a Hoosier State College Certificate, or an Associate in Applied Science degree. The comprehensive curriculum will provide:

- an in-depth understanding of the theory, hardware, and software of computer networking;

- immediately employable skills;

- eighty percent of the coursework toward certification;

- a vendor neutral program;

- a state-of-the-art curriculum developed and supported by 3Com Corporation;

- industry-recognized certifications by the National Association of Communication Systems Engineers (NACSE); and

- NetPrep Senior Network Specialist certificate completion in as little as two semesters.

HSC's NetPrep program will provide students with a vital connection to workplace experiences and internship opportunities. In fall, 20XX, 150 students are anticipated to be enrolled in at least one of the sequenced courses in the networking program at HSC.

Exercise 5-1 answers continue on the next page

Exercise 5-1: Preparing Grant Applications (continued)
(Chapter 5, page 101)

Project Leadership and Partners

Dr. Patrick Smith, the Project Director and Associate Vice President of Academic Affairs at HSC, will lead the project leadership team. David Johnson and Sheila Gorbitz will serve as IT coordinators and create a close working relationship between the four district high schools, the Career Preparation Network, 3Com Corporation, and local district businesses. Résumés for these key staff are located in the appendix. This fall, HSC's pilot project established links between partners by conducting several working committees to develop and refine the IT curriculum and establish internship sites with local businesses. Specific partners and their roles are described below.

Organization	Description	Role In Project
College Community	Hoosier State College	- Increase awareness among high school students of career opportunities and increase high school graduates enrolling in IT. - Develop a dual credit program that begins in the junior year of high school and continues through a degree or certificate program and provides workplace experiences. - Develop partnerships with technology business and industry and/or related professional associations.
High Schools	Hoosierville North Eastland Richton Fields Hoosierville South	- Explore and develop dual credit courses. - Recruit potential students for IT programs. - Include IT courses in high school and college catalogues. - Identify teachers who require IT training. - Grant high school credit for completion of IT courses. - Provide guidance for student transition from secondary to postsecondary programs.
Education Support Organization	Career Preparation Network	- Develop and distribute recruitment materials to high school students and the public. - Serve as a liaison between high schools and HSC to develop IT programs and student transition. - Assist in expanding IT work-based learning experiences for high school students. - Provide professional development opportunities for IT instructors.
Businesses	3Com Local Businesses	- Provide necessary materials and equipment for program curriculum. - Provide workplace experiences and internships for students.

Exercise 5-1 answers continue on the next page

Exercise 5-1: Preparing Grant Applications (continued)
(Chapter 5, page 101)

Goals/Objectives, Project Activities, and Timeline

HSC's proposed project is in alignment with the primary goals presented in Indiana's "Excellence in Education" document. The following project goals specifically address the State Community College Board's agenda for increasing higher education's partnership, opportunities, and excellence and at the same time prepare our district students to enter into the IT profession.

Goal 1. Recruitment: Increase awareness of career opportunities among high school students and increase the number of high school graduates enrolling in Information Technology.

- Develop brochures, press releases, and ads for use in local and district high school newspapers.

- Hold informational meetings and host visitation programs for prospective IT students.

Goal 2. High School/College Program Linkages: Develop a dual credit program that begins with the junior year in high school, continues through a certification program, and provides workplace experiences.

- Students will complete the NetPrep sequence of courses in preparation for certification.

- Student will complete workplace experiences and internships in regional businesses.

Goal 3. Employer Linkages: Create additional partnerships with area business and industry and professional associations.

- Add regional business and industry partners to our partnership pool.

- Form an IT student organization at HSC.

Exercise 5-1 answers continue on the next page

Exercise 5-1: Preparing Grant Applications (continued)
(Chapter 5, page 101)

OBJECTIVES	ACTIVITIES	PROJECT OUTCOMES	TIMELINE
Goal 1. Recruitment			
1.1: Recruit high schools to enroll in Tech Prep programs providing a seamless transition to postsecondary certificate and degree programs.	1.1a Develop marketing program for high school students and parents. 1.1b Host evening informational meetings for students and parents. 1.1c Host visitation programs at HSC for interested high school students. 1.1d Increase IT enrollment.	1.1a 500 brochures, 10 press releases, and 4 newspaper ads will be developed. 1.1b Two informational meetings for students and parents will be held at HSC. 1.1c Two half-day visitation programs will be held at HSC. 1.1d 150 IT students will be enrolled in NetPrep.	1.1a March, 20XX 1.1b March, 20XX 1.1c March, 20XX 1.1d August, 20XX
Goal 2. High School/College Program Linkages			
2.1: Provide high school and college students with a core curriculum in computer networking.	2.1a Review and select IT curriculum materials. 2.1b Develop two high school IT courses to articulate with existing HSC IT courses. 2.1c Develop two new IT courses for HSC. 2.1d Send one instructor from each high school and five faculty from HSC for training in preparation to teach IT curriculum. 2.1e: Develop two additional courses to articulate with the new courses at HSC and to complete a NetPrep secondary school certificate preparing students for employment as an entry level network technician. 2.1f Prepare students for industry standard certification and for advanced coursework leading to certification.	2.1a Text and lab manuals for high school and HSC IT courses will be purchased. 2.1b Two dual IT courses will be established. 2.1c Two advanced IT courses will be developed. 2.1d Nine IT instructors will complete training. 2.1e Four dual credit courses will be implemented. 2.1f 120 students will complete NetPrep sequence of courses in preparation for certification.	2.1a March, 20XX 2.1b June, 20XX 2.1c June, 20XX 2.1d June, 20XX 2.1e June, 20XX 2.1f June, 20XX
2.2 Provide high school and college students with workplace experiences.	2.2a schedule workplace visitations and job shadowing for high school students. 2.2b Expand existing internships in IT to include opportunities in computer networking for college students.	2.2a 60 high school students will be provided workplace experiences in regional businesses. 2.2b Ten additional computer networking internship sites for college students will be established.	2.2a May, 20XX 2.2b May, 20XX
Goal 3. Employer Linkages			
3.1 Establish business linkages for workbased learning and future employment.	3.1a Actively recruit business and industry partners. 3.1b Establish working relationships with IT professional associations.	3.1a Six regional business and industry partners will be added to the existing pool. 3.1b Student organization will be formed at HSC.	3.1a June, 20XX 3.1b June, 20XX

Exercise 5-1 answers continue on the next page

Exercise 5-1: Preparing Grant Applications (continued)
(Chapter 5, page 101)

Appendices

A. Résumés for key staff
    - Patrick Smith, Project Director
    - David Johnson, IT Coordinator
    - Shelia Gorbitz, IT Coordinator

B. Organizational charts
    - HSC Organizational Structure (project location within the organization)
    - IT Project Organizational Structure (staff and reporting duties)

C. Letters of support
    - Local high schools
    - Local business and industry
    - Career Preparation Network

D. 3Com training curriculum
    - Course syllabi
    - Quizzes and tests

E. NetPrep Regional Training Center Agreement
    - Hardware and software commitment
    - Training
    - Certification standards

Exercise 5-2: Editing Narrative
(Chapter 5, page 102)

Sample Edited Responses

Sentence 1
Poor: The proposed project will afford participants the opportunity to master contemporary computer skills.

Good: The proposed project will allow participants to master computer skills.

Sentence 2
Poor: Local colleges are producing highly skilled graduates in light of the fact that community businesses are requiring a stronger technical workforce.

Good: Local colleges are producing highly skilled graduates because businesses demand a strong technical workforce.

Sentence 3
Poor: Outside consultants will conduct an evaluation of the entire project.

Good: Outside consultants will evaluate the project.

Sentence 4
Poor: The end-of-the-year annual performance report will be written at the end of each program year.

Good: The performance report will be written at the end of each program year.

Sentence 5
Poor: Each and every report shall conform to the funding agency's instructions.

Good: All reports shall conform to the funding agency's instructions.

Sentence 6
Poor: The grantee is directed to submit project reports.

Good: The grantee shall submit project reports.

Sentence 7
Poor: It is the duty of the grantee to submit documented financial reports.

Good: The grantee shall submit documented financial reports.

Sentence 8
Poor: The grantee shall submit project reports for the reason that the funding agency's approval is mandatory.

Good: The grantee shall submit project reports for the funding agency's approval.

Sentence 9
Poor: Partners will make annual contributions of $1,000 a year.

Good: Partners will make $1,000 annual contributions.

Sentence 10
Poor: A comprehensive job description listing all duties connected with the proposal manager's position is included in the appendix.

Good: A comprehensive job description for the proposal manager's position is included in the appendix.

Exercise 6-1: Preparing Proposal Budgets (Information Technology)
(Chapter 6, page 119)

Sample Budget

Name of College: Hoosier State College

CEO Name: Dr. Janet J. Passmore, President

CEO Signature: *Janet J. Passmore*

Line Item and Description	Grant Funds	Matching Funds	Total Amount
Salaries	10,000 **10,000**	9,000 **9,000**	19,000 **19,000**
Employee Benefits	1,000 **1,000**	0 **0**	1,000 **1,000**
Contractual Services			
Consultant to develop curriculum	4,000	0	4,000
Cabling for labs	0 **4,000**	3,000 **3,000**	3,000 **7,000**
Supplies and Materials			
Instructional	17,000	0	17,000
Outreach	3,000 **20,000**	3,000 **3,000**	6,000 **23,000**
Conference and Meetings			
Training and travel for instructors	8,000 **8,000**	2,000 **2,000**	10,000 **10,000**
Capital Outlay			
Network Equipment	7,000 **7,000**	700 **700**	7,700 **7,700**
Total	**$50,000**	**$17,700**	**$67,700**

Exercise 6-2: Preparing Proposal Budgets (School-To-Work)
(Chapter 6, pages 120-124)

Proposed Budget

Personnel and Fringe Benefits		Funding Agency	ASD
Oversight Manager ($85,010 x 15%)	=	0	12,752
Project Administrator ($78,008 x 25%)	=	19,502	0
Project Specialist #1 ($40,996 x 100%)	=	40,996	0
Project Specialist #2 ($50,003 x 100%)	=	50,003	0
Financial Manager ($85,010 x 10%)	=	0	8,501
Document Specialist ($36,000 x 25%)	=	0	9,000
Personnel Total	=	110,501	30,253
Fringe Benefits (Personnel x 25%) Total	=	27,625	7,563
Personnel and Fringe Benefits Total	=	**$138,126**	**$ 37,816**

Travel and Per Diem
S-T-W Conference

22 ASB members x $100 per person airfare	=	0	2,200
22 ASB members x $140 per diem x 2 days	=	0	6,160
22 teachers x $100 per person airfare	=	2,200	0
22 teachers x $140 per diem x 2 days	=	6,160	0
1 national speaker x $800 airfare	=	800	0
1 national speaker x $140 per diem x 2 days	=	280	0
2 state speakers x $400 per person airfare	=	800	0
2 state speakers x $140 per diem x 2 days	=	560	0
Subtotal	=	$ 10,800	$ 8,360

Student Work Experience

20 students x $100 (each) airfare	=	2,000	0
20 students x $50 per diem x 14 days	=	14,000	0
Subtotal	=	$ 16,000	$ 0

S-T-W Implementation Project in Schools

2 specialists x 22 Schools x $100 airfare	=	4,400	0
2 specialists x 22 Schools x $35 per diem x 3 days	=	4,620	0
Subtotal	=	$ 9,020	$ 0
Travel and Per Diem Total	=	**$ 35,820**	**$ 8,360**

Purchased Services

Honorarium: 1 national speaker x $1,000	=	1,000	0
Honorarium: 2 state speakers x $500	=	1,000	0
Conference building rent ($1,000 per day x 2 days)	=	2,000	0
Career information center ($50 per sq ft x 400 sq ft)	=	0	20,000
Purchased Services Total	=	**$ 4,000**	**$ 20,000**

Equipment and Supplies

Curriculum materials (22 x $1,000 per school)	=	22,000	0
Career and occupational material	=	0	1,000
Equipment and Supplies Total	=	**$ 22,000**	**$ 1,000**

| **Total Costs** | = | **$199,946** | **$67,176** |

Exercise 7-1: Transmittal Letter and Proposal Delivery
(Chapter 7, pages 135-136)

Sample Transmittal Letter

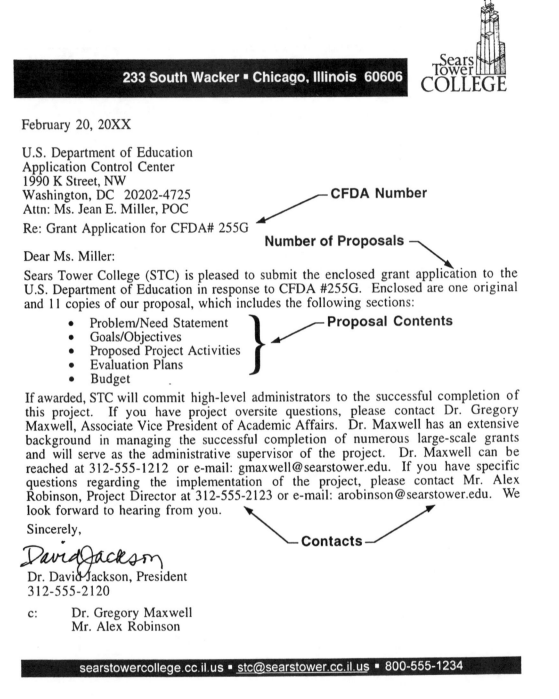

233 South Wacker ▪ Chicago, Illinois 60606

Sears Tower COLLEGE

February 20, 20XX

U.S. Department of Education
Application Control Center
1990 K Street, NW
Washington, DC 20202-4725
Attn: Ms. Jean E. Miller, POC

— **CFDA Number**

Re: Grant Application for CFDA# 255G

Number of Proposals —

Dear Ms. Miller:

Sears Tower College (STC) is pleased to submit the enclosed grant application to the U.S. Department of Education in response to CFDA #255G. Enclosed are one original and 11 copies of our proposal, which includes the following sections:

- Problem/Need Statement
- Goals/Objectives
- Proposed Project Activities
- Evaluation Plans
- Budget

— **Proposal Contents**

If awarded, STC will commit high-level administrators to the successful completion of this project. If you have project oversite questions, please contact Dr. Gregory Maxwell, Associate Vice President of Academic Affairs. Dr. Maxwell has an extensive background in managing the successful completion of numerous large-scale grants and will serve as the administrative supervisor of the project. Dr. Maxwell can be reached at 312-555-1212 or e-mail: gmaxwell@searstower.edu. If you have specific questions regarding the implementation of the project, please contact Mr. Alex Robinson, Project Director at 312-555-2123 or e-mail: arobinson@searstower.edu. We look forward to hearing from you.

— **Contacts** —

Sincerely,

David Jackson

Dr. David Jackson, President
312-555-2120

c: Dr. Gregory Maxwell
       Mr. Alex Robinson

searstowercollege.cc.il.us ▪ stc@searstower.cc.il.us ▪ 800-555-1234

Exercise 7-1 answers continue on the next page

Exercise 7-1: Transmittal Letter and Proposal Delivery
(Chapter 7, pages 135-136)

Delivery Methods and Cost

Delivery Methods	Approximate Costs	Pros/Cons
Couriers www.fedex.com www.airborne.com www.ups.com www.dhl.com	Prices will fluctuate. Check online or call couriers for current rates.	Courier is responsible for delivering the package. Inexpensive compared to using personal automobile or airline. Flight may be cancelled due to bad weather.
Personal Automobile www.mapquest.com	1418 miles @ $.345 per mile = $489 Must also consider costs for tolls, meals, and lost time.	You are responsible for delivering the package. Round trip is more than 24 hours. Must consider inclement weather.
Car Rental www.enterprise.com www.thrifty.com www.avis.com www.nationalcar.com www.hertz.com www.goalamo.com	Prices will fluctuate. Check online or call car rentals for current rates. Cost will also depend on size and model of car. Must also consider costs for tolls, meals, and lost time.	Same as personal automobile.
Airlines www.american.com www.delta.com www.nwa.com www.transworldairlines.com www.united.com www.usair.com	Prices will fluctuate. Check online or call airlines for current rates. Must also consider costs for Washington, DC ground transportation, meals, and lost time.	You are responsible for delivering the package. Flight may be cancelled due to bad weather.
Train www.amtrak.com	Prices will fluctuate. Check online or call Amtrak for current rates. Must also consider costs for Washington, DC ground transportation, meals, and lost time.	You are responsible for delivering the package. One-way travel time is approximately 18 hours.
Bus www.greyhound.com	Prices will fluctuate. Check online or call Greyhound for current rates. Must also consider costs for Washington, DC ground transportation, meals, and lost time.	You are responsible for delivering the package. One-way travel time is approximately 19 hours.
Kinko's www.kinkos.com	Prices will fluctuate. Check online or call Kinko's for current rates.	Text must be in electronic form. Kinko's is responsible for delivering the package.

Exercise 8-1: Evaluating Proposals in Response to Criteria
(Chapter 8, pages 154-164)

Sample Strengths/Weaknesses and Lessons Learned

Criteria #1

The proposal clearly describes the need for supervisory training for small business owners.

Strengths/Weaknesses

Lincoln Department of Development provided a data-based needs statement concerning supervisory training from a survey of small business owners. Jefferson Chamber of Commerce stated "education is the key element to continually improve economic development," but did not provide data-based feedback regarding the need for training small-business owners.

Lessons Learned

Always provide data-based statements to support the need for a grant project.

Criteria #2

The proposal clearly describes a schedule for analyzing, designing, developing, implementing, and evaluating the training.

Strengths/Weaknesses

Lincoln Department of Development provided a schedule for analyzing, designing, developing, implementing, and evaluating training tasks. The schedule showed a logical progression and overlap of activities across time. Jefferson Chamber of Commerce said they recognized the importance of having a detailed project schedule, but failed to provide one.

Lessons Learned

Always provide exactly what is requested in RFPs/RFAs. Whenever possible provide a graphic presentation of activities with a time schedule. Include additional narrative to supplement the proposal schedule.

Criteria #3

The proposal clearly describes time commitments of key personnel who will be responsible for completing the proposed activities.

Strengths/Weaknesses

Lincoln Department of Development provided a table that identified the names of key personnel, their position, and time commitments allocated for completing the proposed project activities. Jefferson Chamber of Commerce provided narrative that did not indicate the names of key personnel.

Lessons Learned

Identify key personnel by name as well as their role in the proposed project. Do not bury key information in narrative. Use tables, charts, and figures to provide a snapshot of important information. Note: this is a quality issue rather than a compliance issue.

Exercise 8-1 answers continue on the next page

Exercise 8-1: Evaluating Proposals in Response to Criteria

(Chapter 8, pages 154-164)

Criteria #4

The proposal clearly describes the involvement that stakeholder groups (administration, staff, board members, small business owners, and the educational community) will have in training.

Strengths/Weaknesses

Lincoln Department of Development used the active voice while Jefferson Chamber of Commerce used the passive voice in presenting information about stakeholder's roles.

Lessons Learned

Always use the active voice in presenting information in grant proposals.

Criteria #5

The proposal clearly describes the project director's experience and training in strategic planning.

Strengths/Weaknesses

Lincoln Department of Development provided specific information about the Executive Director's experience, while Jefferson Chamber of Commerce presented vague information about the Executive Director's experience and training.

Lessons Learned

Always provide quantitative information about key personnel in grant proposals.

Criteria #6

The proposal provides evidence of dedication to the project that indicates that the project will be successful.

Strengths/Weaknesses

Lincoln Department of Development provided specific information about financial support and time commitments for this project. Jefferson Chamber of Commerce did not provide financial and time commitments for this project.

Lessons Learned

Indicate dedication for the proposed project by providing specific financial support and time commitments.

Criteria #7

In a single sentence, the proposal clearly describes the project mission.

Strengths/Weaknesses

Lincoln Department of Development provided a one-sentence description of the project mission. Jefferson Chamber of Commerce uses three sentences and did not describe the project mission.

Lessons Learned

Always provide exactly what is requested in the RFP/RFA, no more and no less.

Exercise 8-1 answers continue on the next page

Exercise 8-1: Evaluating Proposals in Response to Criteria
(Chapter 8, pages 154-164)

Criteria #8

In 30 pages or less, the proposal clearly addresses the following required factors: Required Forms, Need, Proposed Activities, Evaluation Plan, Allocations of Key Personnel, Commitment to Broad-Based Participation, and Budget.

Strengths/Weaknesses

Lincoln Department of Development provided a table of contents that followed the order of required factors identified in the criteria. Jefferson Chamber of Commerce provided a table of contents that did not follow the required factors identified in the criteria and was more than 30 pages in length.

Lessons Learned

Always present information in the order requested in the grant criteria. Use the exact heads and subheads identified in the RFP/RFA. Never provide more pages than requested.

Criteria #9

The proposal clearly describes what materials will be produced during the development phase of the project.

Strengths/Weaknesses

Lincoln Department of Development presented a bulleted list of specific materials to be produced during the development phase of the project. Jefferson Chamber of Commerce provided narrative concerning the project materials to be produced.

Lessons Learned

Provide bulleted lists to highlight important proposal requirements. Always include the specific number of items to be produced.

Criteria #10

The proposal clearly describes what performance indicators will be used to monitor the effectiveness of the program.

Strengths/Weaknesses

Lincoln Department of Development provided a bulleted list of performance indicators to monitor the effectiveness of the program. Jefferson Chamber of Commerce provided performance indicators in the narrative.

Lessons Learned

Do not bury important responses to grant criteria in the proposal narrative. Use a list of items to highlight important information.

Exercise 8-2: Evaluating Two Proposals
(Chapter 8, pages 165-191)

Sample Strengths/Weaknesses and Lessons Learned

Instructors, Inc.
Strengths
- Data-based philosophy tailored for Eagle Eye Analysts
- Presents strategy to analyze needs before training
- Clear timeframe of activities and events
- Strong evaluation plans (use of pretest, training, and posttest to arrive at results)
- Clear project management structure with lines of authority
- Clear presentation of personnel duties and responsibilities
- Clear identification of deliverables
- Clear, concise, easy-to-read presentation of material with citations and references
- Attractive two-column proposal format (some agencies will not allow)
- Good use of textboxes to highlight key messages
- Excellent figures with captions
- Strong appendices

Weaknesses
- Lacks evidence to support expertise in the aerial/satellite photograph analysis.
- Lacks specific detail about teaching methods
- Repetitive use of the term "hands on"

Technical Trainers, Inc.
Strengths
- Provides evidence of expertise in aerial/satellite photograph analysis.
- Clear goals and objectives
- Detailed agenda
- Clear project steps
- Good match between objectives and methods
- Detailed narrative with organizational headings

Weaknesses
- Boilerplate narrative is non-specific and difficult to read
- Lack of information about the expertise of proposed personnel in narrative
- Lack of data to support philosophy
- Figures in back of proposal lose impact

Exercise 8-2 answers continue on the next page

Exercise 8-2: Evaluating Two Proposals
(Chapter 8, pages 165-191)

Lessons Learned

- Include easy-to-understand proposal narrative that is well documented to support specific claims and demonstrate expertise in the field. Use short sentences and paragraphs to reduce reader fatigue. Use graphics and textboxes to support central messages, especially when the RFP/RFA limits the number of proposal pages.

- Avoid using boilerplate (generic) narrative. Know your audience and adapt your message to meet the client's (funding agency's) wants and needs.

- Include methods and procedures that are clear and understandable. Use a timeline that describes when activities will be accomplished. Use the active voice to describe activities and procedures.

- Include well-documented narrative that discusses the strength and expertise of key personnel who will manage the proposed project. Use an organizational chart to show lines of authority. Include résumés of key personnel in the appendix.

- Include strong evaluation plans that describe formative and summative methods to assess project outcomes. Include a discussion about how quantitative and qualitative data will be collected, analyzed, and reported to the agency.

- Provide a proposal that is organized according to the RFP/RFA specifications. Provide only what is required.

- Include support material in a well-organized appendix. Include a table of contents with page numbers prior to appendix materials to help readers locate specific documents.

Appendices

Comprehensive Review Answers

1. In addition to grants, identify two other forms of funding provided by the U.S. government. See Chapter 1, page 1.
   - Cooperative agreements
   - Procurement contracts

2. Name the primary document that funding seekers use to locate information about grant opportunities. See Chapter 1, page 3.
   - *Federal Register (FR)*

3. In addition to the *Federal Register*, name three resource publications used to locate solicitations. See Chapter 1, page 5. (See page 203 for additional resource publications).
   - *Aid for Education Report*
   - *Chronicle of Higher Education*
   - *Federal Assistance Monitor*
   - *Federal Grants and Contracts Weekly*
   - *Nyquist Report on Funding for Community, Junior, and Technical Colleges*
   - *The Grantsmanship Center Magazine*

4. Name two categories of grants. See Chapter 1, page 6.
   - Discretionary grants
   - Entitlement, mandatory, or formula grants

5. Name the Web site where government agencies post all public notices about federal procurement contract solicitations over $25,000. See Chapter 1, page 7.
   - *FedBizOpps (FBO)* (www.fedbizopps.gov)

6. Name two broad categorical groupings of procurement contracts. See Chapter 1, page 7.
   - Fixed-price contracts
   - Cost-reimbursement contracts

Comprehensive Review answers continue on the next page

7. Identify the major differences between grants and procurement contracts. See Chapter 1, page 10.

Grants	*Procurement Contracts*
• Found in the Federal Register (FR*)*	• Found in the FedBizOpps (FBO)
• Project announcements	• Competitive bidding announcements
• Multiple awards	• One award
• Respond to criteria	• Respond to tasks
• Initiated by funding seeker	• Initiated by Contracting Officer (CO)
• Funding seeker determines direction	• CO determines direction
• Publications	• Deliverables
• Limited oversight	• Substantial oversight
• Funding seeker keeps equipment	• Government may keep equipment
• Up-front payments	• Payments made after expenditures
• Major sections	• Major sections
• Abstract	• Executive Summary
• Introduction (optional)	• Introduction
• Problem/Need	• Statement of Work (SOW)
• Goals/Objectives	• Management/Organization/Staffing
• Methods/Activities	• Corporate Experience
• Evaluation Plans	• Facilities and Equipment
• Budget	• Budget (as a separate document)
• Appendices	• Appendices

8. Name six distinct proposal development phases that funding seekers should go through to prepare winning proposals. See Chapter 2, page 25.

  • Activities before the RFP/RFA is released
  • Prewriting activities after the RFP/RFA is released
  • Writing, reviewing, rewriting, and editing narrative
  • Preparing budgets
  • Producing, reproducing, packaging, and delivering proposals
  • Postsubmission activities

9. Name the common components found in most grant applications. See Chapter 2, page 29.

  • Application cover sheet
  • Abstract
  • Table of contents
  • Project narrative
  • Budget
  • Assurances and certifications
  • Appendices

Comprehensive Review answers continue on the next page

10. Describe the difference between funding agency's needs and wants. See Chapter 3, page 35.
    - Funding agency's *needs* are basic requirements included in RFPs/RFAs
    - Funding agency's *wants* are what funding agencies would ideally like to see mentioned in winning proposals

11. List eight activities that experienced funding seekers will complete six months to one year prior to release of RFPs/RFAs. See Chapter 3, page 35.
    - Gather intelligence
    - Make preliminary bid/no bid decision
    - Identify a proposal director and team members
    - Identify partners, subcontractors, and/or consultants
    - Develop a "model" solicitation
    - Establish a preliminary budget
    - Create boilerplate materials
    - Write a preliminary proposal draft

12. Identify three individuals who should be questioned by funding seekers before bid/no bid decisions are made. See Chapter 3, page 37.
    - Point of contact (POC)
    - Past award winners
    - Funding agency proposal readers

13. Identify three questions you would ask a Point of Contact (POC) before release of RFPs/RFAs. See Chapter 3, page 37.
    - Does the proposed project fall within funding priorities?
    - What is the total funding available? What is the average award?
    - Will awards be made on the basis of special criteria (e.g., geographic region)?
    - What is the anticipated application/award ratio?
    - What common mistakes have prevented funding seekers from winning?
    - What should be in a proposal that other applicants may have overlooked?
    - Should the proposal be written for reviewers with non-technical backgrounds?
    - How are proposals reviewed?
    - What is the agency's preference for proposal submission?
    - Would you review a 2 to 3 page prospectus and/or proposal draft?
    - Are there any unsolicited funds to support project ideas?

Comprehensive Review answers continue on the next page

14. Identify the main members of a proposal development team. See Chapter 3, page 43.
   - Upper administration/management
   - Proposal director
   - Writer(s) and reviewer(s)
   - Financial/budget staff members
   - Editor(s) and graphic designer(s)
   - Partners/consultants/subcontractors
   - Word processing and reproduction/mailing staff members

15. Identify the pros and cons of using external grant writers to develop grant proposals. See Chapter 3, page 44.

   Pros
   - External grant writers bring a fresh perspective to the proposed project and usually have a thorough understanding of the grant development process and what it takes to win.
   - External grant writers develop proposals without interrupting the daily duties of staff members.

   Cons
   - External grant writers are usually expensive. Some grant writers charge a flat fee while others charge a percentage of the total award.
   - External grant writers will not be responsible for completing the daily activities identified in the proposed project, if the grant is awarded.

16. Identify three "boilerplate" documents that would be helpful in preparing grant proposals. See Chapter 3, page 45.
   - Institutional mission statements/strategic plans
   - Reports from surveys, community forums, and case studies that document current problems that will be addressed as a result of grant funding
   - Goals/Objectives from approved proposals completed by your organization
   - Various time/task and project organizational charts
   - Successful evaluation strategies used in similar winning grant proposals
   - List of components included in your institution's fringe benefits package
   - Assurance and certification forms from similar grant submissions

17. Name two major activities that should be completed the first day after release of RFPs/RFAs. See Chapter 4, page 51.
   - Analyze RFP/RFA immediately
   - Identify ambiguities and request clarification
   - Adjust/re-evaluate estimated probability of winning
   - Make formal bid/no bid decision

Comprehensive Review answers continue on the next page

18. Name four organizational tools developed prior to holding a proposal strategy (kickoff) meeting. See Chapter 4, page 51.
    - Compliance checklist
    - Proposal prospectus
    - Proposal outline
    - Proposal schedule

19. Describe the major topics discussed at a proposal strategy (kickoff) meeting. See Chapter 4, page 58.
    - Strategies/themes to be used in proposal narrative
    - Budget assumptions
    - Proposal writing assignments
    - Due dates for proposal drafts

20. Identify four skills that winning proposal writers possess. See Chapter 5, page 73.
    - Subject-matter skills
    - Writing skills
    - Analytical and creative skills
    - Marketing skills

21. Identify four "Cs" of proposal writing. See Chapter 5, page 75.
    - Have a thorough understanding of the proposed project *content*
    - *Communicate* information to the reading audience
    - *Commit* to completing the grant writing tasks within a specified time
    - Be *consistent* with format and presentation of information

22. Identify the narrative sections contained in most grant proposals. See Chapter 5, page 77.
    - Abstract
    - Introduction (optional)
    - Problem/need
    - Goals/objectives
    - Methods/activities
    - Evaluation plans
    - Appendices (optional)

Comprehensive Review answers continue on the next page

23. Identify the guidelines for writing good problem/need statements. See Chapter 5, page 79.
    - Document a need that relates directly to the funding agency's interest
    - Identify a problem of reasonable size that can be solved
    - Describe a problem/need within a context
    - Provide a vision for solving the problem

24. Identify the guidelines for writing good project objectives. See Chapter 5, page 83.
    - Clear and concise statements listed in chronological order of achievement
    - Measurable in quantitative terms
    - Manageable, ambitious but attainable (i.e., do you have the time and needed resources to accomplish the objectives?)
    - Practical and cost effective

25. Describe the components found in a good methods/activities section of a grant application. See Chapter 5, pages 83-88.
    - Specific tasks designed to meet project goals/objectives within the funding agency's performance period
    - Key personnel (name, role, and time commitments) to be used in the project as well as indicating the lines of authority within the organization
    - Proposed project team's skills and experience necessary to deliver a successful project

26. Define the two forms of evaluation used in grant applications. See Chapter 5, page 89.
    - Formative evaluation is used to monitor the ongoing progress of a grant project
    - Summative evaluation is used to judge the overall quality or worth of a grant program at the end of the project

27. Identify five documents found in proposal appendices. See Chapter 5, page 92.
    - Organization's mission statement
    - Résumés or job descriptions of key personnel
    - Partners'/subcontractors'/consultants' letters of support and commitment
    - Financial reports
    - Lengthy charts and tables
    - Multi-page reports or papers

28. Describe two types of proposal editing. See Chapter 5, page 94.
    - Substantive editing focuses on correctness or completeness of proposal content.
    - Style editing focuses on clarity and readability of ideas

Comprehensive Review answers continue on the next page

29. Name three government agency assurances or certifications that are often submitted with grant applications. See Chapter 5, page 95.
    - Anti-discrimination
    - Drug-free workplace
    - Lobbing restrictions
    - Environmental protection
    - Health, safety, and welfare of human subjects
    - Public employee standards

30. Describe two reasons for using graphics in grant proposals. See Chapter 5, page 98.
    - Graphics supplement the grant narrative
    - Graphics provide readers with an illustration of key points

31. List three *direct* cost items used in proposal budgets. See Chapter 6, page 103.
    - Personnel and fringe benefits
    - Purchased services
    - Supplies and equipment
    - Travel and per diem

32. List three in*direct* cost items used in proposal budgets. See Chapter 6, page 106.
    - Electricity costs
    - Telephone costs
    - Insurance costs
    - Maintenance costs

33. Describe what is meant by "indirect cost rate agreement." See Chapter 6, page 106.

    Organizations that develop grant proposals on a regular basis will often negotiate an *indirect cost rate agreement* with one government agency that can be used with other funding agencies when applying for grants. Indirect cost rate agreements establish a specific indirect cost percentage ranging from 20% to 60% or higher of the total direct cost. This established indirect cost rate percentage is often honored by other agencies when funding seekers apply for grants.

34. Identify and provide examples of two types of cost sharing used in grant proposals. See Chapter 6, page 107.

    Cost sharing represents a specific contribution percentage from the funding seeker as matching funds (actual cash) or in-kind contributions. Matching funds can come from the organization's general operating funds, other state or federal grants with similar goals and objectives, or from private sector contributions. In-kind contributions include institution donations from direct and/or indirect costs.

Comprehensive Review answers continue on the next page.

35. Describe what is meant by budget detail and budget narrative. See Chapter 6, page 110.
    • Budget detail is a brief written description of line items
    • Budget narrative provides a thorough explanation of cost expenditures

36. List three common proposal budget problems. See Chapter 6, page 117.
    • Arithmetic errors in subtotals and totals
    • Lack of budget detail
    • Unrealistic costs for budget items
    • Budget items are inconsistent with proposal narrative
    • Little or no budget narrative
    • Vague and unexplained source(s) for cost sharing dollars
    • Indirect costs are missing from budgets

37. Identify five items that should be checked before grant applications are delivered to funding agencies. See Chapter 7, page 130.
    • Date and time when the proposal is due
    • Number of proposal copies required by the funding agency
    • Funding agency's address
    • Authorized signatures on the cover sheet and all necessary application forms
    • Proper marking on proposal packaging

38. List three components found in a good proposal transmittal letter. See Chapter 7, page 130.
    • RFP/RFA or CFDA number
    • Number of proposals in package as well as contents of each proposal
    • Address, telephone number, and e-mail address of contact person

39. List two reasons to hold a debriefing meeting with writers and reviewers after proposal submission. See Chapter 8, page 137.
    • Discuss proposal strengths and weaknesses
    • Anticipate proposal deficiencies

40. Identify three activities that should be completed if proposals are not funded. See Chapter 8, page 149.
    • Request a debriefing meeting with the Point of Contact
    • Request a copy of reviewers' comments
    • Request copies of winning proposals

Index